D0584890

www.

30007004127774

CO

C'

400038

Patsy

Patsy

The Story of Mary Cornwallis-West

TIM COATES

BLOOMSBURY

327371

Every effort has been made to trace all copyright holders of copyright material reproduced in this book, but if any have been overlooked, the publishers would be glad to hear from them.

First published 2003

Copyright © 2003 by Tim Coates

The moral right of the author has been asserted

Bloomsbury Publishing Plc, 38 Soho Square, London WID 3HB

A CIP catalogue record for this book
is available from the British Library

ISBN 0 7475 6081 1

10 9 8 7 6 5 4 3 2 1

Typeset by Hewer Text Ltd, Edinburgh
Printed in Great Britain by Clays Limited, St Ives plc

This book is dedicated to
Bridget Cave
and our sons, Sam and Olly

CONTENTS

ACKNOWLEDGEMENTS

I am grateful for the kindness and encouragement of Lady Mary Ashtown, Mrs Josephine Filmer Sankey and Mr and Mrs William Filmer Sankey, who are members of the Cornwallis-West family. Mr and Mrs Roy Rees, Christine Richards Rostworoska, John Koch and Keith Butcher, who are distinguished scholars of the family, have been generous without limit. I should also like to thank Mick Cockerill and Michele Staple of the Stationery Office; and those in Ruthin to whom I talked, particularly the staff of the Record Office and of Ruthin Castle hotel. The archivists and keepers of all the collections I have listed have all been helpful and kind. I would like also to thank Dan Griffiths, the headmaster of Aberfan School, who was extremely understanding and generous and, with the help of his mother and daughter, worked out the words and the translation and found the music of the hymn printed towards the end of the book. And my thanks to the family of Arthur Markham for permission to reproduce his letters of 1916.

Liz Calder and Alexandra Pringle at Bloomsbury said this was a good story, and to that message this book owes its existence. Helen Simpson and Edward Faulkener brought great improvement to the manuscript.

The interpretation of the events and the evidence is my own. No one else should be held responsible.

AUTHOR'S NOTE

Some years ago I had the good fortune to discover an old series of papers and books, called Blue Books, published by the British government. Each was compiled, edited and printed upon an occasion of national significance. The practice of publishing Blue Books began in the 1700s and ended in the 1930s.

There are several reasons for their fascination. The first is that they contain copies of documents passed between governments and government departments during the course of some momentous event, such as a war, civil unrest or an incident which provoked the need for enquiry or perhaps an attempt at civic improvement. The second is that they are entirely of their time, which is to say that they contain nothing of that which we call hindsight. The writers, employees of the government or the crown, or those giving witness to an enquiry, faced with dilemma or outrage, or just a need for simple factual observation, wrote and reported only what they knew and understood. They did not and could not know the lasting outcome or the consequences of the events they were describing, and their judgments were solely those which came naturally to them from their own experience. A reader feels close to the events and shares the anxieties that unfold.

The third attraction is that they are beautifully written. Britain had a quite small civil service in those times, but most of those who rose to positions wherein they were required to write official documents were educated in classical languages. Their sentences and perceptions have precision, discipline and rhythm, to a standard which has become rare. The pleasure of reading these old books induces a tide of envy at the ease and abundant skill in the craft of writing English. It was not only diplomatic officers who were so accomplished: the same generous and gracious language is to be found among many (although not all) of the explorers, generals, admirals, surveyors and other professionals whose work is included in these collections. It is a shame that, lying behind the forbidding cover of official history, they are not more widely read and known, for they are indeed classic and enjoyable.

This preamble's relevance to the story that follows is twofold. Within the great collection of Blue Books compiled during the First World War, which are abundant with revelation, there is a single sheet which says: 'In the matter of Second Lieutenant Patrick Barrett, no more will be said'. The sheet printed with this sentence was headlined 'Army Courts of Enquiry Act 1916' Although the official published parliamentary record contained no more, this statement alone indicated that the matter could not have been a trivial one. Only a search which began at the Public Record Office in London and led to collections, archives, letters and memories in several different countries explained who Second Lieutenant Patrick Barrett was and what more might or might not be said about him.

Secondly, by my immersion in this most profound library of great works, I had become captivated by the idea that history is essentially about what happened to the people who were alive at the time, and that the work of the historian is to help recreate their experience. Most historians will tell you that the role is much more: having recreated the events and identified the actions and motives of the leading figures, the principal duty is to deduce what lessons can be learnt, to distil the significance, and to add to the weight of human understanding. Reading about some occasion in these original papers and then studying a historian's view of the same event, I find in the latter too much interpretation, too much judgment: the distilled product bears little relation to the original. Particularly, it removes the detail of each individual person's excitement or fear. Indeed, often it removes the whole recognisable drama of their lives, and all with which we would identify and sympathise. History, like our own experience, is as much something that happens *to* people as it is something that people *do*. If we are not careful, we elevate the politician to being a creator of history rather than a servant of the people. If only the historian could describe what it felt like, for example, to be in the British embassy in Berlin when war was declared in 1914, or in England when that news came through. Such ability would require first and essentially imagination, because imagination is what a human being needs in order to know what another is thinking.

In the case of Patsy Cornwallis-West many of the documents and letters that recorded her life have been destroyed, for a reason which will be explained later in the story. In relation to Patrick Barrett, however, there is a detailed record of his case which includes records of several important conversations. So in writing this story I have tried to present the reader with the events as they occurred. Wherever I could I have used the documents and records of conversations, exactly as they are to be found in the archive. Sometimes, when those records or moments in the lives of the participants have been lost or the scenes need to be reproduced, I have attempted to recreate them as the evidence suggests they would have been.

There is another aspect to which in these readings I became drawn and it concerns the need to know about a subject's family. Nobody, not even the most famous celebrity, is only a public figure. Notoriety is not enjoyed or endured alone in the face of the press. Everybody has a family. And those who are in such close relationship participate, willingly or not, happily or not, in the experience that becomes public. One cannot understand a person unless one sees how their life and their actions are reflected in the life of their wife, or husband, children and parents. Without understanding the picture of these people, and their own situations, the portrait of the subject is not complete. In the case of Patsy Cornwallis-West, the members of her family were very important to her, and she to them.

Our own experience suggests that that which is written in letters later collected in boxes, cabinets and suitcases, and certainly that which appears in newspaper articles, is rarely the truth in its most intimate and private form. People do not write down the names of their lovers, for their own sake, never mind the embarrassment of their grandchildren. They even sometimes do not faithfully record the names of their children's fathers, or the correct date of a birth, for the most practical reasons; and in more extreme circumstances for the avoidance of humiliation, poverty and danger. So, even if an archive is copious, it needs to be regarded with suspicion. It may not contain many things one should call real truth. The truth needs to be imagined.

This is not a formal biography or a history. It is, however, a true story.

HISTORICAL NOTE

Queen Victoria reigned from 1837 to 1901. She was married to Prince Albert of Saxe-Coburg-Gotha, who died of typhoid in 1861. Edward Albert, her eldest son, the Prince of Wales, sometimes called Bertie, reigned as Edward VII from 1901 to 1910. His wife was Queen Alexandra. Their son George V reigned from 1910 to 1936.

Herbert Asquith was prime minister from 1908 until December 1916. David Lloyd George was prime minister from December 1916 until 1922. Lord Kitchener was secretary of state for war from 1914 until 1916.

Kaiser Wilhelm II of Germany reigned from 1888 until his abdication in 1918. He was a nephew of King Edward VII, being the son of Edward's sister Victoria.

The value of a pound in 1900 was slightly more than sixty times that of a pound in 2000.

Chapter 1

MOTHERS

M ANY PEOPLE ENJOY adultery while deploring it when indulged in by others.

Prince Albert, in public an honourable man and the devoted husband of Queen Victoria, had an affair with Olivia Taylour, daughter of the lord chamberlain. When the Queen found out she was deeply distressed, humiliated and angry. She banished the girl from court, and the matter was hushed up – the records of it are well hidden.

Olivia returned to her family home, Headfort, a fine estate to the north of Dublin. Eventually, at her parents' suggestion, she married the Reverend Frederick Fitzpatrick, rector of Cloone in County Leitrim, a true 'hunting parson'. The young couple had four children, two girls and two boys, who were brought up at Headfort. The third, born in 1858, was baptised Mary, but when very young was nicknamed Patsy; she kept the name for the rest of her life.

After Prince Albert's death from typhoid in 1861, Olivia was able to return to England. The Fitzpatricks bought Warren Hall, which was within the hunt of the Marquis (later the Duke) of Westminster, near Chester racecourse. It was a substantial house, with ample stabling for Frederick's horses, and from there Olivia set out to re-establish her acquaintance with members of the court and the royal family. One friendship soon revived was that with Albert Edward, the Prince of Wales. He had inherited his father's roaming tendencies, and she had a fancy for him. She approved of flirtation and enjoyed it, and so, she knew, did he.

At both Headfort and Warren Hall, the four children – Patsy, her sister, Min, and her two brothers, Jack and Hugo – had a rush-around, delightful childhood, with much happiness and closeness. There was such learning as upper-class Irish parents thought appropriate, plus some riding and sailing in summer, and in winter some skating and tobogganing, Patsy enjoyed this last so much that she commandeered her parents' best silver tea-tray to slide down the staircase.

Britain was then the world's richest and most powerful country, and London and its society were the world's centre. 'The season' meant the circuit of race meetings from Ascot to Newmarket to Doncaster and Chester, yachting at Cowes and dancing at balls in the great houses of the capital. It also meant public appearances by the royal family, and the presentation to them of young debutantes from high-born and wealthy families.

Mrs Fitzpatrick was determined that her daughters should become part of that society. She herself was wild, beautiful, reckless, noble, and a wonderful creator of gardens. If we are supposed to be bound by the horizons of pleasure and experience we set for ourselves, no one told her. She tolerated no restraints. She did what she liked.

All these qualities she passed on to Patsy. Patsy was blue-eyed and as full of life as a swirling breeze on the sea shore. Her fair hair was shot with the red-gold glints of a summer evening's sunset. Thoughout her life men and women alike marvelled at and spoke and wrote of her beauty, her mischievous, gorgeous smile, her slender figure and pretty legs – much to her pleasure and enjoyment. She grew up to become as exciting as any woman in Victorian England.

Patsy Fitzpatrick made her debut in London when she was sixteen. Her grandfather's high office and her mother's friendship with the Prince of Wales, who by now was married (to Princess Alexandra, daughter of King Christian IX of Denmark) and a father (of the future King George V), ensured that she was known and accepted in all the most significant places. She still liked to come down even the grandest stairs on a tea-tray, which caused much amusement. The prince found her charming and irresistible, and he declared her the prettiest and most exotic girl in the whole world. They started a secret affair of the greatest passion.

She was not his first conquest: he had already a taste for actresses and painters' models, which horrified his mother and had terrified his father, particularly because his indiscretions were talked about in public places. (Shortly before his death Prince Albert had berated his son, then a student at Cambridge, for his dalliance with a young woman.) But the Prince of Wales was Patsy's first love, and the relationship between them lasted to the end of his life. Of this matter, there is no longer almost any public record. Even now, the story is told only in private, in hushed conversation, or in quiet asides, without naming names.

When Patsy was seventeen, after a year of dangerous, secret and most exciting romance, the prince suggested that the best plan would be for her to marry. They selected for this purpose a man twice her age, William Cornwallis-West, whom the Queen was about to install as Lord Lieutenant of Denbighshire. By this arrangement the prince and his young mistress hoped that their liaison could continue, away from the prying eyes of the court. William lived at Ruthin Castle in north Wales, not far from Warren Hall and therefore a convenient visiting place. His mother lived in Hampshire, in a house called Newlands, which faces Cowes on the Isle of Wight and which was later to become a rendezvous for the prince and his circle. In addition, the prince helped William acquire a house in Eaton Place, in Belgravia, London.

William Cornwallis-West was amiable, kind and agreeable. He had succeeded his late father as tenant of Ruthin, and was about to take on his father's roles as Lord Lieutenant of the county and colonel of the Regiment of Royal Welch Fusiliers. He also became an MP, and a campaigner for the improvement of state education.

It was the artist in him who fell for Patsy. A mere teenager, she was already sitting for portraits in London by the most fashionable painters: Whistler, Sargent and their friends. She was one of the first to have photographic portraits taken. Her effect on a gathering of artists and writers was that of an expert magician. She was unpredictable, memorable, mysterious and entertaining. She loved to be mad. Everybody fell for her. William became so entranced that he did not care what anyone else thought. That she seemed to want to be with him was enough and more than he could wish.

His mother, however, understood all too readily the character of the proposed arrangement. She recalled Olivia Taylour's outrageous affair with Prince Albert, and saw the same nature in Olivia's daughter. She refused to accept the marriage. She was deeply worried about her son.

Theresa Cornwallis-West was as much a part of the Royal Navy's heritage as a three-masted sailing-ship. From her bedroom window, she looked out over the Solent and Southampton Water. Admiral Sir William Cornwallis had been commander-in-chief in East India waters at the end of the eighteenth century, and had commanded the Channel Fleet in Nelson's day. Although she was not a direct descendant (he had no children), her branch of the family had been entrusted with his house and his memory, and she stood for the values and virtues his name represented. This was reflected in her view of those elected to parliament and even those on the fringes of the royal family: an inferior generation, indolent and timid. She kept the house in shade, reclusive and unchanged, and received only guests whom she found agreeable.

Her late husband, Frederick West, had been a straightforward, unflamboyant landowner. He had acquired land in the area of Ruthin and Chirk in the Clwyd valley, and had bought the stretch between Newlands and the Channel, including the village of Milford-on-Sea. The rents brought Theresa a good income.

She had three daughters; William was her only son. He was trained in law, but was, like his mother, a talented painter. To her dismay he had decided, having completed his legal studies, to pursue his artistic interests in Florence, where he stayed for several years. On his return he gave the impression that he had been free with his affections there, and might even have fathered some children. His escape from any possible resulting commitments came on his father's death, when his mother instructed him to come home and take responsibility for the estates.

He was now in his mid-thirties, and it was certainly time for him to settle down, but Theresa was furious at the suggestion that he should marry the seventeen-year-old daughter of a manipulative Irish troublemaker, however high-born or pretty the girl might be. William was caught between these two strong-willed women. He did his best to ease the animus between them, but without much success. He found it all very difficult and stressful.

William had no idea of the real reason for Patsy's apparent attraction to him. Of course, nobody dared say, or could be completely sure, that this was an arrangement to suit the Prince of Wales, but to Theresa Cornwallis-West, whose instinct to protect her son was aroused, even the possibility of such an arrangement was appalling. She flatly refused to acknowledge the marriage, the girl or her family. She told William that he was a fool and that she wanted nothing to do with child brides.

So a great society wedding took place without the groom's mother. Patsy became Mrs William Cornwallis-West, and not long afterwards fell pregnant.

Perhaps it was the forthcoming birth of her grandchild which softened the elder Mrs Cornwallis-West. Six months after the wedding, she told William that she had reflected and now would arrange a ball for the couple, an acknowledgement of the match. Newlands was dressed for a famous party. The formidable guest list included royalty, great families and officers of both army and navy.

Patsy had no particular interest in Theresa's forebodings; they were a problem for her husband. She had not bothered at all that the gloomy old woman had not come to the wedding; it meant nothing. But a ball was fun, and a welcome distraction from the confining unpleasantness of child-bearing. Besides, Newlands was a very attractive house, which she liked, and to which she felt she could make great improvements. It was true that with a telescope you could see Cowes from the balcony.

She spent much of the evening of her wedding ball flirting with the chargé d'affaires of the Spanish embassy, and when supper was called, at midnight, she was nowhere to be found. Theresa became more and more angry – with William, of course. This was exactly what she had warned him of and she had been correct in her predictions. The atmosphere grew unpleasantly tense. After an age, and with much anxiety in the kitchen, Theresa led the guests in to supper without Patsy. But Patsy was already there, with her Spanish diplomat, laughing and drinking among the desserts. She told Theresa she had been too hungry to wait all that time.

In the morning Theresa told William that, on account of her behaviour, Patsy was no longer welcome at Newlands. He was to come when his presence as heir to the estate required it, but Patsy was banned from Newlands until Theresa died. The two women never spoke to each other again.

William and Patsy divided their time between 49 Eaton Place and Ruthin Castle. By the time she was twenty-one Patsy had three children, Daisy, George and Constance. They were a close family. 'George,' Daisy later wrote in her diary, 'my only brother, is known to the family as Bassie. My sister Constance is Shelagh, father is Poppets and my mother, who has a collection of Irish and English names, is Patsy. It quite shocks our Victorian relatives when we use her name in public. Since she was only seventeen when I was born, and my father was then thirty-nine, we have been more like sisters . . .'

Even today people in Ruthin say how kind Patsy was, and will not have a word said against her, however interesting a topic of conversation she may be. They remember with amusement that she used often to toboggan down the main staircase of the castle.

They also say that the Prince of Wales was a very frequent visitor then. There was a branch railway line from St Asaph into sidings not far from the castle, and it was regularly used by the royal train. When William was away, the servants showed the royal visitor in through their own back entrance to the house, and were rewarded for their silence with gifts. There is a room known as the Prince of Wales room by those who talk. Some even whisper that perhaps one or two or even three of the children were not William's at all, but the prince's. The prince's party more than once included his friend and lawyer, the solicitor George Lewis, who helped with the arrangements for Patsy's care when her son, George, was born.

In London, sweet as a peach and soft as a feather, Patsy dashed from party to party, ball to ball; from races to yachts, from smart house to grand palace. She met and became intimate friends with members of many royal European households when they visited the Prince of Wales. She was the English style: everything she did set a fashion. From a vivacious girl she grew into a charming and famous young woman

In the 1870s it was the custom to ride or stroll in Rotten Row, in London's Hyde Park, and Patsy often took her children there for exercise and to show them off. All three were outstandingly handsome, though not as beautiful as their mother, whom George described as 'the loveliest woman in all four Kingdoms'. (Patsy did not like to think the children might rival her in looks. When she was vexed she accused them of having long noses or misshapen ears.)

One summer's day she heard an officer call out, 'I do wish Mrs Cornwallis-West did not feel a need to paint her face. Sure it is not required.'

Patsy told her maid to call the officer over, offered him her damp handkerchief and her cheek and allowed him to discover that there was no powder or rouge on her face at all. 'It is all my own fair; now perhaps you'll believe I do not paint myself,' she said, and his friends laughed.

The house at 49 Eaton Place was open to artists and Bohemians, who called her a savage beauty and said how exotic she was. Among her closest friends was the actress Lillie Langtry, the celebrated 'Jersey Lily', a neighbour in Eaton Place. Although Lillie was five years the elder, Patsy had been longer in society, and she helped her friend gain the entrée to the highest society. For the season of 1878, Lillie was the sensation. Everywhere, when the fashion was to wear the creations of Monsieur Worth of Paris, Lillie wore the same simple black dress to every ball. It had been made for her by her mother's dressmaker in Jersey.

One evening Lillie and her husband, Ned, were invited to dinner at the Cornwallis-Wests'. The downstairs rooms were hung with Italian paintings bought by William; there were also some of his own, for his talent was quite respectable, and some by Whistler and Millais. There were other guests at dinner, but William's chair was empty, and for his absence Patsy offered no explanation. As the meal progressed the wine bottles emptied, and only then did she say that she regretted that, as she had locked her husband in the wine cellar, because they had had a disagreement, she was unable to have more wine fetched. His punishment was not yet complete.

To the astonishment of the columnists who followed their every outing, Patsy, returning late one evening from the country without a gown for the night's ball, persuaded Lillie to lend her her famous black dress. Having danced the night away in several houses, at dawn she returned the dress; it was in shreds, unwearable. So together they went out to buy more clothes.

Monsieur Worth of Paris – he actually came from Lincolnshire – was the only person to whom the ladies of London and Paris would entrust their couture. He had his favourites. He asked Mrs Langtry and Mrs Cornwallis-West if they would be photographed for the

London shops, in his dresses. He had the revolutionary idea that photographs of beautiful women placed in shop windows might persuade other ladies that they would be equally beautiful if they wore his creations.

Chapter 2

BAD BEHAVIOUR

O N 4 OCTOBER 1879 *Town Talk*, a London newspaper which retailed society gossip under the pretext of moralising, published two articles of particular interest.

The first was about Lillie Langtry, whose husband had previously been rumoured to want to divorce her because she had become the Prince of Wales's mistress.

> I am now informed, on authority which I have no reason to doubt, that Mr Langtry has withdrawn the petition which he had filed in the Divorce Court. The case of Langtry v. Langtry and others is therefore finally disposed of, and we have probably heard the last of it. The 'others' here cited as co-respondents were the Prince of Wales, Lord Londesborough and Lord Lonsdale. It is useless for the sixpenny twaddlers to deny that Mr Langtry ever filed a petition. He did, and, as I have said before, an application was made for Sir James Hannen to hear it privately and he consented. I am told that it is not at all unlikely that Mr Langtry will shortly be appointed to some diplomatic post abroad. It is not stated whether his beautiful consort will accompany him.

The second was about Patsy Cornwallis-West.

It is an undoubted fact that the most aristocratic portion of English society has done more towards making our British classes a byword for scandal and scoffing than all the efforts of demagogues and republicans put together. To think that a lady of exalted position should find it worth her while to be photographed for sale is a disgrace to the upper ten thousand, and I trust that the rumour is true that Her Most Gracious Majesty has issued an express wish that this traffic in the likenesses of photographic beauties shall be discontinued. It certainly does not make foreign countries and critics think much of our Lord Lieutenant of Denbigh that for the sake of gratifying his wife's stupid vanity and realising a few pounds per annum, he allows that lady's photo to be exposed for sale at a price ranging from one penny to two shillings and sixpence. Mr Cornwallis-West is a dignitary who ought certainly to uphold his position as a Lord Lieutenant and he does not do so when he allows Mrs West, the bone of his bone and the flesh of his flesh, to make the public exhibition of herself that is daily seen in our fashionable shop windows. When an official of high rank permits his wife to display her charms side by side with the portraitures of half-naked actresses and entirely naked Zulu women, he can have but little respect for himself, for her or for his position.

Mrs West lives in the neighbourhood of Eaton Square, in the region known as Pimlico. At the back of the house is a yard, and in this yard are four corners, and in each corner is a photographic studio; in addition to this there is a glass house on the roof and fifteen dark rooms on various landings. It is almost impossible to conceive the labour gone through by Mrs West in the course of a day. About seven o'clock she takes her breakfast, and after reading *Town Talk* and the *Denbigh Daily* sent her by Mr W, she proceeds to her extensive wardrobe and attires herself ready for the first photographic artist who happens to call. Jane (that is the name of the lady's maid) has strict orders to state that she is not at home to any one except Fradelle and Marshall or the Stereoscopic Company's young man. When either of these parties arrive they are taken into the front parlour, treated to a glass of something short, and conducted afterwards into one or another of the photographic studios. Sometimes each of all five of these rooms contains an operator at the same time and Mrs West rushes from one to the other in various costumes with a rapidity that is something marvellous. Her changes of costume are so quickly manipulated that any quick-change artist is completely out of the hunt. Now in blue satin, now in red, then in green, and next in white, she seems to be a human feminine chameleon. Sometimes she is taken with a grin, occasionally with a leer; at times with a devotional aspect, and at other times quite the opposite. Having been taken about fifteen times in as many new positions, the photographers are dismissed for a time and Mrs West rests after her laborious exertions, and having partaken of a light luncheon of hard-boiled eggs, dresses herself, and the brougham or victoria, (according to the state of the weather) is brought round to the door, and she drives around the various shops to collect her commission for the previous day. I do not vouch for the truth of the statement, but I am informed that this little commission amounts to thousands yearly, and the joke of the whole things is that these pictures are purchased principally by cads, who show the likeness about to their friends and often times boast that they were given to them by Mrs West herself, and I cannot say that I in any way pity the lady, for she lays herself open to this sort of insult

One of Mrs W's greatest troubles is the fact that she is so outphotoed by Mrs Langtry, and the knowledge that Mrs L has been illustrated by George Purkess in the *Police News* has excited Mrs West to the greatest extent. I have heard that George has been offered an enormous sum by Mrs W to enshrine her likeness amongst his roll of famous men and women, but I am afraid that he has been bribed by the other photographic professional beauty to give her the monopoly of appearing in his charming paper.

Mrs Cornwallis-West has a quantity of pets, all of which are appropriately named after the various articles used in the trade in which she is embarked. For instance, her collie dog is named Collie-odeon, her cat is Iodide of Potassium, whilst the parrot is known as Camera Poll.

The paper went on to describe the spectacle of some half-score of nude men bathing on the Surrey side of Blackfriars Bridge, hobbledehoys of the navvy or 'coster' or barrow-boy class, and several hundred persons – men, women and girls – watching the proceedings with careful interest.

Patsy described the articles to Lillie as 'combative with too much truth'. She proposed that, as both libels were in the same edition, their husbands should sue the newspaper at the same time. 'It's bound to be a judge that one of us knows,' she said. 'God help the editor.' She asked the Prince of Wales to make sure the offending editor was silenced, and he agreed that the matter needed to be concluded. He offered the services of his friend George Lewis.

London's other gossip paper, *Vanity Fair*, could not confine its excitement.

Worthy aldermen and eminent counsel have been in paroxysms of indignation over the wretched creature who has been charged with publishing libels on Mrs Langtry and Mrs Cornwallis-West. All newspaper leaders and public utterances of any kind that refer to the matter will surely reflect this virtuous rage. Mr George Lewis, indeed, the eminent counsel who prosecutes confidently counts upon 'a wave of public indignation' which will 'wash down together these people and their papers!' Such is the public attitude produced by the proceedings against the publishers of the libels; but the private attitude is not quite the same. The case has first of all been received as a delightful excitement of a very unexpected nature, and has been the occasion for a whole series of comments and questions relative to the ladies concerned, and the gentlemen whose names have been mentioned in connection with them: comments and questions of that free nature which Society discusses all the more eagerly in private because they are forbidden in public.

The libels themselves are certainly very unscrupulous and very malicious; but they are concocted of such wonderful rubbish and with such signal ignorance that they carry their falsehood on the face of them. That which relates to Mrs Cornwallis-West is the veriest of libel. It alleges that she has five photographic studios in the 'back-yard' of her house, that she spends part of her day in being photographed, and the rest of it in driving about to the photographers to 'collect' her commissions on the cartes-de-visite and the cabinets that 'have been sold during the previous day'. It is hard to suppose that even the most ignorant reader of *Town Talk* could believe such nonsense as this.

The same may be said of the libel on Mrs Langtry. It consists of a statement repeated several times that Mr Langtry had filed a petition against her in the Divorce Court, and that the Prince of Wales and 'two other gentlemen', afterwards suggested to be Lord Londesborough and Lord Lonsdale, were the two co-respondents. No human being who knows anything of Mr and Mrs Langtry could have believed for a moment that there was any foundation whatever for the allegation that a petition for divorce had been filed at all. No sane person would in any case have associated with any such impossible petition the name either of Lord Lonsdale or of Lord Londesborough, and the notion that the Prince could be suspected of being in a condition to be made a co-respondent in such a case is even still more ludicrous.

It might therefore have been the more dignified course to take no notice of these rubbishing productions. But, however that may be, the case brings out in a very forcible manner the disgrace to which private ladies expose themselves when they accept the position of public women. For a very long time past, not merely the two charming ladies who have been thus libelled, but many others, have been publicly paraded as exceptionally beautiful persons. Their photographs, presumably not without their own consent or allowance, have been in every shop window throughout the kingdom, with their names attached thereto; and their comings and goings have been recorded with a fidelity which shows the interest they have excited. This, which it may be supposed was the pleasant side of the picture, they have, so far as is known, accepted with resignation, if not with satisfaction. But the ball of publicity, once set rolling, goes into strange places. Not merely Society, but the outside rascal, lays hold of it, and makes his rascally comments upon it. It is inevitable that it should be so – so inevitable that it has become a commonplace to say that public men must not be too thin-skinned. Neither, some will now certainly say, must public women. It is inevitable that coarse and silly comments should be made upon them by coarse and silly persons who find them submitted to public criticism. And it is also inevitable that when ladies are concerned these comments should be far more displeasing than any that can be made upon a man. Except in the case of very few women, personal charms and personal virtue are all that a woman has to submit to criticism. You cannot deal with her political opinions or dispute her scientific conclusions. You cannot criticise her theological views, discuss her style, or attack her consistency on the Eastern Question. She brings into the public arena beauty and virtue. When you have said she is beautiful and virtuous, there is an end of the matter.

William Cornwallis-West was most certainly indignant on his wife's behalf, and, indeed, on his own. He decided to confront Mr Oscar Rosenberg, *Town Talk*'s editor and proprietor, and set off for the paper's offices in Museum Street. On the way there he saw a policeman, and asked him to accompany him. On arrival at *Town Talk*, William demanded that Mr Rosenberg state the truth about his wife's daily habits, and about the divorce of their acquaintances Mr and Mrs Langtry, in front of the policeman.

Mr Rosenberg could not do so, as he could name no source of his information for either story. He became anxious. He had apparently considered that any matter might at worst be the subject of a civil proceeding, but now he was faced with charges of criminal libel, for which the police officer immediately arrested him and took him away.

The case was heard in a crowded court, packed with people trying to glimpse the two women. After only a few minutes' deliberation, the jury found Mr Rosenberg guilty of all the charges.

The judge, Mr Justice Hawkins, gave forthright expression to his views. 'You published these atrocious libels in a scandalous and mendacious production. I shall not insult the respectable press of this country by styling it a newspaper. They were published by you with the professed intention of suppressing vice and immorality. The real intention was to pander to the depraved tastes of those who could be found weak and debased enough to buy your publication. In the first instance you implied a case of adultery committed by persons of the highest standing. In the other you sought to hold Mrs Cornwallis-West up to ridicule and scorn in a way which no man has a right to do, entirely for the purpose of your own financial gain.

'The effect of my judgments shall be that you shall be sent to jail for two years under a regime of hard labour. Your publication shall pay all the costs of the cases involved. We shall hope not to hear from it again.'

A ball at Grosvenor House coincided with the ending of the trial. Patsy, in mischievous mood, tipped a spoonful of ice-cream down the back of the Prince of Wales's neck. Always very formal in public, he became angry. Thinking that Mrs Langtry, with whom he had been dancing, was responsible, he left in haste and great anger, and did not speak to her for several days. Neither of the women dared raise the subject with him in order to explain who was really to blame.

A few months later Mrs Langtry found that she was pregnant. Patsy shared her distress. They were unsure which of three men, including the Prince of Wales but not including her husband, was to be the father. Patsy advised Lillie to approach and implicate only the Prince of Wales, because he would make sure Lillie was looked after, as he had done when Patsy's son, George, was born. 'You will find Mr George Lewis, the solicitor, will come and visit.'

That is indeed what happened. Lewis arrived and, in the most charming way possible, made all necessary and comforting arrangements. Mrs Langtry was moved first to Jersey, to her mother and away from her husband, and then to Paris, for her confinement. Mr Langtry was given a diplomatic post abroad, just as Oscar Rosenberg, now a prisoner, had predicted, and did not discover until many years later that his wife had had a child. Such was the power of a royal prince and his ladies.

Some seasons after this, in 1882, Patsy featured again in *Vanity Fair*. Lord Rossmore told the paper's reporter:

I think the loveliest woman I have ever set eyes on was Mrs Cornwallis-West. The first time I saw her was at Ascot, when I was on a coach belonging to the regiment of the First Life Guards. Suddenly, my attention was arrested by the appearance of a lady who was walking in my direction and who was accompanied by half a dozen men.

I thought her the most beautiful creature imaginable and

dressed in white and wearing a big white hat, she was perfectly delightful to look at, and I cried out immediately, greatly to the amusement of my brother officers, 'Good Heavens! Who's that?' A chorus of remarks instantly arose: 'Why, it's Mrs Cornwallis-West'; 'nobody her equal'; 'beats Lillie Langtry hollow'; and then, in unison, 'surely you know Mrs West?'

'No,' I replied, still all eyes for the lady, 'but it won't be my fault if I do not know her very soon.'

The Prince of Wales gave a ball that night to which our party was invited, and greatly to my delight I saw Mrs West there. I simply could not take my eyes off her. She was talking to Mrs Dartoris with whom I was acquainted, so I went up to her boldly. 'Will you introduce me?'

'Hmm,' replied Mrs Dartoris, 'I do not know whether Mrs West wants to know you.'

'Never mind, I'll introduce myself.' So I turned to Mrs West and said with true Derry daring. 'Come on, let's have a dance.'

'Well and I will, yer honour,' she replied with the most tremendous brogue.

Off we went. I was in the seventh heaven, but I noticed that the floor seemed strangely empty. However, I was too happy to trouble about any reasons why other people were not dancing until I bumped into no less a personage than the Princess of Wales. Then the truth dawned on me. Her Royal Highness was dancing, which accounted for the empty floor.

The entirely irresponsible unconventionality of Mrs Cornwallis-West's attitude in such an informal introduction was quite characteristic of her. She was always bright, breezy and buoyant; a famous beauty, even in her girlhood, and full of Irish sparkle.

Lord Rossmore openly adored her, and this made William so angry that he forbade Patsy to see Rossmore. Once, she went to a ball and found that Rossmore was there, and she had to leave, quite flustered, so that William would not find out. Nor was Rossmore the only one: wherever Patsy went, men fell in love with her.

Chapter 3

CHILDREN AND MARRIAGES

AFTER THERESA CORNWALLIS-WEST died William's sister arranged for a large plaque to be carved and placed on the wall of All Saints' Church at Milford-on-Sea.

. . . as a tribute of affection to a Mother, whose high principles and religious spirit enabled her to bear severe trials and sufferings with courage and resignation; although so clever and accomplished as an authoress, musician, poetess and painter, she was ingenuous and trustful . . .

William and Patsy were now able to make Newlands their third home. Patsy had redecorated at both Ruthin and Eaton Place, to make the houses brighter and more cheerful, and she created large and wonderful gardens. At Ruthin, on the old battlements of the castle, she had made formal flowerbeds looking over the moat and the deep valley outside the walls. At Newlands she had the gardens re-landscaped to make more of the lake and the glades and woods beyond it, and she surrounded the house with exquisite rose gardens. The children loved both houses in the country. To live in either was an adventure.

Daisy later confided to her diary that no one could have wished for a happier childhood. 'When I was eighteen,' she wrote, 'and to be married to a German Prince, and become Princess Daisy, we all went to Ruthin to collect some clothes I wanted packed into my luggage. I was in the playroom, which is a dark room that faces the castle wall and my father came to see me. It had been a requirement of protocol of the family of my husband-to-be, the ancient House of Pless, that I could prove that all sixteen of my great-grandparents were of Royal descent. Poppets [the family's nickname for William] had had made a huge painted chart of the families to show that this was true. He had been working on it for weeks, and although the German demand had irritated him he was proud and enjoyed telling us about the details it contained.

'He said, rather formally, to start, that he was certain the house would miss me when I had gone away. I knew that he did not mean the people who were there; he meant the funny old building which was such a lovely home when we were small. He was crying, dear Poppets, and he had chosen this dark room to talk to me, so that I would not see his tears. He told me about when he first met Patsy and how they had married. He told me some rather secret things that he wanted to share at that moment.

'He had previously been in Italy for several years. In Florence, and Perugia and Siena. He told me, and I never knew before, that he was born in Florence. He said that he had had many very close friends when he was there as a young man. He had studied painting and sculpture, at which he is very talented, but has always been unable to devote the time that was needed to exploit his skill (probably because of the time he had given to us). Among his friends, he said, were a number of Italian girls whom he might even have married, but did not. My response to that was that I felt that travelling sounded rather exciting.

'His mother, Granny Theresa, at Newlands, whom I hardly ever met, wanted him to return home to England to manage the estate, so he came back.

'At Windsor, in a royal party, when he had come to court in order, eventually, to be made the new Lord Lieutenant, he saw a young girl. She had striking and beautiful hair. He said that he could not believe his eyes – she was so fresh, with such light in her face. Every day since that one, he has readily been able to recollect the moment. It changed his life. And when she talked to him, he said, it was like a shower of gifts. She was only sixteen, but on the instant he asked her to marry him. He said he thought he might only ever have one chance – that by the next day someone else might have asked her – so instantly he offered her his whole life, without a moment's reflection. He said he was so excited he might have sung; which made us both laugh. I am quite talented at singing, but he is not.

' "Your mother is disgracefully wicked. She loves to be. She and her mother, Granny Olivia, were both wild, Irish and uncontrollable. They had a reputation, even with the Queen, who expelled Olivia Taylour from court for flirting with Prince Albert. Their lives have been the pursuit of revolution. And clothes: who could believe the schemes Patsy has invented to get herself, and now you and Shelagh, the most beautiful dresses in London?

' "I have always adored Patsy completely," he said, "and she has made Newlands such a wonderfully happy and beautiful home. It is hard to believe that the house with the beautiful gardens that she has made looking over the sea and Cowes and the Isle of Wight, is the same gloomy place that Granny brooded over so darkly." '

Daisy spoke of how hard that must have been for him, to have had difficult relations with his mother. He said she had not been the same kind of mother as Patsy at all, and that this was not a time to create philosophies about marriage. Especially now when all he wanted Daisy to know was how much Patsy had meant to him; and how much he would miss Daisy when she was in Germany. They shed tears together; then Daisy collected some of her favourite dolls.

George later wrote of the occasion when the Prince of Wales announced his arrival for Cowes Week in a telegram addressed to 'The Queen of Ireland, Hampshire', which was, of course, delivered to Patsy. 'I shall be attending the Wild West Show', the telegram declared.

He also recalled being sent to Newlands to visit Granny Theresa, the lady whom his sisters were hardly ever allowed to meet, and about whom they were so curious and sought detailed reports. There is a lake, at the front of the house, with good fishing. I asked if I would be permitted to try with a fly, and she had me tied to a tree to avoid drowning. Though young, George was already experienced with a fishing-rod, so there was no need for such caution, which astonished Patsy and his sisters when he told them about it.

The two girls were educated at home. They were both well-read and talented. Shelagh became an expert horsewoman. Daisy was musical. Her singing was of a high standard, and she later often entertained royalty.

George, it was decided, should be prepared for the diplomatic service and was sent to Eton. The Prince of Wales took a great interest in his well-being, and it was to the prince that George protested he would far rather become an engine-driver, an option which seemed not to have been considered. The prince was a good friend to the boy. There were always notes and gifts and summonses to George, often to go fishing and, later, deer-stalking.

At Eton George was good at games; not so much at cricket, but quite fair at shooting He learnt the advantage of a football bladder in his jacket, to cushion the recoil of a rifle-shot, but, when describing this to Patsy, and to please her with his honesty, he assured her he did not use this tactic for school matches. Fishing became his favourite pastime, and later he wrote a book about the pleasures it brought him. (His other book about himself was also mostly devoted to sport and outdoor activities.)

Patsy loved all her children, but George was especially important to her, and she devoted great care to choosing places to take him and amusements they could share. One summer, in the school holidays, Patsy took George to the aquarium at Westminster. The aquarium itself George described as a feeble affair – a few pike and some odd perch in a tank – but the other attractions offered splendid fun. Here one could see Zaza shot out of a cannon twice a day. This was a risky business, as the lady found to her cost one day when she was badly injured landing on the wall. Here also one could see a gentleman in red tights dive from the roof into a tank in which there was about a couple of feet of water. Alas, he, too, tempted fortune once too often.

The aquarium boasted several sideshows, two of which were particularly memorable. The first was Doctor Kennedy, a mesmerist. He took three men from the audience, sat them on the front of the stage, and told them they were fishing. To one he said, 'You are having a wonderful day's sport,' and to the others he said they would catch nothing. The first man made all the motions of hauling in and throwing out again, with a 'completely satisfied angler' look on his face; and the other two became more and more mournful, as they caught nothing. Then Kennedy took another man, poured out a tumbler of oil, and told him it was a glass of beer. The wretched man drank it off and apparently thoroughly enjoyed it. One of the 'halfwits', as George called them when he described the day to his sisters, was told that he was to serenade his sweetheart. This man had no voice at all, but embarked upon a ridiculous, though harmless, love-song, and with a vacant stare descended from the stage, walked towards Patsy and serenaded her, which embarrassed George a great deal.

These wretched people were supposed to be taken from the audience, but the same ones turned up time after time. If they were dull to start with, by the time Kennedy had finished, they were, said George censoriously, 'entirely brainless'.

The outing continued with a visit to Succi, the Fasting Man. The placard announced that he had backed himself to starve for forty days, so Patsy and George paid an extra sixpence to see him, sitting in the front row. There in front of them on a raised platform was an emaciated creature who looked down upon his patient audience. George brought out of a bag two large iced buns he had purchased for their lunch, and he and his mother proceeded to eat them. Such a look of yearning appeared on the haggard face of the Fasting Man, that it was never to be forgotten, and had to be described in minute detail to Daisy and Shelagh. Shelagh said it served Succi right for making a fool of himself.

During a later school holiday, spent mainly at Ruthin, Patsy enabled George to fulfil his old ambition to be an engine-driver. She took him to the slate quarry at Dinorwic on the Menai Strait, and he was taught how to drive a locomotive. The quarry and the port were about seven miles apart and were connected by a railway used for handling the slates. There were large locomotives for the main line and small, almost toylike, ones for the quarry tramlines. George was ecstatic; this experience unexpectedly proved to be of great benefit to him, in later life.

One reason mother and son were so close was that George had inherited Patsy's mischievous streak. At the end of his last year at Eton, he and a close friend, Edward Grey, hatched a plot to embarrass a master they disliked, the Reverend H. 'Hoppy' Daman. They wrote to a weekly sporting newspaper:

> Dear Sir
>
> I observed this spring that a pair of partridges had nested in my orchard, where I keep a cow for the benefit of my nursery. It was a source of intense gratification to me when the old hen partridge hatched out a dozen or more fluffy little fellows. To my horror and amazement one day, shortly after this happened, I saw the cow proceed to devour the whole brood. Can any of your readers inform me whether they have a similar experience of a cow eating partridges?
>
> Yours truly,
> H. Daman
> Eton College

The paper published the letter, and the following week – and indeed for several weeks afterwards – correspondents wrote to the editor, some to the effect that a cow eating partridges was not at all an unusual occurrence, others insinuating that the Rev. Daman's imagination was, to put it mildly, of the meandering kind.

But 'Hoppy' Daman scored in the end, for he wrote to the paper himself.

Dear Sir

My attention has been called to a letter which appeared in your columns some weeks ago written by, I imagine, some foolish pupils of mine. Let me tell you that I have neither nursery nor orchard and that I do not keep a cow.

Yours etc.,

As far as the three children were concerned, life was idyllic. For their father, though, financial problems were looming.

In the 1890s William came up with a plan for developing the estate along the coast at Milford-on-Sea into a collection of spacious villas. Sadly, this adventurous approach to land management proved very costly. He had the intention of creating perhaps a new East-bourne, but it was more in keeping with his generous nature to give plots of land away than to sell them for a proper value.

He brought Richard Birch, whose father had been Frederick West's land agent in Ruthin, down to Hampshire to manage the estate. However, Mr Birch found himself spending more time dealing with problems of the family's overdraft than with buildings along the sea front.

There were several drains upon the family resources. First, the land in north Wales declined in value, and therefore in the income it produced. Second, the project at Milford was, of course, a long-term investment, and consequently a draw on available cash. Thirdly, George, once he left school and joined the army, demon-strated a capacity for spending which astonished everybody, parti-cularly the manager of the bank.

Patsy, now in her mid-thirties and full of enterprise, resolved that the way forward was to marry her two beautiful daughters to the richest men she could find.

For Daisy she selected Prince Hans Heinrich of Pless, heir to the Fürst von Pless, whose family owned enormous estates – Schloss Fürstenstein had no fewer than six hundred rooms – in Silesia in south-eastern Germany. Daisy preferred another man, an English army officer who had no money but who was attractive, and, she thought, in love with her. Unfortunately he was also Patsy's lover of the moment, and in any case Patsy was set on the match with the Prince of Pless. So Patsy arranged through her contacts in the War Office that the soldier should be sent off to South Africa, to the Zulu Wars; sadly, he was killed a few months later.

The eighteen-year-old Daisy bowed to her mother's will, and her marriage to Prince Hans Heinrich duly took place, in the presence of the Prince of Wales, at St Margaret's, Westminster.

It was agonising for William to contemplate his beloved daughter moving so far from home, but Patsy assured him that they would spend as much time in Silesia as at Ruthin. The Pless estates would be as good for shooting as any in England or Scotland. She also pointed out that Daisy would be at the heart of the highest circles in Europe – and therefore in the world.

Hans Heinrich's father, the Fürst von Pless, was one of the most important men in Germany and very close to the Kaiser. The Kaiser, who was a nephew of the Prince of Wales, therefore took a close interest in the young bride. Despite the dislike and rivalry between uncle and nephew, Daisy Cornwallis-West, now Princess Daisy of Pless, always remained for both a treasured child.

In fact, the marriage was a devastating experience for the girl. Although she was at home in the highest circles of British society, and was throughly accustomed to the court's strict etiquette, nothing had prepared her for the iron-rigid and all-pervasive protocol of a great German princely house. She could not so much as open a door for herself, and in none of her new homes could she ever relax and be informal as she had at Ruthin or

Newlands. Nor was she permitted privacy: a maid, a footman, the major-domo or one of the army of other servants was constantly at hand.

Patsy was her daughter's help and co-conspirator. It was Patsy who made a home and a life out of the impenetrable formality. Her charm and fascination induced men and women, from whatever country, to do anything for her, and she was determined to make sure Daisy was happy.

She invited the Kaiser to Newlands. She felt it would help things along, not only for Daisy but for England and Germany, too. Under her influence he unbent enough to plant a tree in her new avenue, and she wrote to Daisy that 'he was perfectly charming and kissed my hand twice, quite hard. Do you know he sits all his days surrounded by people who only tell him good things about himself. Each day they bring him a newspaper printed with Gold ink that has been prepared especially for him containing only stories that will please him, nothing that would upset. His great trouble is whether or not you and Hans will put bathrooms in Pless and not give him the horrible dreary suite of rooms again which always gives him the blues! I said, "Well, Sire, you go to Fürstenstein, you won't get the blues there and you'll find plenty of baths. Daisy is doing up all Promnitz [Castle] and Hans is putting in baths there." He seemed to be enjoying his rest so much, poor man, the first he has had for twenty years. He said that his uncle, the Prince of Wales, had often told him what a charming place is Newlands; but the reality greatly exceeded what the Prince had led him to expect.'

The Kaiser soon learnt to confide in Daisy. She was less obsequious than those close to him and like her mother she spoke her thoughts, something which most – almost all – others dared not do. She was sensitive to the anxious political times and had contacts and friends in the highest and most influential groups, which she used energetically. The Prince of Wales and the Kaiser disliked each other, and Daisy recognised that this alone could lead to much misunderstanding between the two countries. The Kaiser told her

CORK CITY LIBRARY

he could not understand why there was such hatred of him in England. She wrote to him that 'Emperors and Kings scarcely hear the truth, as those who surround them say nothing except to repeat back what their master has said. The fact is that the English are too conceited and the Germans are too touchy.' She offered to carry private messages between the two men, and did all she could to mitigate their mutual hostility.

Daisy's diary gives some vivid glimpses of the life led by a German princess. There was a fancy-dress ball at Schloss Fürstenstein. Patsy and Shelagh came to Germany for the occasion, and they and Princess Daisy wore jewels given to Daisy by the Maharaja of Cooch Behar. The Maharaja wore traditional Indian dress in blue and gold, with a turban and diamonds, and he entertained the company by playing the piano. Grand Duke Michael of Russia wore a Japanese coat with a turban and long sword. The Count of Turin dressed as a Neapolitan fisherman, in a pair of white leather breeches (borrowed from the stables) and a loose red silk blouse, with some red pompoms of Daisy's hanging at the end of it. Patsy wore a black hat, a red velvet bodice, a white satin skirt with exquisite old lace on it and pink roses. Daisy wore blue satin with Indian gold embroidery and a high Medici lace collar, with a little pink velvet cap with feathers. The guests of honour were Mr and Mrs Townsend, the American ambassador in Vienna and his wife.

Having got Daisy suitably married and established in European society, Patsy looked around for a husband for Shelagh. Her eye fell on Hugh Grosvenor, Duke of Westminster, a childhood friend of Shelagh, whom everyone knew as Bend Or. Though a dukedom could not compare to a princedom, he would certainly do: the Grosvenor family were – and are still – the richest landowners in England. Like her sister, Shelagh duly married the man her mother favoured. Patsy was delighted.

However, she was anything but delighted when George fell in love, for his intended was a woman of Patsy's own age and social circle, Jennie Churchill. She was an American who had become one of what George called 'the Edwardians', the Prince of Wales's intimate friends. She became the wife of Lord Randolph Churchill, but both before and after her marriage she was very close to the prince. While Randolph was away fighting an election before the wedding, Jennie had been making hay with the prince and his friends in London and Paris. The wedding had been rushed, and had had only the reluctant approval of Randolph's father, the Duke of Marlborough. Jennie's first son, Winston, was born six months later.

Winston's parentage has never been questioned, but Patsy, when she was being hard about Jennie, whom she disliked and saw as one of many who manipulated the prince's affections, said the question to answer was 'Where was George Lewis, the prince's helping hand, at the time Jennie gave birth? Perhaps he was the prince's child?' George Lewis did, in fact, later become Winston's private solicitor and held the position for many years. It was widely known that Jennie's second son, Jack, was not Randolph's child.

Lord Randolph Churchill had had a topsy-turvy political career. He was secretary of state for India in 1885–6, and was then made chancellor and leader of the House of Commons, which offices he abruptly resigned in December 1886, to the surprise of everyone, including the Queen. He suffered for some years from syphilis, which he certainly did not contract from his wife, and in 1895 he died of 'general paralysis'.

His death opened the way for George to marry Jennie, and he pursued her ardently. Jennie's motives for marrying a man so much younger than herself are unclear. Perhaps she was jealous of Patsy's intimacy with the Prince of Wales, and thought this was a way of hurting her. She certainly thought George had a great deal of money, which was the unfortunate impression created by his behaviour. He recognised, when it was pointed out to him by a business acquaintance, that he had much more aptitude for disposing of money than for gaining it. When George was in his twenties, William had had to raise mortgages to cover his son's debts from racing and other gentlemanly activities. Jennie Church-ill, indeed, was an even more talented and fluent spender.

Everyone tried to persuade the couple that they were not a good match. The age difference was more than twenty years, and Jennie's two sons were George's age. She enjoyed life in the highest intellectual and political society. George preferred to spend a quiet day horse racing or stalking deer in the Highlands. In addition, Jennie had had several other well-known affairs while she was married to Randolph. All these aspects made them an unlikely couple. Besides, when William died they would inherit the whole of his estate, even if Patsy were still alive. It might mean not only that Patsy would lose her beautiful homes but also that she would have nowhere at all to live. George would never have thought about that, but William and Patsy did, and Jennie Churchill might.

All the parties concerned were aware that the Prince of Wales did not approve of the match at all. Encouraged by the prince, who hoped distance and activity might prove a distraction from Jennie, George went off with his regiment, the Scots Guards, to South Africa to fight in the Boer War. They sailed aboard the *Nubia*, a small P & O liner taken over by the army. The men practised their rifle fire on the flying-fish that followed the ship, and the officers enjoyed drinking their way through twenty cases of Perrier Jouet 1887, presented to the Guards by Alfred Rothschild.

There was no distraction, though, for Jennie followed. She hired a ship, the *Maine*, and sailed to Cape Town, where the ship was to serve as a hospital for injured soldiers. She would be near George, and also near her sons: Winston was reporting on the war for the *Morning Post*, and Jack, for whom his brother had obtained a commission in the South African Light Horse, accompanied her.

George thought the men they were fighting were a splendid type, whose sole idea was to protect their country from invasion. They knew little of the political intrigues, or the gold mines around Johannesburg, or the businessmen who controlled them. Their war was a just cause, and he wondered whether the British could say the same.

His role, arranged by the Prince of Wales to keep him from getting too close to the action, was to carry messages for the staff of General Lord Methuen. One day, as he was riding across the railway he saw what looked like a large grey molehill. Approaching cautiously, he found it was the stomach of Mr Bennett Stamford, special correspondent of the *Daily Telegraph*, who was lying asleep on his back after lunch. George warned him he was only partially under cover.

The dangers of the war were sometimes unpredictable. George's childhood visit to Dinorwic unexpectedly enabled him to come to the rescue when, on a train travelling north to the Modder river, towards Ladysmith, the passengers were told that the driver, evidently a Boer sympathiser, had got off and disappeared into the veldt. No one else, not even the stoker, knew how to drive an engine, so George volunteered.

He wrote to Patsy that 'The Engineer officer reluctantly took me at my word, though I'm sure he felt very nervous. Difficulty lay in front of us. To my horror, at the first station I found there was no water to fill our tank, in which there was precious little left. I realised however that there were a lot of trains behind us and if we did not make it to the Modder River crossing we should block the whole of the main line to the Front and it would be difficult to get supplies to the troops. The question was whether we had sufficient water to get to the highest point; for after that it would be plain sailing, or rolling, at least.

'I decided to risk it, but to my great consternation, at Honeynest Kloof, the guard at the back of the train, not realising our predicament, applied the brakes in order to drop out a detachment of troops there, which he could perfectly well have done without stopping the train. Matters looked serious; there was not a drop of water in the tank and very little showing on the boiler gauge. My stoker was a splendid fellow. I told him the position and all he said was, 'I'm game, sir. We can only be blown up once!' Eventually we managed to crawl to the top of the hill, and no furnace was ever raked out quicker by the driver and stoker than the furnace of that locomotive.

'We have also just received news that Winston, who had been taken captive by the Boers, has returned to Methuen's encampment. He must have escaped somehow. I'm sure he will have managed to get word to Lady Churchill. I have also written to her and asked that she pass a message back to you that I am safe.'

George was safe but he was not well and suffered from sunstroke and was sent home.

Patsy and William were profoundly relieved to hear from him. There had been a story in one London newspaper that the *Nubia* had foundered and sunk in the Bay of Biscay. William had stormed into their office for news. There was no way that a newspaper could get a story like that before the days of a Marconi wireless. Such writing was an extremely irresponsible pursuit of a headline and sales. The editor was very apologetic and blamed the source of the information, which he seemed unclear about. William had dealt with newspapermen before, but he was more concerned with establishing that George's ship had in fact not sunk.

When they all got back to England views had polarised about George and Jennie's romance. The couple had decided that they should get married, and absolutely everyone else had decided that they should not. There could hardly have been a more distinguished list of advocates: the Prince of Wales and his most influential circle, George's regiment, Winston and Jack Churchill, the Duke and Duchess of Westminster, the Prince and Princess of Pless, and Colonel and Mrs Cornwallis-West all urged George not to marry Jennie – Patsy said vehemently that he was being utterly foolish. But George and Jennie did get married; nobody went to the wedding.

George tried to make an alliance with Winston. Shortly after the wedding, he wrote to him:

My dear Winston,

I cannot impress upon you how much I appreciate the line you have taken as regards my marriage to your mother. I have always liked and admired you, but I do so ten times more now. I only wish, as I wrote and told my father, that my family could have taken a leaf out of your book. Nothing could have exceeded the sympathy and kindness which you and all the Churchills have shown me. I hope always, as now, to be a real true friend to you and never to come between yourself and your mother. If ever I do, which God forbid, you can always refer me to this letter which is a record of the feelings I have in the bottom of my heart towards you and yours. We arrive tomorrow at 2.15. Will you order lunch for three, unless you have another coming? *A demain*, my dear friend.

Chapter 4

GEORGE

I N 1901 QUEEN Victoria died and Prince Albert Edward
became King Edward VII. The step from being heir to
ascending the throne brought a tremendous change in responsibility. Friendships now had to be treated much more cir-
cumspectly.

Patsy was no longer able to see him so easily. He was not young
and his time was occupied with matters of state. His immediate
entourage was a closed and protective circle and he had, as always,
several ladies in attendance (Patsy was acquainted and friendly with
Alice Keppel, who was his mistress in these years). He was occupied
with many international matters.

For her part, Patsy was concerned with her grandchildren and, in
particular, with George's squandering of the family resources.
When he approached the manager of a large London bank for a
loan to purchase some promising shares, the manager is recorded as
saying, 'My dear sir, you have made a mistake. We want your
money. We do not want to lend you ours!' It was perhaps George's
presence at the racecourses which gave rise to such remarks, and it is
true that he more than once tried to resolve a financial crisis by a
well-placed bet during a sunny afternoon at Epsom.

After some time and various unsuccessful attempts to improve his
financial position, George sought further income and made a
partnership with a Mr Wheater to buy and sell shares. Wheater,

Cornwallis-West and Co had a number of investments, which caused George to realise eventually that Wheater was even more of a born gambler than he was.

There was a copper mine near Córdoba in Spain which, though pleasant to visit, was also dangerous, as parts of it were prone to collapse. George's notes record that the mine would have done better if there had been more copper left when they bought it.

However that was not quite what he said to Winston, who had forwarded to George a cheque from the Duke of Westminster, intended to rescue George yet again from creditors:

19 February '07

My dear Winston,

Many thanks for your letter with cheque enclosed. I am sorry not to have acknowledged it before, but I only received it yesterday as it followed me about to several places. As I told you before, I have no hesitation in saying that I believe most certainly the mine is good as ever it was and better. The returns are improving every fortnight and I sincerely trust that we shall all get our money back.

Yours ever,

George

There were other equally ambitious, and equally unsuccessful, projects. One was pearl cultivation in Australia. Unfortunately, the man who claimed to have invented the technique died before the experiments were completed, and when the envelope that should have contained the secret details of his method was opened the contents were incomprehensible.

Another was the development of an automatic rifle proposed by an Australian named Ashton. George was a proficient rifleman, and not only made some changes to the gun but also paid for a new, more successful model to be built; it was completed in 1907 and named the West-Ashton rifle. But when George offered it to the

War Office Small Arms Committee, they turned it down, on the grounds that 'an automatic rifle would encourage the waste of ammunition by the soldier, rendering impossible the supply of ammunition to an army in the field carrying automatic weapons'. George was so disgusted that he did not keep the master patents, and his method was later applied very successfully – and without payment – in the Lewis gun.

Jennie's schemes were on a far grander scale and were concerned with entertainment. In summer 1911 she hired Earls Court for a pageant, lasting several months, to raise money for a new National Theatre. The attractions included an exhibition called 'Shakespeare's England', designed by the architect Sir Edward Lutyens, which included Tudor houses, the Globe Theatre, and a Mermaid Tavern run as a club for the intelligentsia and idle rich. For the closing ball, Lutyens created a medieval castle for a tournament, the contestants wearing fine armour, correctly emblazoned, and carrying papier-mâché lances.

The cost was immense and many investors lost a great deal. George and Jennie themselves spent nearly £35,000 of borrowed funds. Estimates of paying visitors, which had been used to persuade investors and lenders of the project's viability, proved sadly wrong, but no friends were lost.

In the autumn of that year, the King brought a party of friends to north Wales and stayed at Eaton, the country seat of the Duke and Duchess of Westminster. One day he said to George, 'How's your driving, George?' On being assured of George's competence, he proposed a visit to Granny Olivia, whose house was not far away. To the concern of all those whose job it was to organise the King's entertainment, off they went. The passengers were Patsy, Daisy, Alice Keppel and King Edward, and George drove.

Granny Olivia, now in her eighties, was not best pleased. She had been out walking and her hair was blown about; she had no entertainment or refreshments prepared; and the whole thing was an unwelcome surprise. Eventually, though, she softened and sat and talked with the King about the days when they were both young and at court. He reminded her of how she used to carry on with his father, which made old Queen Victoria 'go sharp', as he said.

'He liked to be flirted with – well, who does not?' she retorted. 'You certainly do.'

'Well, both of us,' answered the King, 'would hardly qualify as people who did not enjoy good company.'

They looked at old photographs taken at Warren Hall when Patsy was a girl and was already a burst of sunshine wherever she went. They talked all afternoon. When the royal party returned to Eaton, his advisers were astonished that he could have been amused for so long. Both Daisy and George remembered that day all their lives. It was as if the King had gathered together the people whom, his family apart, he loved most in all his life.

Daisy later said it was on that day she realised that Granny Olivia had been like a big sister to him when he was young, encouraging him and rebuking him. His affection for her had turned into his closeness to and obsession with Patsy. In the early years he had pursued Patsy around the country, to hideout after hideout. Theirs had been the maddest, the most wicked, sinful, intimate love, and had lasted many years. Such jealousies as might later have angered either of them were overcome by a deep affection.

A long time afterwards, a society newspaper wrote, and spread the story, that Princess Daisy of Pless was the only woman of whom his wife, Queen Alexandra, was ever truly jealous, but Daisy said that was ridiculous and that the Queen was a good friend who had helped in troubled times. The story embarrassed her, though, because it was nearly true: the writer had almost – but not quite – understood the relationships. It was Patsy of whom Queen Alexandra had sometimes been jealous, for the King's intimacy with her was of a kind which exceeded and excluded all others.

The day at Granny Olivia's was a good day, but it was the King's last visit to north Wales. On 6 May 1910 he died, of a surfeit of too many enjoyable things. That was a sad time; his funeral was a great gathering of kind friends, and many reminiscences, like the last movement of a grand symphony.

Daisy was in Germany, and William wrote to her, 'Patsy is very quiet and hurt. She will miss him. And I know that so will you.'

Chapter 5

WAR

OR MANY YEARS there were Germans who believed that
King Edward VII wanted the First World War. They said
that the British army was secretly prepared for winning it
and that the foreign secretary, Sir Edward Grey, artfully chose the
moment for it to begin. In order to screen this planning, Winston
Churchill, and others, made long and frequent protestations of
Anglo-German friendship.

Daisy's view was that 'King Edward, being brought up in sternly
realistic England, had no inferiority complexes. The place of
England and the British Empire was assured and unassailable;
the King knew that without the slightest effort or insistence on
his part he was the most important personage in any assembly to
which he might choose to go. He needed neither crowns nor
clanking swords nor Horse or Foot Guards to remind people that
he not only occupied the greatest throne in the world, but, by
virtue of his own personality, was the first gentleman in Europe, or
anywhere.'

Daisy had come to London in June 1914 for the season and to
arrange some accommodation for her brother-in-law, Prince Fritz.
She and Patsy were searching for a suitable house in the New Forest
near Newlands, and by their dithering cost William the opportunity to sell one of his houses for much-needed cash, and prevented
him even from letting it for a few months in the summer. He wrote

unhappily to Dick Birch, his land agent, 'I wish the women would stop dabbling in matters they do not understand. However, of course we will oblige the Princess.'

It was Edwardian midsummer, and garden fêtes, croquet and cricket matches filled the warm days. Not many people followed the intrigues of anarchists and spies in Serbia

On 28 June 1914, Archduke Franz Ferdinand, heir to the throne of the Austro-Hungarian Empire, and his wife were assassinated in Sarajevo by Gavrilo Princip, a Serb. Austro-Hungary and Germany reacted fiercely. The people of Austro-Hungary, particularly the Viennese, were wild with the excitement of going to war with Serbia, but for a while their neighbours, the Germans, the Russians and the Italians, all pleaded for peace.

In response to Austrian military action against Serbia, Russia mobilised its army on the Serbian border on the next day. As a consequence of the Russian mobilisation, the German army was put into a state of readiness. At the beginning of 1870 in the war between Germany and France, the French had been caught unprepared by the initial German attack. Naturally, therefore, when the German army became active in 1914, the French armed their divisions on the German border. The British did nothing.

The day after the assassination, a close Austrian friend of Daisy's, Count Alfonse Clary, wrote to her.

Karmelitergasse, Prague
29 June 1914

Oh Daisy,

I am writing to you with my most aching heart and tears in my eyes, tears of sorrow, or terrible rage and fury.

They have slaughtered our future leader, him to whom we all looked as our saviour, and her, too, his wife, whose life was only love, who followed him everywhere danger was near: and she died trying to protect him with her body. To think of

44

those noble little children waiting for their parents to come home again.

Three weeks later, on 20 July, the foreign secretary, Sir Edward Grey, George Cornwallis-West's former schoolfriend, wrote to the British ambassador in Berlin.

I asked the German ambassador in London today if he had any news of what was going on in Vienna with regard to Serbia.

He said that he had not, but that he regarded the situation as very uncomfortable.

I said that I had not heard anything recently, except that Count Berchtold, the Austrian foreign minister, in Vienna, had deprecated the suggestion that the situation was grave, but had said that it should be cleared up.

I told the ambassador that I hated the idea of a war between any of the Great Powers, and that any of them should be dragged into a war by Serbia would be detestable. The ambassador agreed wholeheartedly in this sentiment.

On 29 July, Clary wrote to Daisy again:

I hope it will be <u>war</u>, because we cannot go on living with an abscess in our side, stinging our side and poisoning us day by day; it is better to cut it open right away and see if we can get over the operation.

We must crush Serbia utterly; the movement for 'Greater Serbia' must be extinguished for good.

Goodbye. I could not come to England now. I cannot leave my country before all trouble is over.

Bless you, my beloved.

Alphy

The next day, 30 July, Daisy had lunch with Paul Cambon, French ambassador in London, whose brother, Jules, was ambassador in Berlin. Even at that late date, Paul Cambon seemed convinced that Austria and Serbia would fight it out alone and that no general crisis would arise. Unfortunately, his attempts to reassure Daisy had the opposite effect and she became terrified that war would break out at any moment. Immediately the lunch was over, she went straight to Patsy and together they went to the German embassy to obtain tickets so that Daisy could return to Germany and to her children on the next crossing. At the embassy the officials wanted to help her but were uncertain whether she would get over the Dutch frontier. She caught an American liner to Rotterdam and then a train. Although the train was stopped at the border, the sleeping-cars were allowed to continue to Berlin, arriving there on Saturday. Daisy was distressed that nowhere had her husband left a message for her, and she then and for ever believed he had not wanted her to come back to Germany. Now she was an English princess with German nationality and a German title in enemy lands.

Patsy was bereft.

On 4 August the Germans invaded Belgium, which was neutral, so that they could attack France quickly and decisively, from a direction which would surprise the French defences. They moved at speed towards Paris. It was only after the invasion had started that the British government decided which side to join – or even to fight at all. The last time there had been such an attack, in 1870, Britain had decided not to get involved, and had profited greatly from that inaction. But this time Britain declared war on Germany on the very day of the invasion. If the response and assistance were to be any help British troops had to get to France quickly, with all their guns and equipment, and join the French line. There was a frantic rush to get to the front.

Quite suddenly, orders from local army camps became urgent and ominous: all soldiers were to parade within two hours.

For twenty-three-year-old Sergeant Patrick Barrett, this was the first call to arms. An orphan, he had been sent to the Regiment of the Royal Welch Fusiliers at the age of eleven, directly from the St Asaph Cathedral orphanage where he had been raised. First drummer-boy, then apprentice, then private soldier, he had worked his way up to the rank of sergeant only a few months before the war broke out. Slim, shy and good-looking, with only just enough confidence to give orders to the rankers, he found himself off to war with his platoon. There was a great deal of which to be careful: his first concern was to stop the young soldiers forgetting or losing their kit and getting into trouble with the regimental sergeant-major. It was a misfortune for him that the subaltern in command of the platoon was on sick leave.

The Royal Welch Fusiliers' barracks was at Bodelwyddan Camp in Denbighshire, at the foot of the Clwyd valley, on the hillside looking over the sea at Rhyl. The men were assembled and marched to the regiment's private railway station in the grounds of the enormous country house at Kinmel Park.

Patrick's men were excited and nervous, and plied him with questions.

'Where is this Serbia, Sarge?'

'Serbia? I think . . . London, I think. Somewhere – I don't know.'

'London, then?'

'I don't know.'

'Have you been there?'

'Where?'

'London?'

'Of course not.'

'Mr Birch goes to London.'

'Well?'

'On the train from Chester.'

'Well?'

'Are we going to fight for these Serbies?'

'I don't know.'

'You're the bloody sergeant.'

'Am I?'

Patrick went over in his head all the things the sergeant-major had said, mainly about everybody's kit. But he was more bothered about the boys having a fight with all these reservists coming in and pinching their kit. He did not want them having a fight, not now. But they probably would – he would have.

'Not been on a train?'

'Of course, you bloody Welshman.'

'That's your mother down the end of the platform, Gerard. She's calling.'

'She's fussing.'

'Well, you have to say cheerio properly to your mother. Go on, boy.'

'Yes, Sergeant.'

Patrick had never been on a train himself. The noise of the steam was terrible in the little stone station. When he at last got his men aboard he kept counting them to make sure he hadn't left anyone behind on the platform with a girl or a sister, or a mother. And their kitbags: he kept counting those, on the rack.

'Did you see last night, Sarge?'

'What?'

'Christine.'

'Christine who?'

'You know.'

'What about her?'

'In the window, above the fish shop at Bodelwyddan.'

'And?'

'She took all her clothes off.'

'Liar.'

'She did. Right at the window.'

'It's right she did, we were watching.'

Patrick was excited by that. Just thinking about that was exciting.

Christine was very pretty. He'd always thought so. Too rich for him, but very pretty.

'In France all the girls take their clothes off.'

'Don't do that, Kevin Jenkins. You'll crash the train.'

'How?'

'Just don't do it.'

'I'm serious, Sarge. In France all the girls take their clothes off.'

'Leave it alone.'

'They believe in nudity.'

'No wonder the Welsh are being sent to fight them off. We don't believe in nudity.'

'They're invading London all in the nude. French women. And we're being sent to put a stop to it.'

'Close combat.'

'Jones, are you asleep?'

'Yes.'

'Is that true, Sergeant, the French are invading London? I've an aunty in London.'

'No, I'm sure that's not right. I don't think it can be. I don't know where the Serbies are, really.'

'I think there's nudie women in London, too.'

'Don't be stupid. My aunty's there.'

'Bloody train keeps stopping.'

All night the train kept stopping. Patrick looked out, wondering where they were. Sometimes he saw countryside in the warm moonlight, sometimes dark towns. He hadn't been to England before. He thought perhaps it would be a different colour or something. But he felt that the whole country was alert and tense, because there was a war. He dozed and dreamt of the foreign countries they'd been told about in drill. They'd heard about Africa and India and strange wild men with spears. He had to keep counting everything for the sergeant-major.

In the morning they reached London and stared as, in the heat, miles and miles of houses and factories and churches seemed to spread everywhere, all over. The people they could see from the window took no notice of this great train from Wales. The Welch Fusiliers arriving and nobody interested; even worse, the people looked irritated.

The train juddered to a standstill.

'Do we get out? Sergeant?'

The station was bigger than a mountain and smoky like a pit. Patrick had to keep them all together, and their kit all in one heap on the platform. Officers dashed back and forth with orders, then new orders, then more new orders which countermanded the previous ones. After what seemed like hours, the men were fallen in and told to march out of the station.

London was full of soldiers in hot brown uniforms under the summer sun. Patrick and his platoon stepped out briskly in their allotted place in the regiment. They marched to Hyde Park, where they were to spend the night. They did not know what they were to do next. There might be orders to visit the pubs and the sinful brothels, of which they had only ever dreamt, or to dig a trench and fight where they stood. Over the railings of the park, they saw the mad, full roads of the dirty city packed with traffic. In fact they were told to eat bully beef and biscuits and await a special ration of rum. Next morning, at four o'clock, they were to entrain at Victoria. No one was to leave their platoon.

As soon as they said that, Kevin Jenkins was away like a bullet from his rifle, over the fence and off to God knows where, and Michael Rees with him. They hadn't come to London to camp out in Hyde Park – they could camp out in bloody Rhyl, any time. And then the others, too, and most of the reserves, so Patrick had no one left to count. He walked down to where they said Buckingham Palace was, and he looked at that. And Big Ben – he recognised it from a postcard he'd seen at Mrs Birch's on the mantelpiece. 'It's all too big, really, this London thing,' he said to himself, because actually he was lonely. He had enjoyed the train and he was looking forward to having another ride tomorrow. He worried about Jenkins and Rees, because they might get him into trouble.

Jenkins was sick in the night. The reserves had got him drunk and he kept saying he was that ill they'd have to send him home, the first casualty. The smell was foul. It was a hot night so they just moved away under their blankets. You could not see stars for the smoke haze, but the city glowed in the darkness.

'I've got my twelve,' Patrick kept saying to himself, ready for when he was asked in the morning. It was grand, always, to wake up with the sun and make tea on a fire.

Little Gerard, who was only sixteen – he'd lied about it in order to get into the Fusiliers – was crying. He'd gone off with the others, but had lagged behind because he found them a bit frightening. Then he came back and couldn't find Patrick and the others in the dark. So he sat awake until it was light enough to see and then came running over. Patrick saw him coming and was going to get cross, and then he saw the boy was crying. He made him some tea. 'It's just bloody London, Gerard.'

Jenkins woke up with a jump. 'Where are they? I'll get them.' And off they went, cracking jokes about the Serbies and the nudie French women, and how they'd met all these girls last night, and it was the lousy London beer that had made them ill. Bloody London.

At four o'clock in the morning Victoria Station was already full of soldiers trying to keep together, 'trying to hold on to their own things mind you'.

'We'll have them, whoever they are.'

'These buggers here are from Blackpool. We went there on the charabanc, on our holidays. My mam sent a card from there. Our Gran still has it in the front room.'

'Are you the British army?' asked an officer.

'Sir.'

'Well, smarten up.'

Jenkins pulled a face. 'Who was he?'

'God knows.'

'Which train are we, Sarge?'

Patrick was watching the other sergeants to see what they did. But nothing was happening. So they stood at attention, and then just stood, and then they sat down and waited.

Their train did not come. They waited all day. A long wait. But nobody was in trouble, so it was just a day of nothing, and playing cards on the ground. It felt rather important to be army. There were girls hanging about and Rees said it was because they wanted to kiss a soldier, so he went and tried and came back after quite a long while and said it was true. So Patrick said it was OK to go and get a kiss, but one at a time and not to be completely out of sight, in case they got an order to move.

When it was Gerard's turn, he did not want to go, but the others ribbed him until Patrick thought he might cry again. In the end Gerard did go, and he got a long kiss from a pretty girl who'd been watching. They wanted her to come over with her sister, who was there, too, but she would not. The two girls just stood by the news kiosk, kissing the soldiers who came up and asked them. Rees said they would give you more than a kiss, for thruppence, but Jenkins said it wasn't true, because he'd asked.

Gerard asked if he could go and get another kiss, and Patrick said yes. He was away quite a long time.

They spent the night at Victoria Station, and their train came at three o'clock in the morning. The battalion crossed the channel to Boulogne in the middle of the next night. No one in Patrick's platoon had been on a boat before, and it was very crowded. There was a lot of singing. The boat was actually one for carrying cows and sheep, so there was straw on the deck and it got very warm and had a smell which was a mixture of animal droppings on the hillside and the bathroom tar soap in the barracks at Bodelwyddan.

On the train from Victoria they'd each been given a book about how to be a soldier in the British Army. The book had a printed letter from Lord Kitchener, 'Chief Cook,' Jenkins called him. 'Kitchens, you see.' The letter told them that in France they were to resist the temptations of French women. Kitchener could not have thought of anything more erotic than that to say to a soldier. 'Always be courteous,' the letter said, which Patrick thought was something to do with the way you held the handle on a tea-cup. So far, all the tea had been in tins with no handles.

'Those roofs have slates, look,' said Rees as the boat was waiting off Boulogne dockside.

'Even the London houses had slates.'

'They'd better be our slates.'

There was a crowd of women on the dockside watching the boats land.

'Why do they call us Tommies?'

'I don't know.'

'Is it bad?'

'I don't know.'

'Are the Serbies here?'

'How long are we staying?'

'Where's the fighting now?'

'I don't know at all.'

The town at Boulogne poured itself into the sea. The harbour was for unloading fishing-boats, with cranes, directly on to the market stalls on the cobbles that lined the quay. So each cattleboat waited its turn to moor alongside and deliver its small portion of the British army, the soldiers of which had all been instructed to be courteous and avoid the affections of French women.

'I don't think they have beer in France, Sergeant.'

'You ask.'

So young Gerard sat at a table outside a café in the square and looked at the waitress and said, 'Beer?'

'Four beer?' she said.

And they cheered her for understanding them. This was good, to sit outside in the town square and ask for beer.

'It's the Germans, apparently. That's who we're against. Apparently.'

'Well, it's not the French, is it?'

'Apparently not. I don't know.'

'Lieutenant Thomas said there have been loads of regiments already gone from here. We have to get another train. We're in reserve at the moment. Apparently.'

'There's a whole camp, here, where we're staying, he said, up there on the hill. That's where we're heading now. He said we'll be doing some shooting. You know, rifle drill and that.'

'Ask her if she's got a pie or something, Gerard. I'm starving.' So Gerard asked the waitress. 'Pie?' he said. But he got nowhere with that.

The regiment camped on the hill outside Boulogne for two weeks. There was a hard routine of rifle drill and basic training. Second Lieutenant Moreton tried to keep an eye on Patrick's platoon as well as on his own, but for most of the time the men looked to Patrick, not the officers, for guidance.

Rumour said that the army at the front was having a difficult time and the French army was no help. The British were facing the worst of what the Germans had to offer. It sounded as if they were moving from one place to another in order to get into good positions.

In the second week they were given passes to go out in the town, but the sergeant-major was very strict and he had a patrol marching everywhere and sending people back to camp even if they sneezed or something. The sergeants had all been told that they could not risk any trouble at all, so they were not going to. No regimental sergeant-major was going to let his regiment get a reputation for being no good. It wan't a bloody holiday, it was a bloody war. Anyhow, they spent so much time digging trenches – 'At the double!' 'No slackers!' – that they were too tired to do anything except hope for their food at night.

French girls came up to the camp wire and sold cakes and wine and there was some kissing, but the sentries chased them away. So the Chief Cook need not have worried too much.

Then the order came to get their kit ready for the train to somewhere called Mons, wherever on earth that might be.

Like the boat, the train had been used to transport cattle, and the men were carried in cattle trucks which stank of their recent occupants. The best they could do to stop themselves being sick was to pile the kit on the floor and lie as low as possible. They were carrying their rifles as well and were careful not to bang all the ammo boxes around for fear of them going off.

Patrick had been told to make sure they'd ditched all their bottles of wine, 'and no messing about, because this is bloody serious'.

'How do you know what a German looks like?'

'He's got a spike on his head.'

'Are they any good?'

'They're no good. We're the best.'

But when the train suddenly clattered to a stop it was grey and dark and there were hundreds of ordinary French people hurrying along with things brought from their houses, trying to get away. Families tried desperately to stay together and the children were crying and screaming. They were pulling carts piled with blankets and warm clothes. The Fusiliers couldn't move for the people running up and down the platform, pushing, and they couldn't line up. It was raining heavily. Not far away there were loud explosions, of shells, lighting up the sky. There was already a jam of people, and the soldiers pouring off the train were making it worse. Women yelled at them and gestured fiercely that they should get out of the way. The crowds were on both sides of the train, and on the track.

Then the crowd parted and Patrick saw what looked like a whole British regiment coming towards them along the platform. Bearers were carrying the seriously wounded on stretchers, and men with no boots and blood all over them were trying to get away from the shelling and the machine-gun fire they could hear across the fields.

The officers shouted and the buglers gave the call for the soldiers to fall in. They did so in a field, off the road, and were given orders to get across to a hedgerow where they could get in a position to cover the other regiment's retreat. Just like that, in the dark. They had not got all the stuff off the train and they were getting into firing positions. But Patrick had made sure his men had got their ammunition boxes and their kit safely with them. He was pleased about that.

There was an artillery regiment ahead of them, and the gunners had to get their cannon across the field. The horses were not in harness, so the men pulled the guns themselves, frantically, to get them into good firing positions before they got stuck in the mud and the wet soil.

When the Fusiliers were in position, they were ordered to fire everything they could as fast as they could. So they kept firing and reloading and firing again in the direction of the enemy, over and over. The noise was terrible, and the big guns started shelling from behind them over their heads. The idea was to show the Germans that a huge army corps had arrived to protect the railway line and the station, and to try to make them withdraw.

There was three hours of this before the bugles sounded the ceasefire and they realised that the enemy shelling had stopped. A big cheer went up, but straight away the order was for the big guns to retreat and for the infantry to cover them and then retire as fast as possible down the road where the civilians had been. It was completely dark now, and they could see the shells exploding away in the east. Everyone was soaked through, but, apart from the ringing in their ears, they were all right.

The platoon was not allowed to stop marching for hours. It seemed like all night. The road was full of holes, which made the march exhausting. Then, in the middle of the night, they got an order to stop in a farmyard where there was a barn, so they went in there and rolled up in their blankets and slept.

At five they were up and off, and the order was to keep going as fast as they could. They knew the Germans were behind them somewhere, so they had to keep going. All the time, too, there were these poor civilians going past, carrying what they had brought from their homes. The men could not talk to them, or help them, because it was important to keep moving on.

Someone said the British had already surrendered at Saint-Quentin, so now it was a question of keeping away from the Germans, because they were killing everybody in their way. There was nothing else to do.

Jenkins saw an abandoned cart by the roadside. They pulled it up on to the road and put all their kit and coats and rifles on it with the ammunition boxes. They gave rides to French children as they went along. 'Keep on the road south' was the only order they got; 'and don't stop.'

The kids went and pinched things from deserted farmhouses as they went along, so soon they had quite a stall on the cart. There was cheese and eggs and more blankets. Patrick saw that Rees was beginning a small hoard of wine bottles in a crate on the front of the cart. 'Well, why not, Sarge?' he said. 'If the bloody Germans are coming after us, there's no good leaving it for them.'

Sergeant Patrick Barrett still had all his men. No one lost yet, and they still had most of their stuff. It had felt wrong using up ammunition like that last night, but that was the order. Whatever they'd done seemed to have worked because there was no firing now. Not close behind them. You could hear shelling to the east but it was a long way off. The whole battalion was stretched out in front and behind them, nearly all three thousand soldiers, all along the road. And streams of French civilians from the villages.

On 29 July Sir Edward Grey wrote to Sir Maurice de Bunsen, the British ambassador in Vienna.

London

Count Mensdorff, the Austrian ambassador, has told me that the war with Serbia must proceed. Public opinion in Austria was at such a pitch that her government could not continue to permit her to be exposed to the necessity of mobilizing again and again, as she had in recent years. She had no idea of territorial aggrandizement, and all she wanted was to make sure that her interests were safeguarded.

I said that it would be quite possible, without continually interfering with the independence of Serbia, or taking away any of her territory, to turn her into a sort of vassal state.

Count Mensdorff deprecated this.

In response to some further remarks of mine as to the effect the Austrian action might have on Russia, he said that Serbia had always been regarded as being within the Austrian sphere of influence.

The first weeks of September 1914 brought sweltering days and torrential storms at night. The British Expeditionary Force, in retreat, marched day after day southwards from Mons towards Paris. Twenty miles, at least, at a time. Who was to know what plan, if any, there was in this? The belief among the soldiers, those who had survived, was that the whole division was going to regroup and attack from a carefully selected position. The desperate tiredness and aching hunger were necessary, and to be expected as part of the necessities of battle. Perhaps the German troops who were following them were simply being drawn into a trap in which they would be mortally surprised and slaughtered like those they had cruelly slain in their path.

Patrick marched in confidence that the war was under control, and his men drew strength from his certainty. Anyhow, he did not know what else to think. Orders were still coming down from battalion headquarters and they seemed to make sense, even if they were repetitive. 'Keep going south, as far each day as you can.'

The stories they heard from people they met on the road frightened them. So many people had died. The machine-guns were terrifying. Hundreds of soldiers and civilians had been left by the wayside, unable to walk or even stand. There was so much hurt.

Gerard asked if there would be fighting soon.

'Are you keen for a fight, young Gerard?' asked Patrick.

'I think we ought to be fighting.'

'It's no use fighting if you're not in a good position. You need to win.'

Nobody wanted to ask if they were running away. They sang sometimes, moving along, as they had practised at Bodelwyddan, like a choir of Welsh men and boys.

They came to a town called Meaux. There were British troops everywhere. The road crossed a river and then a canal only a few yards further on. The Welch Fusiliers were all together – it was the first time for a fortnight – and there was food cooked and waiting for them. The men asked Patrick if it was all right to swim. They had not washed much since they left Boulogne. Their orders were to dig in, in deep trenches, so they had an hour in the river for swimming and washing and then they started digging.

The heavy artillery started up from a hill behind them, firing huge shells northwards at the Germans. The British were going to attack in the morning. They could see that the infantry division stretched right along the canal. It was going to be a huge advance. Behind them in the fields there were two cavalry regiments running the length of the line, with their horses and guns. The soldiers had never seen anything like that. You could imagine what it would be like to be in the way of a cavalry charge. A hundred horses racing and jumping across the hedges, wild with freedom, bayonets ringing and sharp.

At three in the morning, a whisper along the line woke them up, and then the machine-guns started. The noise was frantic. The Germans were in a wood about two hundred yards in front of them, so the guns pounded the wood, and shells from the heavy artillery blasted into the enemy positions. The Fusiliers were to stay ready until they got orders to charge into the wood. For an hour the guns kept firing.

Then came the bugle-call and they ran forward across the canal bridge and across the river and into the wood, bayonets fixed to their rifles. All the way along the line everybody rushed forward. As he ran, Patrick kept shouting everyone's name: 'Gerard, Neil, Thomas!' He found a wounded German behind a tree and stuck his bayonet into him, and then another. And the others were doing the same. The only Germans left were the wounded; the others had already run. On and on. 'Michael, David, Kevin!' There were bullets flying everywhere, but he kept going, shouting names and bayoneting, and kicking German bodies to make sure they were dead. 'Go on, Harry, Gerald, Gerard, go on!'

They reached a cart track, and Patrick looked around to count his men, but he could not see all of them. They saw the others hurrying across the clearing with the machine-guns firing ahead of them, so they had to keep going into the wood. There were more machine-guns firing at them and he saw British soldiers falling as they went forward, and he kept going, with his bayonet, shouting and shouting through the wood.

After a frightening hour of this, they came to the far side of the wood, and looked out on the fields. The machine-guns were still firing from within the trees down the field. There were bodies all over it. German soldiers were trying to get away; others were dead and dying. The Fusiliers were ordered to stay under cover of the wood, and keep moving left. Patrick was not sure if he still had everyone with him. They were being shelled and the explosions in the wood and along the field threw vast clouds of mud and earth into the air, and bodies, too. The order was to keep moving left; he could hear the bugler blowing the call. They were obviously doing well and advancing. So on they went.

There was a village ahead and they were told to move into the village and take it. Two machine-guns were set up and they fired and fired until the infantry were told to crawl in. Suddenly to their left an enemy gun started up, and within a minute there were bodies and blood everywhere. Their own machine-gun turned on the enemy, but probably fifty British were hit before the German gun was silenced.

They got into the village, which was a mess of rubble and smashed timbers and bodies of civilians and soldiers and dogs and horses. Patrick was almost sick at what he saw. The shelling had moved further north. The Germans were retreating ahead of them, and the Fusiliers were being followed by the next wave of attack troops. A lieutenant told Patrick and his men to make the village secure for the night. Patrick did not know who most of the soldiers were who came with him. Three of his own were dead. Neil Jones, Michael Rees and David Hibbert.

'Three of us,' said Gerard.

They were to stay the night, but there was a constant flow of British troops through the village in pursuit of the Germans. Thousands of soldiers came through, and at three the next morning Patrick and his platoon followed them forward.

From Sir Edmund Goschen, British ambassador in Berlin, to Sir Edward Grey In accordance with instructions contained in your telegram of 4 August, I called upon the secretary of state that afternoon and enquired, in the name of His Majesty's Government, whether the Imperial Government of Germany would refrain from violating Belgian neutrality. Herr von Jagow at once replied that he was sorry to say that his answer must be 'No', as in consequence of the German troops having crossed the frontier that morning, Belgian neutrality had already been violated. Herr von Jagow again went into the reasons why the Imperial Government had been obliged to take this step, namely, that they had to advance into France by the quickest and easiest way, so as to be able to get well ahead with their operations and to endeavour to make some decisive blow as early as possible. It was a matter of life and death for them, as if they had gone by the more southern route they could not have hoped, in view of the paucity of the roads, and the strength of the fortresses, to have got through without formidable opposition, entailing great loss of time. This loss would have meant time gained by the Russians for bringing up their troops to the German frontier. Rapidity of action was the great German asset, while that of Russia was an inexhaustible supply of troops.

I pointed out to Herr von Jagow that this fait accompli of the violation of the Belgian frontier rendered, as he would readily understand, the situation exceedingly grave, and I asked him whether there was still time to draw back and avoid possible consequences, which both he and I would deplore. He replied that, for the reasons he had just given me, it was impossible for them to draw back.

In compliance with your instructions I gave his excellency a written summary of your telegram and, pointing out that you had mentioned twelve o'clock as the time when His Majesty's Government would expect an answer, asked him whether, in view of the terrible consequences which would necessarily ensue, it were not possible, even at the last moment, that their answer should be reconsidered. He replied that, if the time given were twenty-four hours or more, his answer would be the same. I said that in that case I should have to demand my passports. The interview took place at about seven o'clock.

In a short conversation which ensued Herr von Jagow expressed his poignant regret at the crumbling of his entire policy and that of the chancellor [Theobald von Bethmann-Hollweg], which had been to make friends with Great Britain and then, through Great Britain, with France. I said that this sudden end to my work in Berlin was to me also a matter of deep regret and disappointment, but he must understand that under the circumstances, and in view of our engagements, His Majesty's Government could not possibly have acted otherwise than they had done.

I then said that I should like to go to see the chancellor, as it might perhaps be the last time I should have an opportunity of seeing him. He begged me to do so.

I found the chancellor very agitated. His excellency at once began a harangue which lasted for about twenty minutes. He said that the step taken by His Majesty's Government was terrible to a degree; just for a word, 'neutrality', a word which in war time had been so often disregarded, just for a scrap of paper. Great Britain was going to make war on a kindred nation who desired nothing better than to be friends with her. What we had done was unthinkable; it was like striking a man from behind when he was fighting against two assailants. He held Great Britain responsible for all the terrible events that might happen.

I protested strongly against that statement, and said that, in the same way as he and Herr von Jagow wished me to understand that for strategical reasons it was a matter of life and death to Germany to advance through Belgium and violate the latter's neutrality, so I would wish to understand that it was, so to speak, a matter of 'life and death' for the honour of Great Britain that she should keep her solemn engagement to do her utmost to defend Belgium's neutrality if attacked. That solemn compact simply had to be kept, or what confidence could anyone have in engagements given by Great Britain in the future?

The chancellor said, 'But at what price will that compact have been kept?'

I hinted to his excellency as plainly as I could that fear of the consequences could hardly be regarded as an excuse for breaking solemn engagements, but his excellency was so excited, so evidently overcome by the news of our action, and so little disposed to hear reason, that I refrained from adding fuel to the flame by further argument.

As I was leaving he said that the blow of Great Britain joining Germany's enemies was all the greater that almost up to the last moment he and his government had been working with us and supporting our efforts to maintain peace between Austria and Russia.

I said it was part of the tragedy which saw the two nations fall apart just at the moment when relations between them had been more friendly and cordial than they had been for years. He would readily understand that no one regretted this more than I.

At about 9.30pm Herr von Zimmermann, the under-secretary of state, came to see me. After expressing his deep regret that the very friendly official and personal relations between us were about to cease, he asked me casually whether a demand for passports was equivalent to a declaration of war. I said that such an authority on international law as he was known to be must know as well or better than I what was usual in such cases. I added that there were many cases where diplomatic relations had been broken off, and, nevertheless, war had not ensued, but that in this case he would have seen from my instructions, of which I had given Herr von Jagow a written summary, that His Majesty's Government expected an answer to a definite question by twelve o'clock that night and thus in default of a satisfactory answer they would be forced to take such steps as their engagements required. Herr Zimmer-mann said that that was, in fact, a declaration of war, as the Imperial Government could not possibly give the assurance required that night, or any other night.

In the meantime, after Herr Zimmermann left me, a flying sheet issued by the *Berliner Tageblatt* was circulated, stating that Great Britain had declared war against Germany. The im-mediate result was the assemblage of an exceedingly excited and unruly mob before His Majesty's embassy. The small force of police which had been sent to guard the embassy was soon overpowered, and the attitude of the mob became more threatening. We took no notice of this demonstration as long as it was confined to noise, but when the crash of glass and the landing of cobble-stones they threw into the drawing-room, where we were all sitting, warned us that the situation was getting unpleasant, I telephoned to the Foreign Office an account of what was happening. Herr von Jagow immediately informed the chief of police, and an adequate force of mounted police, sent with great promptness, cleared the street. From the moment on we were well guarded, and no more direct unpleasantness occurred.

After order had been restored, Herr von Jagow came to see me and expressed his most heartfelt regrets at what had occurred. He said that the behaviour of his countrymen had made him feel more ashamed than he had words to express. It was an indelible stain on the reputation of Berlin. He said that the flying sheet circulated in the streets had not been authorised by the government; in fact, the chancellor had asked him by telephone whether he thought that such a statement should be issued. And he had replied, 'Certainly not, until the morning.' It was in consequence of his decision to that effect that only a small force of police had been sent to the neighbourhood of the embassy, as he had thought that the presence of a large force would inevitably attract attention and perhaps lead to disturbances. It was the 'pestilential *Tageblatt*', which had somehow got hold of the news, and upset his calculations. He had heard rumours that the mob had been excited to violence by gestures made and missiles thrown from the embassy, but he felt sure that that was not true (I was able to assure him that the report had no foundation whatever) and even if it was, it was no excuse for the disgraceful scenes which had taken place. He feared that I would take home with me a sorry impression of Berlin manners in moments of excitement. In fact, no apology could have been more full and complete.

On the following morning, the 5 August, the Kaiser sent an aide-de-camp to me with the following message: 'The Kaiser has charged me to express to your excellency his regret for the occurrences of last night, but to tell you at the same time that you will gather from those occurrences an idea of the feelings of the people respecting the actions of Great Britain in joining with other nations against her old allies of Waterloo. His Majesty also begs that you will tell the King that he has been proud of the titles of British field marshall and British admiral, but that in consequence of what has occurred he must now at once divest himself of those titles.'

I would add that the above message lost none of its acerbity in the manner of its delivery.

On the other hand, I should like to say that I received all through this trying time nothing but courtesy at the hands of Herr von Jagow and the officials of the Imperial Foreign Office. At about eleven o'clock on the same morning, Count Wedel handed me my passports, which I had earlier in the day demanded in writing, and told me that he had been instructed to confer with me as to the route I should follow for my return to England. He said that he understood that I preferred the route via the Hook of Holland to that via Copenhagen; they had therefore arranged that I should go by the former route, only I should have to wait till the following morning. I agreed to this, and he said I might be quite assured that there would be no repetition of the disgraceful scenes of the preceding night as full precautions would be taken. He added that they were doing all in their power to have a restaurant car attached to the train, but it was rather a difficult matter. He also brought me a rather charming letter from Herr von Jagow couched in the most friendly terms. The day was taken in packing up such articles as time allowed.

The night passed quietly without any incident. In the morning a strong force of police was posted along the route to the Lehrter Station, while the embassy was smuggled away in taxi-cabs to the station by side streets. We there suffered no molestation whatsoever, and avoided the treatment meted out to my Russian and French colleagues. Count Wedel met us at the station to say goodbye on behalf of Herr von Jagow and to see that all the arrangements made for our comfort had been properly carried out. A retired colonel of the Guards accompanied the train to the Dutch frontier and was exceedingly kind in his efforts to prevent the great crowds which thronged the platforms at every station where we stopped from insulting us; but beyond the yelling of patriotic songs and a few jeers and insulting gestures we had really nothing to complain of during our tedious journey.

The Fusiliers followed the rest of the division forwards, but saw no more fighting for three days. They were behind the front line. Others had stayed behind to bury the dead. They buried Germans and British in separate pits which they dug alongside the wood.

There was some food now. Apparently they were not far from Paris, and Gerard said it was all being cooked by French chefs. But their clothes were in rags and their boots were coming apart. All Patrick could think was that they had to keep their rifles working properly and make sure they had plenty of ammunition.

On the fourth day there was another order to prepare to attack and they were now about half a mile behind the front line, so they were ready for it. But this time the front line never moved. It was as if the Germans and British both attacked at the same time and faced each other along a line some five miles long, and they just killed each other every time they stood up. The machine-guns fired and fired for hour after hour. There was a cavalry charge to the right of Patrick and his men, and within minutes of appearing every horse and every soldier was dead.

So Patrick never got the order to advance, and they were told to stay and hold the second line in case of a German breakthrough. More reserves came up from behind and moved forward to replenish the front line. There must have been trainloads coming from England, all with clean clothes and new boots and packs and rifles.

Instead of moving up they were told to move back and get ready to go on a train: they were being sent somewhere else.

Patrick now had a section of twenty men. There were those who had been with him before and some others who had lost their units in the battles. There was not much kit left, but they still tried to keep a cart going, full of whatever food and drink they could find, and to carry things. The men had made a sign: 'Sergeant Barrett's cart'.

Battalion HQ had gathered as many as they could find of the Royal Welch Fusiliers to go on the same train. A padre held a service before they got on the train, for those who had died and for those who had been taken away injured. There were a few on the train they had not seen for a while, and they sang Welsh hymns together. A lot of friends had died. Nobody wanted to talk about that. The singing helped a bit. And there were all those it was good to see were still alive.

They took the sign from Patrick's cart on the train with them. No one was told where they were going, but the journey took two days and the train stopped at a place that everyone called 'Wipers'.

From Jules Cambon, French ambassador in Berlin, to Herr Gottlieb von Jagow, German foreign minister

Berlin, 4 August 1914

Sir,

More than once your excellency has said to me that the Imperial Government, in accordance with the usages of international courtesy, would facilitate my return to my own country, and would give me every means of getting back to it quickly.

Yesterday, however, Baron von Langworth, after refusing me access to Belgium and Holland, informed me that I could travel to Switzerland via Lake Constance. During the night I was informed that I should be sent to Austria, a country which is taking part in the present war on the side of Germany. As I had no knowledge of the intentions of Austria towards me – once on Austrian soil, I am nothing but an ordinary private individual – I wrote to Baron von Langworth that I requested the Imperial Government to give me a promise that the Imperial and Royal Austrian authorities would give me all possible facilities for continuing my journey and that Switzerland would not be closed to me. Herr von Langworth had been good enough to answer me in writing that I could be assured of an easy journey and that the Austrian authorities would do all that was necessary.

It is nearly five o'clock and Baron von Langworth has just announced to me that I shall be sent to Denmark. In view of the present situation there is no security that I shall find a ship to England and it is this consideration which made me reject this proposal with the approval of Herr von Langworth.

From M Cambon's subsequent report to the French Government
While this letter was being delivered I was told that the journey would not be made direct but by way of Schleswig. At ten o'clock in the evening, I left the embassy with my staff in the middle of a great assembly of foot and mounted police.

At the station, the Ministry of Foreign Affairs was only represented by an officer of inferior rank.

The journey took place with extreme slowness. We took more than twenty-four hours to reach the frontier. It seemed that at every station they had to wait for orders to proceed. I was accompanied by Major von Rheinbaben of the Alexandra Regiment of the Guard and by a police officer. In the neighbourhood of the Kiel Canal the soldiers entered our carriage. The windows were shut and the curtains of the carriages were drawn down; each of us had to remain isolated in his compartment and was forbidden to get up or touch his luggage. A soldier stood in the carriage before the door of each of our compartments, which were kept open, revolver in hand, and finger on the trigger. The Russian chargé d'affaires, the women and children and everyone were subjected to the same treatment.

At the last German station about eleven o'clock at night, Major von Rheinbaben came to take leave of me. I handed him a letter for Herr von Jagow which included the following remarks: 'Today, as the train in which I was passed over the Kiel Canal, an attempt was made to search all our luggage as if we might have hidden some instruments of destruction. Thanks to the intervention of Major von Rheinbaben we were spared this insult. Yesterday I had the honour of writing to your excellency that I was being treated almost as a dangerous prisoner. Also I must record that during our journey, which from Berlin to Denmark has taken twenty-four hours, no food has been prepared nor provided for me nor for the persons who were travelling with me to the frontier.'

I thought that our troubles were finished, when shortly afterwards Major von Rheinbaben came, rather embarrassed, to inform me that the train would not proceed to the Danish frontier if I did not pay for the cost of this train. I expressed my astonishment that I had not been made to pay at Berlin and that at any rate I had not been forewarned of this. I offered to pay by a cheque on one of the larger Berlin banks. This facility was refused me. With the help of my companions, I was able to collect, in gold, the sum which was required of me at once, and which amounted to 3,611 marks 75 pfennigs. This is about 5,000 francs at the present rate of exchange.

I am assured that my British colleague and the Belgian minister, although they had left Berlin after I did, travelled by the direct route to Holland. I am struck by the difference of treatment, and as Denmark and Norway are, at this moment infested with spies, if I succeed in embarking in Norway, there is a danger that I may be arrested at sea with the officials who accompany me.

Jules Cambon

At Wipers, the Royal Welch Fusiliers were now old hands. Gerard was already looking for a suitable cart when they were fallen in in the fine town square. 'Take Menin' was the order, so they set off ready and with purpose down the road to Menin. They dug trenches about half a mile to the west of the town, having been advised that there was a small German presence there.

There was no need for shelling; they were to move forward with tripod machine-guns. It was quite likely, they were told, that there would be no fighting, because the occupying force was meagre and would retreat. It was raining heavily, so they took shelter for the night in barns and other farm buildings off the Menin Road, hoping that their mere presence would be enough to empty the town of enemy troops by morning.

At 2am they were shelled, and machine-gun fire thrashed into the buildings where they were sleeping. When they crawled out into the night, they could not see the enemy in the darkness and the torrential rain. The attack was devastating. They had nowhere to hide. All they could do was fire at where they believed the enemy guns were. The buildings were no protection, because the shells had the range exactly and were smashing them to fragments. The gunfire coming at them was overwhelming and literally filled the air. They had no light, so all they could see was the chaos of an explosion with its terrible roar and flash.

Within an hour a third of the regiment had been killed and the remainder of the men were trying to make their way in scattered retreat across the muddy fields towards Ypres.

Next morning the survivors regrouped and dug deep trenches in the mud on a hill outside Zandvoorde, in line with the main army east of Ypres. They could now see the strength of the Germans opposite. It was as if the entire nation had come to face them. They had ten times the men and ten times the guns of the British army.

Patrick was still trying to count his men. Gerard was there; his arm was bleeding and he was covered in mud. They'd lost a lot of the things on the cart bringing it across the fields, but they still had some ammunition and some food, and some bottles of wine they'd stuffed in their coat pockets. Two of them had even brought a machine-gun and its stand. They posted two sentries, and the rest tried to get some sleep. But at five o'clock the big guns started up, shelling the trenches on both sides. There was so much mud you had no chance to move.

They mounted the machine-gun as low down as they could make it. Patrick said they must wait until the enemy were really close before they opened fire. They could already see them massing across the fields, but Patrick said, 'Wait. The longer we wait, the more of them we can hit before they get our gun.'

Then on their right, the British cavalry charged. It was a fantastic sight: hundreds of horses dashing out through the filth with bayonets flashing towards the enemy. They were fast but not fast enough, for the machine-gunners cut them down, horses and men. They were brave and did some damage, but soon only half of them were charging across to the left. And they'd left the whole of the Fusiliers' right flank exposed.

The German infantry moved slowly towards them. Patrick knew he had to kill enough of them to make them stop. He waited until they were only two hundred yards away and he could see that they were all schoolboys and there were thousands of them, and he started firing, and so did another machine-gun down the trench to his left. They fired and fired and killed hundreds but those behind kept coming forward, each new wave climbing over the bodies in front of them. Patrick did not have enough ammunition for this: he was running out.

An officer rode past behind and Patrick screamed for ammunition, but the officer said, 'You'll just have to use your spades,' and he rode away.

Then the Germans brought up a machine-gun to their right and fired into the trench, and killed everybody. Nobody could get away; there was no protection on the right. Gerard tried to hold on to Patrick, for love, but two Germans came down and bayoneted everybody in the trench.

Sir Maurice de Bunsen, British ambassador in Vienna, to Sir Edward Grey

1 September 1914

On the 5 August, I had the honour to receive your instructions of the previous day, preparing me for the immediate outbreak of war with Germany, but adding that, Austria being understood to be not yet at that date at war with Russia and France, you did not desire me to ask for my passport or to make any particular communication to the Austro-Hungarian Government. You stated at the same time that His Majesty's Government of course expected Austria not to commit any act of war against us without the notice required by diplomatic usage.

On Thursday morning, the 13 August, I had the honour to receive your telegram of the twelfth, stating that you had been compelled to inform Count Mensdorff, at the request of the French Government, that a complete rupture had occurred between France and Austria, on the ground that Austria had declared war on Russia, who was already fighting on the side of France, and that Austria had sent troops to the French-German frontier under conditions that were a direct menace to France. The rupture having been brought about with France, in this way, I was to ask for my passport, and your telegram stated, in conclusion, that you had informed Count Mensdorff that a state of war would exist between the two countries from midnight on the 12 August.

After seeing Mr Penfield, the United States ambassador, who accepted immediately in the most friendly spirit my request that his excellency would take charge, provisionally, of British interests in Austria-Hungary during the unfortunate interruption of relations, I proceeded, to the Ballplatz, to the Foreign Office. Count Berchtold received me at mid-day. I delivered my message, for which his excellency did not seem to be unprepared, although he told me that a long telegram from Count Mensdorff, in London, had just come in but had not yet been brought to him. His excellency received my communication with the courtesy which never leaves him. He deplored the unhappy complications which were drawing such good friends as Austria and England into war. In point of fact, he added, Austria did not consider herself then at war with France, though diplomatic relations with that country had been broken off. I explained in a few words how circumstances had forced this unwelcome conflict upon us. We both avoided useless argument. Then I ventured to recommend to his excellency's consideration the case of the numerous stranded British subjects at Carlsbad, Vienna, and other places throughout the country. I had already had some correspondence with him on the subject, and his excellency took a note of what I said and promised to see what could be done to get them away when the stress of mobilization should be over. Count Berchtold agreed to Mr Phillpotts, until then British consul at Vienna under Consul-General Sir Frederick Duncan, being left by me at the embassy in the capacity of chargé des archives. He presumed a similar privilege would not be refused in England if desired on behalf of the Austro-Hungarian Government. I took leave of Count Berchtold with sincere regret, having received from the day of my arrival at Vienna, not quite nine months before, many marks of friendship and consideration from his excellency. As I left I begged his excellency to present my profound respects to

Emperor Francis Joseph, together with an expression of my hope that His Majesty would pass through these sad times with unimpaired health and strength. Count Berchtold was pleased to say he would deliver my message.

Count Waterskirchen, of the Austro-Hungarian Foreign Office, was deputed the following morning to bring me my passport and to acquaint me with the arrangements made for my departure that evening (14 August). In the course of the day Countess Berchtold and other ladies of Vienna society called to take leave of Lady de Bunsen at the embassy. We left the railway station by special train for the Swiss frontier at 7 pm. No disagreeable incidents occurred. Count Walters-kirchen was present at the station on behalf of Count Berch-told. The journey was necessarily slow, owing to the encumbered state of the line. We reached Buchs on the Swiss frontier in the morning of the 17 August. At the first halting place there had been some hooting and stone throwing on the part of the entraining troops and station officials, but no inconvenience was caused, and at the other stations on our route we found that ample measures had been taken to preserve us from molestation as well as to provide us with food. I was left in no doubt that the Austro-Hungarian Government had desired that the journey should be per-formed under the most comfortable conditions possible, and that I should receive on my departure all the marks of consideration due to His Majesty's representative. I was accompanied by my own family and the entire staff of the embassy, for whose untiring zeal and efficient help in trying times I desire to express my sincere thanks.

Maurice de Bunsen

Chapter 6

INVALIDS

P ATRICK BARRETT WAS one of few survivors of the
contingent of Royal Welch Fusiliers at the battle of Zandvoorde. He was moved by train to a hospital at Le Touquet,
on the north coast of France, which had been set up by Shelagh,
Duchess of Westminster. She had spent quite a while there, making
sure it had all that was needed. It was a large modern building in the
woods outside Le Touquet. The Duke of Westminster was worried
that the German advance down the French coast might mean the
hospital would be taken over by German forces. But for the
moment it was safe.

Patrick had severe bayonet wounds in his right leg. One blade
had pierced right through. His body was riddled with shrapnel. He
had two serious bullet wounds. Shock had left him silent and
weeping when awake. Mostly he slept, and in his sleep he talked
and cried out.

The nurses and officers at the hospital found no papers on him,
but could tell from his uniform, or what was left of it, that he was a
Royal Welch Fusilier from the camp at Bodelwyddan. They knew,
too, that he must have been in the retreat from Mons, in the battles
of the Aisne and the Marne, and finally at Zandvoorde, which was
one of the first battles in the area around Ypres. Three thousand
men of the Royal Welch Fusiliers had left north Wales in August.
By October only eighty were left.

Shelagh saw on a list that he was from Denbigh, and at Christmas, when it was safe for him to be moved, arranged for him to go on a ship back to England and then to his regiment.

He was entrusted to the care of Mrs Richard Birch, whose house, Bryncelin, was near Bodelwyddan. She had told the Fusiliers' commanding officer, Lieutenant-Colonel Delmé-Radcliffe, that she would take six wounded soldiers and they would be tended at her and her husband's expense, until they were fit to return to the regiment.

Bryncelin was quiet and peaceful. It looked over the moor toward St Asaph and Rhyl and the sea. From the back window, the view led down to the barracks at Kinmel Park, with its beautiful house. Kinmel had once belonged to old Mr Hughes, who had taught George Cornwallis-West a great deal about trout streams and poaching, but now it was used as the headquarters of the regiment. There were sheep outside, but inside you could only hear the old clock; in the kitchen, the cat purred in front of the stove.

It was a big house, easily big enough to hold six soldiers, one or two to a room, and it had its own stables for Mr Birch's horses. He had been allowed to keep one horse for his work, which involved riding across the county. The others had been sold to the army for the war effort. Mr Birch was still Colonel Cornwallis-West's land agent. He often had work for the soldiers at the camp. They helped with lambing and harvests and sometimes with fencing and digging ditches or clearing hedges. Mrs Birch was kind, and always gave the soldiers a good meal. Before the war she had run a schoolroom above the stable for children from the army camp and from the houses and farms on that side of St Asaph.

Mrs Birch was in her thirties and had no children of her own. She was dark-haired and attractive, as the soldiers instantly noticed, rather quiet, and good-natured. She had a reputation for being clever and for reading books. Her father had been the headmaster of the school at St Asaph, and she was an only child. She was the one to ask if you needed to know something. She would have known where Serbia was.

Dick Birch liked going to London. He also had his work for Colonel and Mrs West in Hampshire, at Newlands, where the colonel, who was now in his seventies, relied on him to conduct most of the business. But Birch's role was far more intimate than that of the usual land agent: he was a witness to the colonel's will, and knew everything the family did. William and Patsy were generous in the way they looked after Birch and his wife.

In London Birch always stayed at Cox's hotel in Jermyn Street, just by the back door of St James's Church, Piccadilly. It was the most discreet private and luxurious hotel; with an entrance you could only find if you knew exactly where to look. William paid for Birch to have a room at Cox's, whenever he needed to stay there. It was the relationship of dependent employer and most trusted employee: they were close friends.

The news the Birches had heard about the regiment was terrible. Ever since August when the first trainloads went, some to France and some to camp near Southampton, there had been stories of hundreds of men being killed or missing. All the families for miles around had a husband, a son or a brother fighting in France. Everyone in the county knew everyone else, and it was so hard to know what to say to people when one did not know whether their men were dead, or injured, or missing. Of course, all the men were volunteering – they had to – but the deaths were terrible. Colonel Delmé-Radcliffe had arranged for news bulletins to be checked carefully before they were passed, and they had a chapel for families who came to the barracks.

The six soldiers who arrived at Bryncelin in January 1915 all had serious injuries. Two had deep bayonet wounds, one had a broken foot, one had lost two fingers, one had an awful cut right across his head, but the worst of all was the one who just lay on his bed and did not speak. His leg was bandaged so thickly he could not have moved if he had wanted to. He was Sergeant Patrick Barrett, and the Birches knew him: he'd been to the house before. He had sometimes come from the orphanage to Mrs Birch's schoolroom before joining the army. He'd been a drummer in the regiment when he was quite young and been promoted to sergeant only last summer, just before August. Now, as he lay in the room at the top of the stairs, Mrs Birch had to make him food he could eat with a spoon, because he would not leave his bed. He just lay looking at the wall.

Dick Birch said they should leave him alone and he would sort himself out in his head, but Mrs Birch wanted to talk to him, so she told him about the town and the local gossip and the regiment. It was not that she was emotional with him, more that she was thorough. She did not think his brain would get better by lying there in silence, brooding about all the fighting.

She sat with him, off and on, for day after day and then one day he suddenly spoke. 'You're very kind, Mrs Birch,' he said. 'I'm sorry if I've been difficult.'

She hugged him. 'I don't know what happened, Patrick, but I think you had a very bad time. It's safe here, and you can rest.'

'I would like to do work here, for you and Mr Birch, if I can.'

'I'm sure you will, and we'll be very grateful, but I don't think you can walk at the moment, so that will be first.'

Chapter 7

PATSY

W HEN THE WAR started Patsy was in her fifties. Royal
romance was a distant pleasure. She was still beautiful,
slight and fresh-faced so that she could be taken for a
woman in her twenties. For many years her life had been con-
centrated upon her children and the family homes. There had been
secret lovers, and escapades, but nothing that might place at risk the
world of her family. She was now at the age when the satisfactory
arrival in adulthood of one's children is a pride and a sufficiency.
She was and had been, more than anything, a good and fascinating
mother, and William loved and admired her for that, and so did her
children.

No mother can cope with war. When one's children are away
and the news is unclear, one worries; but when they are away in
enemy country, the fear becomes a cutting, continuous pain.

Daisy had gone back to Germany because she had to be with her
husband and their three boys. Her mother ached for her but,
because it was to Germany Daisy had gone, could look to no one
for sympathy. It was ridiculous to contemplate that they were on
opposite sides in a war. Patsy regarded it as a stupidity entirely
brought about by inadequate diplomats and soldiers. She, like many
women – including Daisy and Shelagh – decided that the only
useful contribution she could make was to care for and give
devotion to injured soldiers. So her overflowing energy was

donated to nursing. William had a role to play as colonel of the regiment, and Patsy was happy to be the colonel's wife, but she was lonely for the times gone by and frightened by the events and the news.

In the years since Daisy had gone to live in Germany, Patsy had learnt to dread the thought of German hospitals. When Daisy had her third child the doctors had left a surgical instrument in her womb, and she had had to come to London to have it removed. She nearly died.

Naturally the war had changed what people thought about and wanted to talk about. Daisy and Patsy were of the most admirable group of society, well liked and thoroughly respected for their good works, but now people who did not know them well were not sure what to say about the beautiful daughter who had become a German princess. There were many tales of spies and traitors, and idle chat can so easily become malicious.

Daisy had become energetically involved in the problems of nursing injured soldiers; she had got into quite deep trouble with the German High Command over a visit she made to some prisoners of war. Her husband, Prince Hans Heinrich, had to face difficult questions because she was portrayed as behaving in an anti-German manner. In the end the Kaiser intervened: he told those who had been repeating such accusations that the Princess of Pless was his friend, and that her actions were not to be questioned. Even so, Daisy's movements were restricted. She was confined for a long time to a hotel in Berlin, where she could be watched. Nevertheless, she then gave support and help to German wounded, and entered into kindly correspondence with soldiers from both countries. Like her mother and sister, she had to give all her energy to helping people.

Patsy said, 'What difference does it make which side they're on? If a soldier is hurt, he needs help. Of course he does. Only a fool would think anything else.'

The minister at Ruthin was thoughtful and he wrote Daisy a letter. Patsy was deeply grateful to him for that.

> The Cloisters,
> Ruthin,
> North Wales,
> 24 August 1914

Dear Princess of Pless,

Mrs West has just told me that it is possible to get a letter to you. I should like you to know that we are all thinking of you here in Ruthin. We have special prayers in St Peter's which include all those tending the sick and wounded, either our own or others, as you are doing. And we shall, next Sunday, ask God to take special care of you and yours. It is difficult for us to realise it all here in peaceful little Ruthin but our sympathy with you in this hour of trial is very sincere. It seems only a few Sundays back that you were singing in dear old St Peter's.

May God bless and keep you and yours.

Yours very sincerely,

Lewin Price,

Warden of Ruthin

Ruthin Castle was built in the thirteenth century by Edward I of England, who wanted to keep a watchful eye on the Welsh. It was a fortress, an outpost of England in Wales, and always had been. Patsy had made it also an outpost of London in the wilderness. A cycle of seasonal parties, coinciding with race meetings in the neighbouring counties, filled the house with weekend guests rich and royal, year after year.

Now William had opened its doors to any passing general and travelling politician, so it became an unofficial club for the Western Command of the army. The fires were kept proudly blazing with Welsh coal from the estate, for the rain of north Wales is a good match for the rain in Flanders in winter.

General Sir John Cowans came to attend a meeting of generals of Western Command. He was quartermaster-general of the army, a member of the Army Council and one of the most senior and important officers in the country. Working for Lord Kitchener, he was responsible for the supply of food and clothing to the troops. He had been for a long time a close friend of the Cornwallis-Wests, and was very close to both Patsy and Daisy. Patsy was pleased and excited that he was coming. She wanted to show him what was being done in the county to help with the war. She decided that after she had collected him from Chester station, on the way back to Ruthin, she would take him for a brief visit to Bryncelin, to meet some of the wounded soldiers.

Patsy loved driving. Ever since cars were sold, she'd had one. She was often photographed by the car magazines. She sped around the lanes in Wales and in Hampshire.

At Chester station Cowans was surrounded by soldiers. Two had come with him from London on the train and another two had driven two special army cars up from London to meet him. It was their duty to protect him and take him wherever he needed to go. He also had his adjutant with him.

Patsy kissed him. 'Dear Jack, tell your friends that you're coming with me,' she whispered. So the two army cars prepared to escort them and she said to the driver of the first, 'You needn't drive slowly because I'm a woman.'

She sent a telegram to Mrs Birch before they set off. 'Will arrive in army convoy with absolute top brass.'

Jack climbed into Patsy's car.

'Come close and tell me everything,' she said.

'It's good to get out of London – I hardly ever can. The war is awful, to be honest. A terrible mess.'

'Why?'

'Because the government wasn't ready for the fighting. It's true they had planned for mobilisation and so forth, but the military campaign is poor. You know the people; I should be careful what I say. Poor Herbert Asquith. He's such a nice, intelligent man, but as prime minister he's lost. He's playing a civilised game of cricket, and the Germans are ferocious.'

'I know him a little. He has a mistress, I think. Do people know that?'

'Yes, and he is so distracted it's pitiful.'

'Well, it's normal, I think. You can't win a war if you're helplessly in love. You can't do anything.'

'Kitchener is deciding everything. He listens to no one, except perhaps Winston. We do exactly what Kitchener says, but there's no money and there's no army.'

'I don't like Kitchener. I've met him, too, and I found him very cold. Jack, you'll have to tell them what to do. You're the one. You've got to finish it all and get Daisy home.'

'Have you heard from her? I had a note to say she is still in Berlin, but obviously she couldn't say much about anything.'

'We also get notes from her,' said Patsy. 'And I send messages with anyone who's going to France, "Give this to any Germans you meet," I tell them. Oh God, I hope she's safe. Hans Heinrich is in France, I think.'

'We have to get the Americans to join on our side. So far they're helping with supplies. All my blankets are coming from America, and soon there will be guns. President Wilson is a bit difficult, but they'll deal in anything if we can get money to them. It's a war about supplies – that and getting some young men in to lead the army, instead of old buffers.'

'Like Owen Thomas. Do you remember him? He's an old, fat Welshman, and he's been a brigadier-general since Owen Glendower. He speaks Welsh to everyone and they've put him in charge of recruitment round here, God help us! I'm sure he'll be sending the sheep next.'

'What is George doing?' asked Jack.

'Avoiding creditors, I should say. They'd follow him to France if they could – he was at Antwerp with Winston, as you know, and I think he's going out there again next month. I miss everyone being here. Still, at least we'll have a party tomorrow night with the generals, and all look properly grim. We have all to stay close together, Jack. You'll love Mrs Birch. She's so kind, and has been so generous to these poor boys. Her husband has worked for Poppets for years and years.'

They arrived at Bryncelin like the army on the move. The soldiers were searching the grounds before the cars had stopped.

Patsy made the introductions. 'Mr and Mrs Dick Birch, General Sir John Cowans. I've so wanted you three to meet. You are my three best friends in the world. And each of you is doing what will win this wretched war and bring Daisy home. Jack is getting the Americans to help us and supply us with blankets and guns, isn't that right, Jack? And Mrs Birch and Dick are looking after the poor soldiers who have been wounded in the fighting, as well as looking after the entire county. I wanted to get you together and say how special you are.'

Dick said that he had to leave on business, but that he was honoured to meet Sir John. Dick was going to London by the night train and he was riding over to Chester. They wished each other success in their efforts. The guards allowed him to gallop off on his horse.

Mrs Birch made tea and talked about the state of the young men. As she talked, Patrick Barrett hobbled in on his crutches. It was the first time he'd come downstairs. Mrs Birch was astonished, and they had to help him to a chair. He did not say anything. He just stared, mainly at Patsy, but also at General Cowans and Mrs Birch. They talked a little about the regiment, but it was difficult because of Patrick sitting there in silence. He seemed to give them his experience without saying anything. It was not that he was stupid; he was completely apart from them.

'Jack says we need young men now, to lead the army – no more Owen Thomases,' said Patsy.

'Really,' said Mrs Birch, not knowing how to respond. She had known Owen Thomas a long time. 'There's so much that needs to be done.'

'Will you show us round?'

'Of course.'

And they went round so that Cowans could shake hands with each of the soldiers and tell them how proud he was to meet them. He did it well. He was very charming. Then it was time for him and Patsy to leave.

'Thank you for coming,' Patsy said when they were outside. 'The Birches are so good to us.'

'You get too distant sitting in an office in London. One is conscious of the work of the army, but I'd forgotten what it's like to be close to them, to be part of the community.'

'Now you can drive my car.'

'Oh good. Now, listen. I've a proposition to make to you.'

'Well, I thought I'd have to wait for ever.'

'You must come to London and we'll go and see *Pygmalion*.'

'Jack, that's a marvellous idea. I shall get away from wretched Wales for one day at least, and we can see Stella and George.'

At dinner Patsy told the generals about Ruthin. 'It has a moat, of course – you can see that – and when you explore the walls you'll find the stone grave of Mary Grey, who was hanged for murdering her cheating husband in 1290. She haunts us. When you go past the grave, the tradition is that you must lift a stone and then replace it, otherwise she'll come and find you.

'But the castle has many more exciting secrets than that. Under us, and no one knows where, there's a hidden parade ground, where Baron de Grey marshalled his cavalry ready for the assault on Owen Glendower, and they were trapped in there and have never come out. No one has ever found the entrance to their cavern.'

'Oh, Patsy,' protested William, 'don't say things like that. No one will sleep in their beds. You're too frightening. You're worse than all the stuff we've been hearing this afternoon.'

'Well, so,' she said, 'but we can go hunting for holes in the ground in the rose garden tomorrow, to see if we can find them.'

The elderly general sitting next to Jack Cowans whispered to him, 'Patsy West has more secrets than even this old castle.'

'I believe you.'

'They say,' said the general, 'that young George is actually the son of old King Edward.'

'Do they? George who married Winston Churchill's mother?'

'That's right, but the marriage was not a success and they were divorced last year. He's just got married again, hasn't he?'

'Yes, to Mrs Patrick Campbell.'

The general nodded. 'Ah yes, I remember. Everyone was very surprised, because Mrs Campbell and George Bernard Shaw had had a close attachment for a long time. He wrote his new play *Pygmalion* for her – you know, the one that's caused all the stir. But Stella Campbell must be Patsy's age, surely?'

The two men looked down to the end of the table, where their hostess was smiling mischievously at her neighbour.

'She's very lovely,' said the old general.

'She is.'

'I've even heard that Princess Daisy is a daughter of the old King, and that Patsy's marriage to the colonel was . . . organised, because she needed a husband.'

'I've never heard that.' Cowans was still watching Patsy, glad she could not hear what they were saying.

'And the verger told me that the Duchess of Westminster, Shelagh, is too – it happened while Colonel Cornwallis-West was away in America.'

'I didn't know he went to America,' said Cowans.

'Well, now. The royal train came to Ruthin a few times, you see. But she's very kind, and everybody likes her. She is very good to the people here. 'There are stories about the colonel, too. He has children in Italy, you know, from the time before he was married.'

'I don't think that's a secret,' said Cowans. 'I think they just prefer not to talk about it. I understand those children are properly cared for.'

Winston Churchill, first lord of the Admiralty, had watched the early weeks of the movements of the British Expeditionary Force in northern France with an eye to what the navy should do to support them. The German advance through Belgium came northwards in order to outflank the combined French and British armies. This meant they would advance on the port of Antwerp, which was still held by the Belgians. So Winston made a naval attack with a brigade of troops, to defend the fortresses.

On the day war was declared, George had gone to London to buy a new uniform. His business partner, Mr Wheater, said that the war gave them the opportunity to make their fortune, but George felt his duty was to offer his military experience, even though it was thirteen years since he had last been in action. His division of reservists was put under control of the Admiralty and sent to Belgium to help Winston, as if they were sailors, which George found rather comical. Young privates kept rushing up asking permission to go ashore, when they were standing in a field. It appealed to his sense of humour.

He was at the theatre with Stella when a telegram came, ordering him to join the division on its way to Dover. He rushed to Victoria Station where he hired a train, which he paid for, and in this way set off for war. On the line the signalmen assumed he must be very important to have his own train, and put all the other engines into sidelines: even the top brass had to sit and watch as George sped by. At Dover, as he had missed the ship he should have been on, he was given a ride on a submarine, which he called a 'jolly box of tricks', and once they were across the Channel he joined the march from Ostend to Antwerp.

They had had only two battalions of troops, ill equipped and untrained, and they travelled in London buses, brought to Belgium by the navy, but Winston was not daunted and filled the railway line to Antwerp with every empty railway carriage and truck he could find. For several days, train after train rolled into and out of Antwerp under the careful watch of the German commanders. They assumed that hundreds of thousands of British troops were now positioned in the old city and its fortresses.

The Germans shelled the city for over a week, and saw very few troops moving out. George rode to view the forward positions on a bicycle he borrowed from a Belgian. As he neared the trenches he saw a number of large, round, dark objects, and decided he should approach them carefully. They were, he discovered, very acceptable Cheddar cheeses, well worth interrogating. Nevertheless, he quickly retreated, with all his men, as soon as he saw the strength of the German force. This was unfortunate, because he was spotted on his bicycle by an American newspaperman who knew who he was, and knew Daisy, and wrote in the *Salt Lake City News* that the Cornwallis-Wests were cowards and probably German spies and would be the downfall of the British Empire.

The naval force at Antwerp retreated and returned to England, but George was injured and ill with bronchitis and invalided out of fighting for the future. The story from the American newspapers reached London before he did. He was quite a celebrity because of his marriages to Jennie and now Stella, so the news went round London that he had been tried and executed in the Tower for being a spy. That made him angry, because the British papers, quoting American ones, said that he and Patsy and William and Daisy and Shelagh, and even Granny Olivia, who was now ninety-one, were all spying for the Kaiser. It was very unpleasant. George Bernard Shaw was kind to him and told him how silly newspapers are, and he was grateful for that.

Jack Cowans kept his word, and in mid-February took Patsy to see *Pygmalion*. Although it had been running for a while, it was still the show everybody wanted to see, and the line 'Not bloody likely' brought the performance to a halt every night. In the play,

Professor Higgins, a gentleman in his senior years, falls for a Cockney flower-girl and tries to teach her refinement so she can pass as a gentlewoman. She is Eliza Doolittle, who charmed all London as played by Stella Campbell.

Stella and Patsy were good friends. In the star's dressing-room after the performance they were delighted to see each other again. George poured champagne for his mother.

'Do you know who I saw in the audience, George?' she asked.

'Don't embarrass us.'

'Dick Birch, with his London lady, Annie.'

'Did he see you?'

'Yes, but he knows that I know about him and that I won't cause him any trouble.'

'Stella hasn't met Mrs Birch.'

'Oh, Stella, you must,' said Patsy. 'She's a good person. She's looking after wounded soldiers while her husband is away in London gallivanting.'

'Maybe she's gallivanting, too,' suggested Stella, 'with her soldiers.'

'Oh, do you think so? That's clever.'

'Now, Patsy, tell me what you enjoyed about the play.'

'You were wonderful, though we must have nothing to do with that old rogue Professor Higgins. He was up to no good – I could see that from the moment he entered, and I nearly called out, "Watch out for him, Stella!" But I did like those dresses for Ascot. They were very smart.'

'Have you done any fishing lately?' George asked Jack.

'No, none at all. I'm so busy that I hardly leave the office.'

'I absolutely understand. It's a big army you have to feed.'

'What about you?' asked Jack.

'Well, actually, yes. I've been down in Hampshire, you know, on the Test. It's very good down there.'

'I'm jealous.'

'But I have to go off with the regiment for training next month. I doubt if we'll get much sport in France – there wasn't any at Antwerp.'

'No,' said Jack

Churchill's expedition to Antwerp had been a minor triumph. It had delayed the German advance on northern France by over a week, which had enabled the army to move troops up to Ypres to defend the line there and prevent the Germans getting to the coast. Jack Cowans knew how important Antwerp had been for Winston, but he had also seen the stories about George and the family being called spies.

He said to George, 'If Stella's going to America with the play, why don't you go with her? Apart from the newspapermen in Salt Lake City, and perhaps the rest of Utah, you could get us some quite good propaganda. It really would be a useful thing to do. And I'm sure you'd get some fishing.'

George was very grateful for the offer; and from the War Office, Cowans arranged for him to go to America with Stella. It served Cowans's purpose to have a friend there whom he could call on for help, and it kept George away from his creditors; also from those wretched stories in the London papers, about him being a traitor, which did not help anyone.

Chapter 8

PATRICK

P ATRICK COULD NOT cope with nights. He was all right until about five in the morning, but then he awakened and tensed with fear. He lived in that trench with the others. Everything was covered in mud. The machine-gun had fired up and down the trench for several minutes, tearing his friends to pieces, throwing mud and bones and blood up into the rain, and the noise was agony enough.

Then, when the gun stopped, two young German soldiers came down to bayonet the bodies. Patrick had lain as still as he could when they drove the bayonet through his leg, because they were not really watching what they were doing. It could not have been easy for them to do, in the mess. And then he just lay there. He did not think anyone else was alive at all. He could feel that Gerard, whom he was gripping tightly, was ripped to pieces and finished. He did not dare even raise his head. The Germans did not try to move into that trench: it was too full of bodies and mud to clear out while the shelling was going on. So Patrick lay still and tried to breathe without making a sound.

After two hours of fighting the Germans had advanced too far and been slaughtered by British machine-gun fire. They ran back in retreat across Patrick's trench. The Tommies came back in to retake the position and they brought stretchers in case anyone was still alive. There were three or four other survivors from other regiments in other trenches, but only Patrick in that one. Nobody said anything, because they were still under fire, but he was carried back as fast as possible to the battalion's makeshift headquarters in a barn.

He went over these memories every morning when he woke at Bryncelin and heard the sheep outside on the hill. The noise of the machine-gun was still in his head.

He couldn't talk about what had happened, not to these people. He wanted to talk to his friends in the trench, to ask what they had seen. It was not a thing he could share. He didn't want sympathy for what happened. He wanted the others who knew what it had been like to be there. But they were dead. He was on his own, left from what happened.

Mrs Birch was very nice. She wanted him to talk, he knew that, and he did not want to be rude by being silent; it was simply that he could not tell her about it. It was too awful a thing to ask someone else to listen to. It was better to bear his burden alone than to make someone else bear it, too.

She made things very comfortable. He'd never had food like she made. He'd lived at the army camp since he was a child, and it was so delicious to have the meals she made.

He cried a lot. He found it was the most comforting thing, to lie on his bed and cry. So through the days he cried and slept, and at night he lay awake.

Anything which distracted him from thinking about the massacre in the trench seemed pointless. He worried for all the soldiers who were still going through it. The papers always had articles about what the generals had said and so forth, but they did not seem to be about the same war. Talking about the spirit of the brave troops was not the same as looking up at a machine-gun firing at you, or seeing the bloody Germans coming across the field.

Then Mrs Cornwallis-West came on a hot day and took all the soldiers out for a ride in her smart car. At first Patrick didn't want to go, but the others said, 'Nonsense,' and squeezed him into the back seat of the car. The soldiers came to life like a platoon and were

joking and singing. They knew Mrs West was famous or something, but she seemed to be more for having fun than being serious.
She laughed at them and boasted about her car. They drove off to
the hills.

'I know a good place for a picnic,' she said, and she took them to
where the road curved down to the sea and there was a flat field of
grass where you could sit and look at the Moelwyns, the mountains
of Snowdonia, and behind them at Snowdon itself. The boot of the
car was full of pies and cakes and beer and also champagne, which
most of them had only heard about.

The others went off to explore and climb and Patrick was left
with Patsy. They sat for a while in silence, looking at the mountains
and listening to the stream. For quite a long while they sat. Then
Patsy said, 'My daughter is in Germany. She is married to a
German.'

Patrick was really surprised. There was much to say in reply,
but he was so out of practice at talking that he said nothing.
He reflected that he thought he hated the Germans, but perhaps
he didn't really. Most of those soldiers were like him. He had
killed dozens of them. A lot of them were just young boys like
Gerard.

Eventually, he managed to ask, 'Where does she live?'

'In a castle called Fürstenstein, in a great forest.'

'Why does she live in a castle?'

'Because she married a prince.'

'That sounds like a fairy story,' he said.

Patsy didn't answer. She had a way of looking at you with her
eyebrows slightly raised, as if she wanted you to keep talking, as if
she were already surprised by what you were going to say.

This would be a good place for a castle,' he said. 'Perhaps.'

She still didn't answer.

The others were coming back from their climbing, so they had
to stop talking.

They went back to Bryncelin still singing and laughing. Patsy waved goodbye from the driveway. 'No casualties,' she called to Mrs Birch.

Patrick wanted to talk to her more. He wrote her name, 'Patsy', which he knew from hearing Mrs Birch talk about her, on a small piece of paper and hid it in his pocket. He thought she was the most beautiful woman he had ever seen his life. She was slim, with the most striking reddish glints in her golden hair, and such a sweet face. He supposed she must be quite a lot older, but she looked the same age as any of the girls in St Asaph, but much, so much, more exciting and pretty.

He went over each minute that they had spent alone together. He wondered if she really was interested in what he thought.

He decided to write to her and he practised what he would say: 'Dear Mrs Cornwallis-West, Thank you very much for a most interesting conversation.'

He felt instinctively that she wanted him to contact her. He was certain of it from the way she had behaved. Only a small part of him said, 'Don't make a fool of yourself; she'll laugh at you.'

So he wrote, 'Dear Mrs Cornwallis-West, Thank you very much for the outing to Snowdon, which has been very good for my recovery. It would be very enjoyable to have another outing. Yours sincerely, Patrick Barrett.'

Patsy folded his letter and put it safely away in a drawer. She wrote back: 'Dear Patrick, I was very pleased to get your letter. Perhaps we shall be able to have another drive out soon. I hope you are continuing to recover well. From Patsy Cornwallis-West.'

Patrick found her letter in the hall, where the postman had left it, before anyone else saw it. He opened it carefully with a knife along the top of the envelope. He read it over and over again, trying to work out what she meant, and he kept it in his own drawer in the bedroom.

★   ★   ★

It was a hot day in June when she came again. By now the other soldiers had recovered enough to begin training and were at the regimental camp during the daytime. She said, 'Well, I can take Sergeant Barrett, if he would like to come.'

Mrs Birch went and fetched him, and he and Patsy drove off.

'How is your leg now?' she asked. 'Are you sleeping better?'

Patrick said, 'I'm a bit better, thank you.'

'Tell me about when you were in France.'

Somehow, he could talk to her whereas he couldn't to Mrs Birch. So, for the first time since he had come to Bryncelin, he told someone what had happened.

'This was awful for you, wasn't it?' she said. 'You're brave to tell me all that. I'm sure you can't bear to think about it. I haven't heard anyone tell about those things.'

'I don't think anyone knows what it's like over there. They don't talk as if they understand.'

'Do you talk to Mrs Birch?'

'Well, no.' Patrick felt that Patsy wanted him to prefer her to Mrs Birch. And he didn't want her to think that he was dependent on the Birches. 'I don't talk about any of that. It doesn't seem right.'

'Why not?'

'Because we have to do what comes next, to get better. We can't change what happened.'

'Do you really think that?' she asked.

'Well, yes. But on the other hand I think about the others, Jenkins and Hibbert and Rees and Gerard, who was only sixteen, and all the others. I'm sorry, but I cry when I think about them.'

'I like it when you cry,' she said.

'Do you? What do you mean?'

'It just feels good when you cry.'

He didn't understand what she meant, but he couldn't ask any more.

They were sitting by the road in the sun, drinking champagne, after Patrick had practised walking with a stick.

'Have you got a family?' asked Patsy.

'Well, I suppose I must have, somewhere. But I was in the orphanage before I joined the regiment.'

'You've never had a mother?'

'There were sisters, nuns, at the orphanage. Sometimes Mrs Birch is like a mother – or a big sister, at least, I suppose. I don't know.'

'You've done terribly well,' she said.

'Not actually,' he said. He was embarrassed, so the words came out wrong.

'Very few could have done what you've done. I try to think of people I know who could have restored themselves as you have, and I can think of no one. You should be an officer.'

'I haven't had the education.'

'I think you have.'

The champagne was making him more confident. 'Gerard could have been an officer. He was clever.'

'Then you should do it for him.'

'They wouldn't let me.'

'They would now, with your experience. That's what I mean.'

'Mrs Cornwallis-West?'

'Yes?'

'Will you come again and take me for an outing?'

'There's a proposition.'

'I don't know how to ask.'

'I'm not sure about that. Well, you must think about applying to be an officer. You must find out about the examinations.'

That made him feel very happy.

When they got back to the house Patsy said to Mrs Birch, 'I should quite like Patrick to see our doctor, if you think that is possible. I think it would be helpful to have him look at the wound.'

That's very kind. I'm sure it's a good idea, even just to talk about what are the right exercises for his leg. I think he has improved a lot, with his confidence.'

'I promise I shall make an appointment within two weeks and take him myself.'

'Are you sure you have the time, Mrs West?'

'Of course. I feel I must help what you've done for him. He's made remarkable progress. It's wonderful to see.'

Patrick came to the car and this time as she was leaving she kissed him on his mouth. Very quickly. It could have meant nothing.

For the doctor's appointment Patsy arranged for an army car to collect Patrick and bring him to Ruthin. She introduced him to her husband. 'Colonel Cornwallis-West, this is Sergeant Barrett.'

'I am pleased and honoured,' said William. 'My wife has told me that you are a distinguished veteran of the French campaign. The regiment needs young men of such great quality. Come and tell me about yourself.'

Patrick could not speak. It was not that the old man was frightening or overbearing, it was that Patrick was overcome with a memory of the rush into the woods at the Aisne, and how the regiment had tried to fight its way back from its long retreat. It had seemed no great achievement, merely what had to be done to survive. He was dizzy and needed to sit down, but found himself staring at the old soldier.

'Please forgive me,' he said. 'I sometimes get confused as a result of my wounds. There are shrapnel wounds as well as the bayonet cut, and it hurts. Please forgive me. I've discussed this with Mrs Birch and I've decided to apply for a commission with the Fusiliers.'

William was delighted. 'Bring brandy,' he told a servant. 'This is a brave soldier who was injured in battle,' and he made a great fuss of Patrick. 'Fetch the doctor.'

Patsy smiled. 'The doctor's already on his way here to look at the sergeant's wounds,' she said.

'You'll be a great officer in the history of the regiment,' predicted William.

The doctor was an elderly man, with gentle hands. As he examined Patrick's bayonet wound and the shrapnel damage, he said, 'I see from the records that you were at Shelagh's hospital in France. Did you know that Colonel's West's younger daughter, the Duchess of Westminster, built that hospital? That's why it's called the Westminster.'

'No, I didn't know that.'

'They've been looking after you, the family?'

'Yes.'

'The Westminster did a good job on your leg. The secret is going to be walking, I should say. Just keep walking, a bit more each week. Also you had a terrible experience. Don't try to be brave yet. Stay away from things that frighten you. Your mind is wounded as well, and just as badly, so be careful of it. It will strengthen gradually, but you must give it time. Mrs Birch has been very good to you. You're very lucky to be staying with her. I shall call by and tell her I've seen you.'

As Patsy drove Patrick back to Bryncelin, through the woods by the river running along the valley, he said, 'Mrs West, I wanted to say how grateful I am.'

She stopped the car. 'Why?' she asked.

'Because I like you.'

'Good.'

He put his hand up to her face and kissed her. They stayed together like that, without saying anything, for a long time.

'You have a lovely house,' he said

'Are you jealous?'

'I don't know.'

'I want you to be. I want you to be jealous of everything about me.'

He didn't understand, didn't know what to say.

Patsy smiled at him. 'I'm sorry, that was a silly thing to say.'

'No,' he said, but he still didn't understand.

'What did Mrs Birch say about you applying for an officer's commission?'

'I didn't tell her it was your idea. Is that all right?'

'Yes, of course.'

'She was pleased. She said I should talk to the sergeant-major at the camp straight away. So I saw him and he gave me the examination papers to read. I have to take classes. The papers are difficult.'

'I can help you with them. Will you tell her you kissed me?'

'No.'

'Will you always keep it a secret?'

'Do you think I might be able to kiss you again?'

'We'll see. But you have to promise that it's a secret.'

'A war secret?'

'Yes.'

'For ever,' he agreed.

'Then kiss me,' she said.

They left the car and she made him walk along the pathway to exercise his leg. It made him laugh to be so happy. Now he did not let his mind go back to the fighting, because he had new things to think about. He cared so much that she should be all right and that they could be together even for a short moment. It was like being given a present. When he looked at her he could not believe how beautiful she was. Each time he saw her, that took him by surprise.

She was excited, too. He was so frail. She wanted his complete happiness to depend on her, and when she looked at him that was how it seemed. She loved his face and his look of astonishment. He was very precious to her.

'I must take you home now,' she said. 'No one must even guess at our secret. And if anyone ever does we must both be surprised and hurt that they should think such a thing. Do you understand?' she said.

'I'm not sure.'

'Well you'd better be, otherwise I'll eat you.'

'I'll keep my secret the way we're taught to do under enemy interrogation. Never carry papers. They tell us, ' "Blank out your mind. You know nothing, and never did. Act stupid." '

Chapter 9

AN OFFICER

PATRICK TOOK THE course for his application to be an officer. Before the war, they told him, it would have been almost impossible for someone like him, an orphan and from the ranks, to become an officer. The war had made it possible, but it was still very difficult. He would have to prove he had the qualities that distinguished an officer in the British army from other people. It was not only a question of learning, although there was a great deal of that, but also a question of character. He would have to show the character of an officer in everything he did.

To be recommended for promotion, a soldier not only had to demonstrate courage and good leadership in battle but also had to reach a suitable standard of education and pass the written examinations. The practical tests were not difficult for Patrick, but his time at school had been limited. His reading, writing and spelling were poor.

On his course the other applicants were much younger. They were boys fresh from school who already had the learning that, they explained, you needed for an officer's personality. But Patrick had battle experience, so when they talked about the practical skills of war and soldiery he knew a lot. Moreover, he was silent and self-contained, so he had a certain dignity in what he did. He was never raucous or juvenile, and there was no history that anyone could hold against him. On the contrary, his experience in France, and his wounds and the shell-shock from which everyone knew he suffered, earned him respect. 'Shell-shock' was the name people used for symptoms like his, when he began to cry and could not bear to talk.

He had to learn about the British Empire, and he discovered where Serbia was, and Bulgaria and also Turkey, where the army was trying to occupy the Dardanelles peninsula. They learnt about the empire in India, and the problems of China and Tibet.

It was the first school he'd ever been to where he was old enough to listen to and understand what was said, but mostly he was interested in the army and the discussions about manoeuvring positions and trench construction and mortar fire. He learnt how to read maps properly and see from the contours which positions were visible and which were invisible, and which would make the best gun emplacements.

He thought about Patsy every second of every day. The classes at Bodelwyddan meant he was often away from Bryncelin, and Patsy was cunning at making arrangements for them to meet. So they had official time together, when she collected him from Bryncelin in order to follow the doctor's routine of walking and exercise, and unofficial time when she would arrange a secret rendezvous by parking the car in the woods above Kinmel Park.

She was so busy with war charity work all over the county that it was quite easy for her get time with him. Sometimes she made him hide on the floor of the car as she drove through a village, waving to the people.

He liked to give her presents, a posy of flowers, or little notes which were no more than his name, just a tiny something, every time they met. He was filled with secret happiness. It nourished him, so that often he felt no need of food.

Mrs Birch was pleased with Patrick's progress. The work of becoming an officer had absorbed him. He was much less distressed. His leg seemed to be healing, though sometimes at night she knew he was awake because she heard him moving around. For an hour or more each evening she helped him with his homework, and she, too, had learnt a lot from it. She noticed that he was eating less than when he had first arrived, but she did not know why. She thought him a good, kind person. She hoped he would get what he wanted.

She told him, 'You ought to ask Mrs Cornwallis-West if she has any advice about applying for your commission.'

'Do you really think so?' he asked. He hated deceiving her.

Patsy began to make plans. She would talk to Lieutenant-Colonel Delmé-Radcliffe at the camp. William would write to Sir John Cowans at the War Office, so would Mrs Birch, and so would Patsy herself. She would write out letters for Patrick to send, thanking everyone for their support.

Before long there was a regimental dinner at Ruthin, and she took Lieutenant-Colonel Delmé-Radcliffe aside and told him she hoped Sergeant Barrett would get his commission.

'I was in France at the same time as Barrett,' Radcliffe said. 'I just got a bullet in my arm – nothing like what happened to him. I was on the way home when we heard what happened in Zandvoorde. It was dreadful. Nearly all our men there were killed in two days. I heard about him: the subaltern in command of the platoon was on sick leave, and Barrett more or less took charge – he kept a good platoon. I'm sure he'll be an excellent officer. I wish I'd thought of it myself. I'll keep an eye out for the application. I'm sure it will only be a question of his medical; that will be the slow part.'

'My husband is going to write to Sir John Cowans at the War Office, in support of the sergeant's application.'

'When I get it, I'll write, too. These promotions are more common than they used to be, but nevertheless everyone is very careful about them. A reference from Colonel West will be very helpful.'

'How are things at the camp, Colonel?'

'Very busy, madam, you know. There is an immense amount of training of new recruits.'

'Have you heard about the new supply depot at Wrexham?'

'There's been some talk, but I think it's a War Office development, not the Fusiliers'.'

'I know General Cowans was hoping to find someone local to be in command.'

'Oh, really? I don't think I'd be told about that.'

'I could mention your name, if you were interested,' Patsy said

'Well, that is extremely kind, madam. I can say I think I would be.'

'I'm sure to see him in the New Year. I could say that we had a chat.'

'That would be extremely generous, madam. I shall keep my eye out for young Barrett. He has done well to recover.'

'I'm very hopeful he'll turn out to be the right type,' she said, 'and so is Colonel West.'

Patrick sat with his books in the meadow by the river, reading the sample exam questions to Patsy: ' "State at the head of your paper the branch of the Service to which you belong." '

'Patsy,' she said. 'You belong to me. You are in my service.'

'Infantry.' He went on slowly, ' "Question one. General Idea. A Brown army has invaded Whiteland and driven the White army in a westerly direction off the map. Whiteland, however, has territorial forces, which are assembling in the south and south-west.

' "The Brown commander-in-chief has decided to use the Charlbury–Stow-on-the-Wold–Cheltenham line for his supplies." '

'I know the answer to this question,' said Patsy.

'We don't know the question yet.'

'They've given it away. Those are places in England, near my sister Min's house.'

'So who is the Brown army?' Patrick asked her.

'I don't know that yet.'

'So hush until we get to the end of the question. "Until certain necessary repairs on the line are completed, supplies are being forwarded from the railhead at Yarnton by motor lorry. On 20 April, this mobile column was heavily attacked from the south by White territorial troops. All communication since the message giving this information has ceased. Patrols from Windrush failed to get further than the New Barn Inn, where they were fired upon. All traffic west of Burford has stopped. What action do you propose to the C-in-C in order to resolve the situation?"'

'Well, which side are you on?'

'It doesn't seem to say.' Patrick searched back through the question.

'That's the first thing to sort out. Perhaps the Browns are the Welsh?'

'Wait. There's more here.' Patrick continued reading. '"Note: after the men have had their evening meal the following supplies are available. For the 21st, they have that which the men are carrying, and that which is in the cookers. For the 22nd that which is in the train, and two further days' supply can be obtained from any of the communications posts.'

'Well, that's reassuring – we won't go hungry. We have four days to think of an answer. How lovely.'

'We seem to be on the White side.'

'I should hope so,' Patsy said, 'especially if we're fighting in Wiltshire.'

'Ah, it gives the answer at the end: "Probably the first thing you would think of is: 'What does this attack mean? Is it merely a raid by a small party, or is it concerned with the movement of a large hostile force? Is it a determined attempt on our lines of communication or is it only a pinprick?' With the meagre information at your disposal it is difficult for you, as commanding officer, to answer these questions, but it is clearly your duty to try and find out. The next question you would probably ask yourself is 'What ought I to do?'' It goes on for four pages.'

'I think you should call for help.'

'I think that's what it says, in the end.'

In October 1915, Colonel Cornwallis-West wrote to Sir John Cowans: 'I am very unwilling to bother you in the midst of all your work, but I am asked especially to recommend Sergeant Barrett, of the Royal Welch Fusiliers, for a commission. His commanding officer, Lieutenant-Colonel Delmé-Radcliffe has, I am told, already written to you about him. I believe this man, whom I know, to be thoroughly worthy of promotion.'

Cowans's office was always very efficient. They immediately wrote to Radcliffe, asking for a copy of the application, even though in the normal course of events it would have been no concern of the quartermaster-general. Radcliffe replied that he was obliged to wait for the medical officer's certificate, which might, he had been told, take another month. He did, however, enclose a copy of his letter of recommendation: 'My letter will give you an idea of what an excellent man Sergeant Barrett is, and I hope he will get a commission in my present battalion when the medical officer passes him fit for work at home.'

Patsy suggested to Mrs Birch that she should write to Sir John Cowans, asking him to keep an eye on Sergeant Barrett's papers, which, she said, 'were struggling to climb the very steep hill to the War Office'.

Cowans knew that all these letters were really from Patsy. There was nothing anyone could do that was not being done, but she enjoyed making him aware of what she wanted. In the end she wrote directly: 'Be very kind, Jack, and get him appointed to the 12th Battalion at Kinmel Camp, as I can help him in many ways. And all the officers he has served under are there and they all take an interest in him and are anxious to help him on. I am <u>always</u> bothering you, Jack. Love from Patsy.'

Patrick and Patsy were together almost every day in the autumn, while the sunshine lasted. There were favourite places, some in the mountains, some overlooking the sea. 'This can't go on,' said Patsy. 'But it can't stop, either – not for another day. Please, another day. What will we do if someone finds out? I love your hands. I love your eyes and your hair, I love every fraction of your face. The way you said those things, the words you choose, your smile. I love to be alongside you, for you to hold me. You won't like me tomorrow. Just one more sweet soft kiss, just gently on my lips, on the edge of my tongue. I'm lost, I have no more control, cling to me.'

She wanted him to need her, to be dependent on her. She wanted him to be her possession, for him not to think about anything else; to be obsessed, without cease, to be slave to her every whim. To do any ridiculous thing she required of him, and never, never to stop. For it to be beyond his promise, so that he could not control himself, and to give her pleasure of whatever kind she wished.

He wanted her always to be there with affection, with encouragement, with admiration; always to be tolerant of his weakness. He wanted her to listen to him, or, if she teased him, which she did, always to be gentle. He wanted her to be a little vulnerable, whereas she was normally certain about what to do. He liked to hear about what she had done. She knew so many things, particularly how to be good with people, and with that she always surprised him. Yet she was interested in him and what he had done and what he thought. He mattered to her.

They wanted different things, but each wanted the other to provide them. Like two posts leaning against each other, each depending on the other not to fall. Falling would hurt. Neither was ever certain that this would not be the day when the other was not there. They were always frightened about that.

'Test me on this paper,' he said.

They were sitting on the hillside at Llanarmon, looking down over the whole of the Clwyd Valley. It was a fine, warm October day.

She read out the question. ' "You are a brigade commander. Several hundred head of cattle are captured, and you are ordered to select from them a sufficient number to provide two days' supply of fresh meat. To what points do you pay attention when choosing the animals? How many animals would you pick and what steps would you take to ensure their proper care and custody?" '

He answered, ' "Twelve head would be picked. The cattle would first be examined for good health, for which the following points would be noted: movements brisk; eyes bright and . . ." '

' "Full",' she prompted.

' "Eyes bright and full, muzzle cool and moist, dung normal –" '

'Oh, Pat, for goodness' sake, don't be unpleasant.'

'That's what it says in the book: "normal, coat glossy".' He had it off by heart. ' "The animals should be chewing the cud. The twelve animals would be selected from the healthy stock aged between two and five years old." '

'How can you tell their age?' she asked.

'I don't know. It doesn't say.'

'Well, you obviously need to know.'

'I'd ask the farmer.'

'In French?'

'No, of course, we always have farm boys with us. Of course.' He went on, ' "To ensure their proper care and custody the animals should, during a march, be driven along roads different from those used by the troops." '

'What does that mean?'

'I've no idea,' he laughed, 'but that's what it says. "And they should be fed and watered early, again in the middle of the day, and again on reaching camp."'

'That's so good, my sweetheart. Remember: "eyes bright and full", like mine.'

Chapter 10

LOVERS

THE NEWS THAT Patrick had been gazetted Second Lieutenant Barrett in the Royal Welch Fusiliers arrived by telegram at Bryncelin on Christmas Eve 1915. 'Gazetted' meant that the appointment was listed, with other government appointments, in the *London Gazette* for that day. Mrs Birch immediately sent a telegram to Mrs Cornwallis-West at Ruthin Castle, for she knew Patsy would be thrilled and deserved thanks for what she had done for Patrick.

Shelagh and her children had arrived at Ruthin some days before, to help prepare for Christmas. Stella and George were back from America, and would arrive on Christmas Day. There would be a party in the evening for the regiment.

Patsy set out as soon as the telegram came. She was already missing Patrick, and she knew she would hardly be able to see him over Christmas. She told Shelagh she would be away for only a couple of hours.

At Bryncelin there was a tremendous celebration. The soldiers Mrs Birch had nursed, those who had not yet gone back to France, came round for Christmas Eve with some of their friends, so the house was full of soldiers. Dick Birch had a bag of pheasants from the estate, which they were going to roast the next day and which needed to be plucked and drawn.

Patsy managed to get Patrick alone for a moment. 'Congratulations, Lieutenant.' She gave him his Christmas present, a small framed copy of a painting called *The Reunion*, on which she had written, 'Will it be like this for us, Pat, dear?' And he gave her a small book of poetry.

Patsy said, 'I have only a moment, but I wanted to come and see you.' She put his hand on her breast. 'After Christmas we'll be lovers. Do you want that?'

'Yes.'

'Good.'

Patsy gave Mrs Birch and Dick their presents, and then apologised for being hasty. She had been so pleased to get the telegram and wanted to come straight away, but now she had to get back to the family. She told Mrs Birch that she should be very proud.

Mrs Birch said that after Christmas she and Dick would take Patrick up to London to buy his uniform. Patsy told her that she was herself planning to stay at Shelagh's house in Lancaster Gate, to look after the children while Shelagh was away at the hospitals. The Birches must be sure to call in while they were there.

Patsy hoped the London trip would offer opportunities to be alone with Patrick. She thought of another way: 'When you get back, I have some work that I'd like him to do at Ruthin, if you think it would be all right for him to stay over one weekend. I'd be grateful for his help.'

'I'm sure he'd enjoy that,' said Mrs Birch; she was overflowing with pride.

In December 1915, the combined forces fighting under British command on the Gallipoli peninsula in Turkey withdrew, defeated, with the loss of 250,000 men. It was devastating. The expedition had been launched in the spring by Churchill, as a way of opening a second line of attack on the east of the German Empire alongside the Russians. It was a campaign of huge bravado, but ill considered and inadequately prepared. There was a presumption, clearly stated by Kitchener, that the Turks would not fight, and an even more dangerous calculation by Churchill that the objectives were worth a certain 'necessary loss'.

The quartermaster-general, however, famously ran his office like a beautifully assembled timepiece. Any day the objectives might change, but the routines worked faultlessly. Food and blankets were the main priorities all the time, for a million men on the move and numbers ever on the increase.

Cowans avoided getting involved in politics, but he watched what was going on. Mostly, the politicians made him angry. There was too much confusion, no clarity of purpose, too much posturing, and the losses were huge. It was a world falling apart: but not in his office. There they knew that the war could be lost if supplies failed, and they had a tacit understanding that this was becoming a war which no one might win but which someone might lose.

Cowans saw the letters from the Cornwallis-Wests and their friends about a young soldier in the Royal Welch Fusiliers. He made sure that they were passed to the right place with his endorsement, and that he was told what happened. So he knew that Patrick Barrett had been promoted before they knew in Denbigh.

He had always been very close to Daisy, both before and since she got married, and counted Patsy one of the best people in the world. They had always been good to him, and, now that he was in a position to, he wanted to help.

Patsy was given a new car, a Rolls-Royce, for Christmas. She had been asked to have her photograph taken alongside it for a magazine. It was gorgeous, with seats like leather chesterfields.

On 7 January 1916, the Cornwallis-Wests took a box at the pantomime at Rhyl. William and Shelagh and the children went in the charabanc. Patsy went via St Asaph and picked up Patrick, whom William had invited to join the family. Patsy was early. It was the first chance she and Patrick had had to be together since Christmas.

'Did you stop loving me?' she said.

They kissed. And then they made love, for the first time, in her new car, on the way to the pantomime at Rhyl.

That night, when she got back to the castle, Patsy wrote him a note.

Dear Mr Barrett,

If, by chance, you are writing to that dear boy we were talking about, will you give him my love and tell him I often think about him? But I cannot write to him until I see you on Saturday, and get his address for certain.

Yours, most sincerely,

Patsy Cornwallis-West

PS: Please do not tell anyone about the boy. It's just my secret.

Patrick took the note up to his room and put it in his drawer with the other things she had given him.

When he went back downstairs, Mrs Birch asked, 'Are you sure you want to go to Ruthin at the weekend? I don't know why she wants you to do things. She can employ anyone to do labouring for her. She doesn't need an officer in the British army to do that kind of thing.'

'I don't mind.'

'You're not to be officer-class, now, and part of her set. She likes to have certain people around her. You're our set, not hers.'

'I think she likes to make sure I'm still exercising my leg. She makes me work hard on fitness when I see her.'

'She's not to take up your time; you have enough to do with your studies.'

'I think she's only trying to help.'

'I know Patrick, but all the same . . . This is a dangerous time for you. You mustn't let your promotion go to your head. You're not to be boastful.'

'You've been so good to me,' he replied. 'I don't always deserve your kindness.'

They hugged each other.

He didn't want to let either woman down. He saw that Mrs Birch was very attractive. She had a lovely face and dark hair. She was not much older than he was, and she was always so generous to him. Her toughness was rather like his: it came from inside her. Running the house and the farm required her to have great determination and not to get exhausted, and he realised how patient she had been with his wound and sickness. He saw her as a schoolteacher who was honest and worked hard. He wanted to please her.

Suddenly he began to feel dizzy and disorientated, as he had when he met Colonel Cornwallis-West at Ruthin. It was the stress of the people in a conflict of which he might be the cause, and he could not cope with it. It was like a physical grip on him. It really hurt. It was as if his mind had organised itself to cope with violence but could not take personal arguments, and it punished him by putting him back in the trench. He was sweating and had to grip his hands together. And the reason was the guilt he felt about Mrs Birch not knowing about him and Mrs West. That in turn was recreating the fear and the shock. Besides, the evening at the pantomime and in Patsy's car had made him very tired.

'Can you tell me what it is?' she said.

'I'm sorry, I just can't keep control of myself. I'm going to weep.' And he did, sobbing and moaning with convulsions.

'I'm sorry' was all he could say, so she led him over to the sofa and held him very tightly. He found it comforting. Mrs Birch let him fall asleep.

On Saturday afternoon Patrick went up to Ruthin. William was away in Hampshire and Patsy had let the few maids still working have the weekend off, until Sunday evening.

She showed Patrick to his room, which was next to hers, and

told him to make himself at home. She would be downstairs in the drawing-room by the fire.

When he went down, he undressed her in front of the fire and then undressed himself. They made love on the tiger-skin rug.

In the evening she fed him in the kitchen and they made love there and then went from room to room of the castle, and they tobogganed down the stairs, until, exhausted and happy, they collapsed in her bed and lay close together.

During the night it snowed, and from the cold balcony they watched the moonlit fields below the castle turn white. In the morning they wrapped up warmly and walked down to the river.

She made him sleep for a long while before she sent him home.

He took with him a note from Patsy: 'Dear Mrs Birch, On 14 February William will be away in Hampshire with the regiment. There are now so few servants here that I get quite frightened being on my own. Would you mind if I stayed with you that weekend? I would be so grateful. Patsy C-W.'

'What work did you do?' Mrs Birch asked.

'Oh, not much. I just brought up some logs into the house. I think all the menservants have gone now, so she only has the maids.'

'What did she talk about?'

'Just my exams, that sort of thing.'

He was like a sullen schoolboy. She wondered why. She said, 'She shouldn't use you for that kind of work – you're an officer. You didn't have any bad moments, did you?' She was worried that if Patrick had had one of his crying fits Patsy might have told someone about it.

'No, she likes me.'

'What do you mean, she likes you?'

'Nothing. She likes me, that's all I mean.'

'What does she want to stay here for?'

'As she says, the house is empty. I should think she gets nervous.'

'You're behaving very strangely.'

'No I'm not.'

But the deception troubled him deeply. It hurt him to lie to Mrs Birch.

When Patsy arrived on Saturday evening, Mr and Mrs Birch were out.

Patrick was nervous. 'She's been asking me all week what we did at the weekend. She's been in a strange mood all the time.'

'I don't think it's because of me,' said Patsy. 'It's because of something completely different.'

'What do you mean?'

'It's because of Dick Birch.'

'Why?'

'She's suspects that he's having an affair with a woman in London. She's been asking people what he does when he goes there.'

'And is he?'

'Oh yes. He has been for ages. Her name is Annie.'

At dinner they talked about the regiment.

Then Patsy said 'I was very grateful that Lieutenant Barrett could come to Ruthin at the weekend. All the men have gone now and we only have a couple of maids. He was very helpful. I'd like him to come again next weekend.'

Mrs Birch looked at her closely. 'I'm not sure why you asked him to come on his own. He has a life to lead as an officer now.'

This was quite abrupt. Dick and Patsy were both embarrassed. Patrick tensed.

'He's not a servant,' she went on, 'and he got his commission because of his own hard work. He can be very proud of himself. I'm very proud of him, too. But he's an officer now.'

'You're right to be proud.' For once, Patsy was unsure of herself.

'Yes, you are,' said Dick Birch.

'She knows what I mean.'

Dick changed the subject. 'I'm going down to Hampshire myself. The regiment's using the colonel's land at Milton.'

Mrs Birch left the room and went into the kitchen. Patsy followed her.

Mrs Birch said, 'He still has a great deal of studying to do. He must be ahead of his work before he goes back to Bodelwyddan. He knows it's important. He's told me so, but he may be frightened to tell you. Besides, he must still be careful of his health. He mustn't be put under pressure. Sometimes he's put under too much pressure. He's told me that, too.'

'Of course.' Patsy managed to look as if she didn't know what Mrs Birch was talking about. She had been planning to go to Patrick's room during the night, but now she decided not to.

Instead, she wrote him a note and she handed it to him as they went downstairs to breakfast in the morning. It said, 'Boy, dear, I may be wrong, but I don't think I am. Mrs B. doesn't want you to come to me next Saturday, and will stop it by saying you aren't strong enough, or by writing to the major, or something. But I want you so much to come, dear. Don't mind how I treat you today: you will know the real me, Patsy, all the time and understand.'

She could see already that he had withdrawn into himself. He looked as if he hadn't slept. He was frightened.

Dick had ridden out to see to some work before church, so there were just the three of them at the breakfast table. Patrick was silent. Eventually he grew so distressed that he got up and went back to his room.

'This is because of you,' said Mrs Birch angrily. 'You make too many demands on him. Your friendship with him is difficult for him to cope with. He may have been commissioned, but he's just an ordinary soldier trying to do his best. You shouldn't be asking him to go on visits with you. You can see for yourself the damage you're doing him. He needs me to look after him – you must leave him alone. He tells me what you want of him, but he can't cope with it. He doesn't know how to tell you, but he doesn't want to go on visits with you. Or, if he does come to Ruthin, he wants me to come, too. He doesn't want to be alone with you – he's told me. It's killing him.'

Patsy believed that Mrs Birch was overprotecting Patrick and stifling him. He was twenty-four, and had had more, and deeper, experience than most people three times his age; he did not need that kind of protection. He needed loving, and the encouragement to find a life of his own. It was time for him to get away from Mrs Birch. He must understand that, and Patsy knew that she could help him find his way. But she also knew that she could never say that to Mrs Birch; it would be appallingly unkind, when one thought of all she had done for Patrick. Mrs Birch's distress was probably caused by Dick Birch's adultery, and all this about Patrick was her way of expressing her unhappiness. Patsy would never make light of those feelings.

Patsy was annoyed but she was also frightened, because she could not tell, from what Mrs Birch had said, how much the Birches knew about her and Patrick or how much they had guessed. She hated gossip like that, and wouldn't be able to bear it if it spoilt her love or Patrick's.

She went back to her room to get ready for church and started to write Patrick another note.

Boy, dear,

I'm only thinking of you and your happiness. I see you chafing against the tight hand over you. You're beginning to feel yourself again and the man in you is speaking: yet you feel she has nursed you. She has told me you told her that you don't want to go with me when I pay visits. I can quite understand it, if you don't – I was only thinking of you. But personally I would so, so love, to have you quite to myself at Ruthin, and will arrange either for this Saturday, or next. She proposes to come, too. But please I want you alone. So I will, I think, make it the following Saturday. God bless you, darling. I hate to see your poor, tired, worrying face this morning and so want you to have Peace.

Someone knocked. She hid the letter and opened the door. It was Dick Birch.

'Patsy, may I have a word? That night you were with George and General Cowans at the theatre . . . You wouldn't say anything here about that, would you?'

She gave her mischievous smile. 'It's my hold over you, Dick Birch.'

'No, but seriously?'

'Of course I wouldn't.'

'My wife is being very difficult.'

'So I can see.'

'I'm going to London now. I can hardly keep it a secret from you. I'm finding it a strain here, she's so unpleasant. I think I may enlist.'

'I'm sorry it's all so difficult.'

'That's kind of you, Patsy. I'm sorry to have to leave now. You don't come and stay with us often, and I feel I shouldn't go.'

'Please don't worry, dear Dick,' said Patsy.

'All right, then. By the way, I'm sure I'll see George.'

'Give him my love and tell him to send his mother a telegram. I miss him.'

Dick left, and she went back to her letter. 'I began this before going to church. Mr Birch has just interrupted to tell me he is going to London this afternoon (for the reasons I explained). Boy, I trust you and so believe every word you say. I feel as if you could never tell me a lie, and yet . . . ? Well, dear, we must have a few words somehow alone today. Patsy.'

Patsy heard hardly a word of the church service. She was anxious and afraid. She was so in love with Patrick, but she was beginning to think he really might want to break with her. She didn't believe, from what he had said the day before, that Mrs Birch thought they were lovers. It was more that Mrs Birch wanted to take Patrick under her control, and Patsy did not want that and she did not think it was right for Patrick. Mrs Birch was behaving as if she had power over Patsy, which she most certainly did not. Nevertheless, it was very distressing.

She passed Patrick the note as they came out of church.

There were other guests for lunch and tea, who had been invited to meet Patsy. They talked about the regiment and the county, and whose families had lost fathers and sons. However, in the evening, when they had gone, Mrs Birch started again to complain to Patsy.

She said, 'You've been using him. It's made him ill.'

Patsy was furious, but decided that she would not get into an argument when it was unclear what it was she was arguing about. It was beneath her.

She merely said, 'We've had a marvellous weekend. I love coming here, especially in spring. I'm sorry, but I'll have to leave very early tomorrow morning. My husband will need me.'

The she went up to her room and wrote to Patrick again. 'Boy, she has said some cruel, hard things to me today. I think, dear, I shall go to Chester tomorrow morning. She has been very rude; but I will tell you all when we can be at peace in my flower boudoir. I will teach you to love really beautiful poetry. Write to me often. I am so weary of life sometimes. Can't you post your letters at the camp, not here in the bag, where it's not safe? Just write as you feel, express it – spell it as you like – I shall understand. Patsy.'

She took the letter and slipped it under the door of Patrick's room. If he wanted to come to her in the night, he knew where she would be.

Mrs Birch was sitting with Patrick, and they both saw the note slide under the door. Before Patrick could react, she went quickly to the door, picked up the note and read it.

Chapter 11

MRS BIRCH

WITHOUT SPEAKING, MRS Birch threw the note on to the bed and went downstairs.

Patrick read it and then went downstairs, too. He found Mrs Birch in the kitchen, sitting staring into the fire.

As soon as he went in, she demanded, 'What does she mean?'

'She's just being friendly.'

'No, Patrick, don't you lie to me. What does she mean, it's not safe to post your letters here? What does she mean, "we can be at peace in my flower boudoir"?' She was in a rage. 'What have you let her do?'

'Nothing.'

'Patrick, don't try to deceive me. This isn't a letter about nothing. Why is she telling you that I've been cruel to her? Rude, have I been? So she'll teach you to love poetry, will she? Is that what you want?'

'No, of course not.'

'Then why does she say it? Do you know who says things like that?'

'No.'

'No, you don't, thank goodness.' She looked at him hard for a moment. 'Have you touched her?'

'No, I haven't.'

'Never?'

'Well, she gave me a kiss at Christmas.'

'A kiss?'

'Well, yes, when she came when we had the telegram from London that day, about my promotion.'

'She kissed you?'

'Yes.'

'Did you kiss her back?'

'No, I couldn't do that.'

'Do you think she wants to kiss you again?'

'No, of course not.'

'Does she think that I have been wrong for you?'

'Well of course not.'

'Then why does she want to hide things from me? Why does she want to get you on your own? That hurts, Patrick. Do you understand?'

'Yes, I do.'

'I looked after you when you were so ill that you nearly died, and now she wants to take you away and be alone with you – like a possession. How can she be so cruel? And it's me she calls cruel. How can she say I've been cruel, and call me rude?' She was crying.

Patrick was scared to go near her.

'So what are you going to do?' she asked angrily through her tears.

'I'll have to explain to her that she must leave me alone.'

'Leave you alone? What has she been doing?'

'Well, not leave me alone, exactly, but not to write letters like that, even though she's been very kind.'

'And how are you going to explain that to her?'

'I'll write to her, politely thanking her for what she has done, and explaining. I'll practise it first and then I'll write it out.'

'You tell her you don't want to love poetry.'

'Yes, I'll say that, but politely.'

Patrick thought of his agreement with Patsy that if ever they were accused of anything they would both deny that anything had ever happened between them. He hugged Mrs Birch. He said he was sorry Mrs Cornwallis-West's letter had made her so unhappy. He was sure Mrs Cornwallis-West would understand that she had upset Mrs Birch, and he was sure she had never meant to.

Mrs Birch hugged him back. Then she told him, in detail, what he must say in his letter to Patsy.

In the night, Patsy went to Patrick's room, but he wasn't there. From the top of the stairs she could hear voices and Mrs Birch crying downstairs, so she went back to her room.

She left very early in the morning, before anyone else was up.

The next day was 14 February. Patrick walked down to Bodel-wyddan Camp, and found an empty classroom. Carefully he drafted a letter to Patsy. He made several corrections, then wrote it out again and posted it in the camp's postbox. He had made a copy for himself, and took it home to show Mrs Birch.

Dear Mrs Cornwallis-West,

I expect this letter will surprise you very much. I have been awake most of the night thinking over all you have said and wrote to me. You must not mind the mistakes because I have not got my books with me. I have always tried to live an honest and a upright life and I have so far succeeded – though I have been a common Tommy. I must speak my mind on paper which I do not seem able to do when I am with you.

I do not like the way you have wrote about Mrs Birch. I came to Bryncelin a very sick man and she nursed me back to life. And she and Mr Birch gave me a home life for which I have always prayed. She does not have a tight rein on me, and I do not know what you mean by the man speaking in me. It will be a great sorrow when I have to leave the only home I have ever had, and her wonderful Motherly care for me. I respeck her for all the good work she is doing, and I do not like the way you speak about my letters not being safe in the postbag at Bryncelin. Considering how very nicely she speaks of you, to me, it hurt me very much. My heart is in my work and I want to get on and make a name for myself and show you and all those who have been kind to me how I value their help.

I do not think I could ever look Colonel Cornwallis-West in the face because you kissed me; he was very good to me. I do not want to understand Potry, I only want to live a good life and serve my God and King. I do not understand why you call me darling, when Mrs Delmé-Radcliffe, Mrs Donald, Mrs Leach, Mrs Davies-Cooke, Mrs Bibby and Mrs Birch, never do, and they do not want to teach me Potry. I honour and respeck you very much and some day hope to be able to do something for you. Your notes frightened me very much, you see my Religion, as you know, compells me to go to Confession, and it is the first time in my life that for your sake I shall not be able to confess properly, so will you please understand how miserable I am.

Will you please make some excuse for not asking me to Ruthin, at Bryncelin, if you do not do this I shall tell them I intend working all Sundays for my Promotion? I shall always pray that God will give you the good health to continue the good work you are doing. You must please forgive me for writing plainly my thoughts and believe me always ever yours gratefully,

    Patrick Barrett

'What do you mean, "the man speaking in me"?' asked Mrs Birch.

    'It was something she wrote to me.'

    'When?'

    'On Sunday she wrote me a note in the morning,' he said

    'There was another of these?'

    'Yes.'

    'I want to see it.'

Patrick was frightened again. He'd thought he had done well with his letter. He went to fetch the note, and while he did so decided to hide Patsy's presents and all the other letters behind his chest of drawers.

Mrs Birch read the note quickly. 'What does this mean, "Dick Birch is going to London, for the reasons I explained"?' she asked.

Patrick said nothing.

What does it mean? What has she explained about Mr Birch?'

'Just something about going to Newlands.'

'Patrick, you're lying, I can see that. What did she explain about Mr Birch? Are there any more of these letters?'

'No, that's all.'

'I don't believe you. Show me the drawer.'

'There's nothing else there.'

She swept upstairs and went though every drawer, with him watching. 'What else is there?' she demanded.

'Nothing'

'Don't start crying. Now, what did she say about Mr Birch? Has she been writing letters to him as well? Patrick? Answer me.'

'She didn't say anything else about Mr Birch, just that he was going to Newlands. She'd told me that on Saturday.'

'Oh, Patrick, I'm sorry.' With an effort she calmed herself and said gently, 'You've done well. That's a very good letter, and it's brave of you to have written it. I'm sure it will make things much easier for you. You'll have peace here now.'

He couldn't deceive her any more, he couldn't keep secrets any more – he could feel the lies and the deceit destroying him inside. All he could do was give in and not fight any more. He whispered, 'Mrs West told me that Mr Birch has a lady in London and that's what was upsetting you.'

There was a long silence, then Mrs Birch said very quietly, 'That story is not true, Patrick. It does upset me to hear it, especially from her, but I've heard it before and I asked Mr Birch if it was true, and he told me that it was not. And I believe him.'

'I'm sorry I said that,' he said

'No. It's better for us both if you can tell me things like that. Do you believe Mr Birch?'

'That's horrid for you.'

'It's horrid that people say things like that. It makes me look foolish. Like a fool.'

Alone in his room that evening, Patrick thought about what Mrs Birch had said. He decided to write to Patsy again.

> Dear Mrs Cornwallis-West,
>
> I know you will be glad to know that whoever told you that Mr Birch was keeping a lady in London it is not true. I thought you would be glad to know, as this was one of the things that made me so miserable as I love Mr Birch very much and respect him more than anyone I know.
>
> Believe me yours gratefully,
> Patrick Barrett

Patsy felt more destroyed by the second letter, than she had been by the first. When she saw his writing on the envelope she had hoped he might be writing to say sorry for his first letter, or to give her an explanation. She knew the first letter had been written at Mrs Birch's instigation. She could not imagine what conversation had given rise to the second, because Dick Birch was away.

She was deeply hurt, and angry, too. She had been attacked and wanted to defend herself. Patrick's letter was rude and impertinent. It implied behaviour on her part that was a flight of his fanciful imagination. It should not have been written by anyone to a lady, least of all by an officer to the wife of his regiment's colonel. She showed the letters to William, and told him that the young lieutenant had got carried away by the kindness and attention he had been shown. They agreed that he should be told he must not write letters like that. They felt it was best to stay out of the matter and allow a senior officer to talk to him. The following weekend, General Sir Henry Mackinnon, head of Western Command, would be staying at Ruthin. Patsy said she would ask his advice and explain that it was a private matter.

General Mackinnon was delighted to oblige.

'I have had the strangest letter from an officer at Kinmel,' she said. She told him about Patrick's long illness, and that she and William had helped him get his commission, and then handed him Patrick's long letter.

'Oh dear' was his reaction. 'We do make up some unusual officers these days. I hope we can make amends to you. It would be best dealt with, I think, by his commanding officer. Do you think poetry should be more of an army thing?'

She laughed.

'But,' he went on, 'I don't think one can quite let it pass. Something ought to be said.'

'Will you let me talk to Colonel Delmé-Radcliffe?' she asked. 'I'd prefer to keep the matter straightforward.'

'You know him, don't you? Very well, that might be best.'

Patsy duly asked Radcliffe to visit her at Ruthin for a private discussion.

She showed him the letter and said, 'You know I've been worried about the boy. I do feel it's time he got away from that house, and perhaps went back to work. Mrs Birch has been wonderful, but he needs to regain his independence.'

Radcliffe felt more strongly about the letter. He thought, as Patsy had expected he would, that it was an outrageous letter for an officer to write, under any circumstances of any kind. It was exactly the opposite of proper officer conduct. What might or might not have given rise to it made no difference at all; that was nobody's business or concern. It was embarrassing for the regiment that such a thing should happen, he said, and he was most grateful to Mrs Cornwallis-West for giving him the opportunity to deal with it without making the matter public.

As he was leaving, William told him, 'Mrs West is very upset about that letter, but I'm sure you will know how to deal with it. I feel her kindness has been turned against her.'

Chapter 12

DISCIPLINE

DURING THE NEXT few weeks, Delmé-Radcliffe followed Patsy's suggestion and applied for Patrick to be moved away from the area. He also, on his own initiative, put in a request for the young man to be stripped of his commission.

Had she known about the latter, Patsy would have been horrified. She hoped that, if he left Bryncelin, not only would he be removed from Mrs Birch's influence but she might be able to resume contact with him. It was no part of her plan that his commission should be taken away: she knew how distraught Patrick would be.

Colonel Radcliffe also informed General Mackinnon that he intended to move Barrett. He thought it wise to do so, as Mrs Cornwallis-West had apparently discussed the matter with the general first. While it was all to be done properly, they were keen to oblige the lady. The request was also passed through the proper chain of command to Brigadier-General Owen Thomas.

General Mackinnon acknowledged and concurred with the action Radcliffe proposed.

Patrick heard nothing from Patsy, and nothing more was said at Bryncelin. Mrs Birch did not talk to him about it. She hoped that the matter was closed. There were no more invitations for Patrick to go visiting or to stay at Ruthin. Dick Birch knew nothing about the letters or about what had happened on the night after he left for Hampshire.

Patrick hoped that soon Patsy would get a message to him to say, 'Don't worry, Boy. You did what you had to, and well done.'

For a month nobody at the camp said anything. Then, one Tuesday, Patrick had to deliver a report to his superior, Captain Grey, at Kinmel. When he got there he was told to go to Colonel Radcliffe's office. He was marched into the office, and found himself facing not only the colonel but two other officers, Captain Grey and Captain Howard.

Colonel Delmé-Radcliffe said, 'You want to see Captain Grey, and I want to see you, too. What do you mean by writing the way you did to a lady?'

Barrett replied, 'I don't know what you mean, sir.' It had never occurred to him for one instant that Patsy might show the letters to an officer of the regiment. He had not thought she would be angry with him. He had no way of answering the questions.

'Accusing Mrs Cornwallis-West of being in love with you. General Sir Henry Mackinnon knows all about it, and is angry and disgusted. You – *you* – to think Mrs Cornwallis-West is in love with you.'

'Well, sir, I have only done what I thought was right and what my heart told me, and I only wanted to be left alone to do my soldiering, and although they have given me a commission I'm not a gentleman and I don't know how to write to ladies.'

'I am not concerned now with your soldiering. What about this drivel you have written?'

'I only want to be left alone, and Mrs West wouldn't leave me alone.'

'Do you intend to leave it at that?'

Patrick said, 'I have letters she wrote to me.'

Delmé-Radcliffe was becoming very angry. 'I don't care what she has done to you or what she has written to you. What concerns me is the drivel you wrote. If you can't write better than that, well, leave it alone. Do you intend leaving it at this?'

Patrick was completely out of his depth. He had no idea what an officer should or should not do. The only thing he could think of was to tell the truth. 'Well, sir, I will show you the letters.'

'Have you got them here?'

'No, sir, they're at Bryncelin. I'll go and get them.'

'How long will that take?'

'I do not know, sir.'

Captain Howard intervened. 'It won't be possible for us to look at them tonight, Colonel, because there's a dinner.'

'Very well,' said Radcliffe. 'Barrett, you will be here with those letters at ten o'clock in the morning.'

Patrick was dismissed and went home as fast as he could. He was overwhelmed with fear, even terror, at what was happening. He knew he had to get the letters and then somehow face Delmé-Radcliffe with them in the morning. 'When the colonel sees them, perhaps he'll understand why I had to write,' he thought. 'But I'll have to show them to him now, because that's what I said I'd do.'

He ran back to the house. By the time he arrived, he was on the point of collapse. He could not speak, as if he were in seizure. He had never been in such trouble in the army in his life. The constriction in his chest was so bad that he could hardly breathe.

Mr and Mrs Birch were horrified when they saw him. He staggered up to his room, but they could not leave him, and had to go and sit with him until he could tell them what had happened. He was straining for breath. He could not run away and hide, because he had to go back to camp the next morning.

Eventually he became calm enough to unburden himself. 'With Mrs West, there was more than I told you. But now she's complained to Colonel Radcliffe about the letter I wrote, you know. And I told him that it's not fair that she should complain. He went mad at that. The thing is that there is more than I put in the letter, and she's angry with me for what I did. What I did, writing that, was wrong, in a way. I've let her down, by writing what I did. I've got to take the colonel all the letters I've had from her.'

'Which letters?' asked Dick Birch.

Patrick went over and retrieved them from behind the chest of drawers. 'All these. I hid them so that you wouldn't find them. They're her letters to me and the presents she gave me.'

Mrs Birch looked through them all.

'Now do you see?' she said to Dick. 'Now do you see what this woman is? She's infatuated — it's absolutely shameful. Just look how she's been using him. It is disgusting, it's filthy! And now, because he had the courage to ask her to stop, she's done this, she's maliciously passed Patrick's letter to the army, knowing that they'll destroy him. Oh yes, she knows exactly what they'll do to him. They won't even think about what she might have done herself, they'll just throw our Patrick on to the slag-heap. What can he do? Come on, what should he do now?'

Dick tried to think calmly, but his wife's anger made it difficult. It was odd what he felt about the letters. Actually, he found them quite exciting; even the idea of Patsy writing those letters was quite sexual. That was another reason why it was hard to concentrate.

'Let me try to talk to the colonel. We should try and persuade him to take a different course. I don't think we should give Mrs West's letters to him, not without her permission. She might think they've been destroyed. I don't think we should do anything that might make things worse, with her and the colonel.'

'Don't be so stupid,' said his wife fiercely. 'How could things possibly be worse? Look what she's done to Patrick. She's deliberately, and with hatred, worked out how to ruin him. She's a machine-gun, and she's tried to finish what the Germans could not. He's a hero of the war — all her generals and politician friends have made fools of themselves in the war, but Patrick Barrett distinguished himself. She's not going to change that, because I'm going to be the one who stops her. I'll show her letters to the King himself if I have to, and then perhaps she'll learn how to behave like a proper human being. When I finish with her, she'll never dare show her face around here again, and everyone will know just what Patrick Barrett has done for his country.

'Patrick, I'll be straightforward. You're attractive. Ladies like you – I like you. But that doesn't mean Patsy Cornwallis-West can take over your life and treat you like one of her possessions. That's what she's tried to do – any woman can see it. But she thinks the other men, all those stupid commanding officers, and idiots like my husband, will find it amusing. Just one of Patsy's hobbies, which won't be allowed to embarrass her because she's Patsy and you're just a Tommy who told her to leave you alone. My husband is thinking that she's our employer and we'd better be careful. Well, I don't care. We'll make our living somehow. They aren't the only people we can work for. I'll risk that for you, Patrick, as you risked your life for me. And so will Richard Birch when I explain to him what his life is going to be like if he doesn't. He's had trouble coming to him for some time. Now, Dick Birch, what are we going to do?'

Mrs Birch was filled with a tumult of rage at what she believed Patsy had done. That a 'society' woman should use her class and connections to extricate herself from a problem she herself had caused was utterly wicked. Destroying a young man's life, to save her own, was worse than despicable. Mrs Birch felt tremendous affection for Patrick, and an overwhelming need to protect him and give him love. Mrs Cornwallis-West had breached all bounds of decent behaviour. Moreover, Mrs Birch did not believe that Patrick could ever have had the sort of affection for Patsy that Patsy's behaviour implied. No, his deepest feeling was for her, Mrs Birch, and this all arose from Patsy's jealousy of her.

Dick said, 'Patrick, I think we had better make copies of the letters and keep the originals here. You can tell Colonel Radcliffe you've written to ask her permission before handing them over – I'll write to her now to say that. I'll also try and get a message to the colonel to ask if I may go and see him.'

'You go and do that now,' snapped his wife, 'but I'm going to contact General Cowans tonight. I'm going to make sure he knows Mrs West has been giving instructions at Kinmel about how Colonel Radcliffe is to treat the soldiers who don't behave according to her wishes. I'll send him a telegram at his office, so everybody there, all his secretaries, will know what's going on.' She growled at him, and he left the room.

'You know about her, don't you?' she asked Patrick.

'She used to be famous, I think.'

'She still is, in London, and I'll tell you why. She's a whore, a common prostitute, who made herself available to any officer or duke she could get her hands on – they had to ask people to stay away from her. Poor old Colonel West, he's been embarrassed all his life, because she's made a complete mockery of him. George, her son, isn't the colonel's child, he's the son of the old King, Edward. I don't know why the colonel didn't throw her out, except that the King kept paying them to look after his son. Her daughter married the Duke of Westminster and now he's left her, because he knows what kind of a family they really are, and the other daughter, she's married a German, and what does that tell you? That woman Mrs West has no right to go cavorting with generals in the War Office, because she's passing secrets to the Germans.'

Chapter 13

CONSEQUENCES

D ICK BIRCH TRIED desperately not to let matters get worse. He wrote a note to Radcliffe and telephoned the base to ask for a messenger to come and collect it. It said, 'If I could see Lieutenant-Colonel Delmé-Radcliffe for a few minutes this evening in reference to the unfortunate affair of Barrett's, I hope I may be able to help the colonel form a better judgement.' But the messenger told him that there was a regimental dinner that evening, and the colonel would therefore not be available.

So Dick wrote to Patsy:

My dear little Lady,

I came home tonight and found Barrett in a terrible state. He was up before his colonel this morning and confronted with a letter he had written you, and unless he can give a satisfactory explanation he will have to give up his commission. My wife is determined that that shall not be, and will go to any lengths to clear him if possible. She has in her possession four letters of yours, which she proposes showing his colonel and everyone else necessary, and which she insists will justify what Barrett has written to you. I do hope, for everybody's sake, that there will be no washing of dirty linen – it really is not worth it. To please me, if for no other reason, will you write to Colonel Radcliffe, tomorrow, and ask him to take no further notice of this matter? Failing this, your letters will be shown to him. Do please wire and say you have done it. My wife is distraught and will stick at nothing, so please do stop it.

Yours,

Dick

This was the first Patsy had heard of the matter for several days. She replied not by telegram but by letter.

My dear Dick,

Your note is ridiculous. I cannot see how you could connect me with Patrick Barrett's new illness, which worries me greatly. I have only ever been concerned for his well-being. It hurts me to say so, but I have felt for some time that there is a limit to how long he should stay at your house, for his own good, and that feeling I have conveyed to his superiors. If there are letters, I am sure you will wish to have them returned to me. I cannot imagine your wife would want to read my nonsense. Please keep me informed about Barrett.

Patsy

Dick replied from his office that night. 'Patsy, this is more serious than I have made you realise. I cannot control my wife's anger. She is determined to take action against Delmé-Radcliffe for the way he treated Barrett, and also to show your letters to people who could hurt you. She is writing now to General Cowans. I cannot dissuade her.'

When Patsy read this she thought she had better send a note to Cowans herself. She said:

Jack, dear,

This is wearisome, but there is a problem regarding young Barrett, whom you so kindly helped to gain his commission.

You will have to guess, my darling, what the problem might be. However, I beg you now to do what I say. First, take no notice of either Mr or Mrs Birch, who are kind and have cared for him, but believe I am a bad influence on him. I think she has written to you, but Barrett's colonel is already dealing with the matter. Second, help me make sure he is moved to a different base immediately. Surely you can manage those small things for me?

I long to see you. I am tired of Wales. I shall drive to Newlands in the morning. Might you be able to come?

Your own

Patsy

Sir John Cowans was working late and replied immediately from the War Office. 'Patsy, my dear, I have not heard from the lady you mention. It has been a very tiresome case and rather let us all in. If I get anything from her at all, I will do as you suggest and refer her to the man's colonel. Many thanks for letting me know, but anyway I should not have walked into a trap.'

Before setting out for Hampshire the next morning, Patsy wrote again, realising she had forgotten to tell him something of great importance.

Jack, dear,

I didn't even know that you remembered about Barrett. Jack, you know I'd never willingly hurt anything, not even a fly. This woman's husband has written that the boy is seriously ill and that if he is stripped of his commission it will kill him. He is alone in the world, without a penny. Jack, I implore you to send him away from that bad influence, but for my everlasting peace of mind don't take his commission from him. Poor boy, he seemed so proud of it, and so grateful to me and always so respectful. It is only that woman's evil mind and evil, mean jealousy. Don't, please, dear Jack, I beg of you, punish him as badly as that. I can't bear even to even think of it – that I should live to ruin a young life. Oh Jack, for my sake don't do this. I don't know what's going on, as Colonel D R has told me nothing – I shall write to him, too, asking him not to strip Barrett of his commission, whatever else they do to him – and I have not heard from anyone about it except from the woman's husband.

Ever yours
Patsy

The War Office order for Patrick to be transferred to Litherland Camp, in Liverpool, the transit camp for the army en route to France, had already been sent at Colonel Radcliffe's request. It had arrived at regional headquarters in Chester, ready for transmission to Kinmel, but was awaiting the next post, otherwise it would have reached the camp the following morning.

Lieutenant-Colonel Delmé-Radcliffe conducted the interview with Barrett in his own office, with two other officers present. It was a formal meeting.

The colonel said, 'I believe you have some letters for me?'

'Sir, I have brought copies of them.'

'What?'

'I have brought copies of Mrs West's letters, sir.'

'Do I understand you correctly? You were ordered to bring Mrs West's letters, and you have not done so. Is that what you are saying?'

'Sir, I have brought copies of Mrs West's letters, which explain why I wrote her the letter you have seen.'

Radcliffe was furious. He got up and began pacing round the room. ' "Explain" is not what your orders were, Lieutenant. "Bring" is what your orders were, and I have no interest whatsoever in an explanation. Here is the matter. There are letters to be destroyed. Your letter was an outrage to the regiment. The reasons you wrote it do not interest me. That you wrote it is all that matters. You are despised for writing it. I despise you. Whatever happens to an officer, there are some things he never does. He never brings shame or embarrassment to a lady, nor does he attempt to, nor does it so much as cross his mind to do anything that might bring her shame or embarrassment. He neither blames her nor lets her be blamed.'

'Yes, sir.'

'You wrote that Mrs West kissed you.'

'Yes, sir.'

'That is why you are not a true officer – nor ever will be, by God! By what twist of that scrap of brain did you think you could write that Mrs West kissed you, after all that Mrs West and everybody else here has done for you? What the devil do you mean by saying you could not look Colonel Cornwallis-West in the face, and accusing Mrs Cornwallis-West of calling you darling, and naming other ladies – including my own wife – in that letter? I wish I might never see you again. The orders for your posting should be here any day. What are you going to do? What do you intend to do? Do you intend to take this matter further? Well, man? What are you going to do?'

'Obey my orders, sir'

'Destroy all the letters. I never want to set eyes on you again.'

Patrick picked up the copies and left.

Radcliffe instructed that, as soon as the order arrived from the War Office, Barrett should be posted immediately: there was to be not even an hour's delay.

He wrote to Patsy to confirm that Barrett's move would take place very shortly.

Mrs Birch found Patrick on the steps of the house. He was hugging himself and sobbing. She called the army doctor, who certified at once that Barrett was unfit for service, having collapsed, mentally, from his wounds and from the effects of shell-shock. He was to be out of service for at least two months. The interview with Colonel

Delmé-Radcliffe had set him back to where he had been in November 1914, after Ypres. He could not speak.

Later, a car arrived from the camp. The sergeant driving said he had orders to take Patrick to Litherland. Mrs Birch could not believe her ears: in effect, Patrick was being ordered back to France. Fortunately, the doctor was still there, and he and Dick Birch convinced the sergeant that Patrick was medically unfit to be moved. But it was a close-run thing. Dick had to stand and block the doorway while the sergeant listened to what the doctor said. Mercifully, the doctor was able to pull rank.

When the car had gone, Dick tried to contact Patsy, but she was already driving down to Hampshire.

Mrs Birch sat her husband in the kitchen.

'Do you know what she told Patrick about you, the weekend she came here to stay?'

'No.'

'She told him you have a mistress in London. He told me that on the Sunday night. I said I'd heard it before and I did not believe it. Is it true?'

'No.'

'I'll ask you again, but before I do I want you to understand what is at stake. Listen to me. I am going to fight for Patrick Barrett. I am going to bring trouble on Patsy Cornwallis-West, on Colonel Radcliffe, and on every other person who has done this to him. I am going to find them out, however important they think they are, and I am going to ruin them – I shall spend all our money doing it, if necessary. And I'm telling you that I no longer want you to work for the Cornwallis-Wests. So, if you have got a mistress in London, the best thing you can do is leave now. If you go, I shall be quite glad, because I can do this my own way. I want your money, and you will be one of the people I ruin. I will not see you again. But if you stay you will come with me wherever I go and do whatever I say. You will fight with me. You will never, ever, on any occasion or under any circumstances, let me down.

Patsy Cornwallis-West. Painted when she was eighteen years old. Patsy was at the time of
this portrait the mistress of Edward VII and at the height of her fame as one of the great
'professional beauties' of London society.

The family homes at Ruthin (*below*) in Denbighshire and Newlands (*above*) in Hampshire where Daisy said 'No one could have wished for a happier childhood'. At both houses Patsy created the most wonderful landscape gardens.

Colonel William Cornwallis-West MP, Royal Welch Fusiliers,
Lord Lieutenant of Denbighshire, painter. Although he had an
adventurous youth in Italy, William was devoted to Patsy and
supported her in an astonishing way despite her most
outrageous behaviour.

George Cornwallis-West. Randolph Churchill called him 'the most handsome man in England'. Probably a son of Prince Edward Albert, George was married to two of the most famous women of the age: Jennie Churchill, Randolph's wife and Winston's mother, and then Stella Patrick Campbell, the actress.

Daisy. Pictured here at seventeen, she was shortly to be married into the Royal House of Pless. Daisy became one of the leading social figures in Europe.

Shelagh. A great beauty and a fine horsewoman. Shelagh married Bend Or, the Duke of Westminster.

THE DAILY MIRROR, Friday, January 5, 1917.

GERMANY TO MAKE NEW PEACE OFFER—RUMANIAN SUCCESS

The Daily Mirror

CERTIFIED CIRCULATION LARGER THAN THAT OF ANY OTHER DAILY PICTURE PAPER

No. 4,119. | Registered at the G.P.O. as a Newspaper. | FRIDAY, JANUARY 5, 1917 | One Halfpenny.

LIEUTENANT BARRETT AND "THE OTHER LADY IN THE CASE," WHO WAS COMPLIMENTED BY THE COURT.

Second Lieutenant P. Barrett, whose character is completely vindicated.

The beautiful Mrs. Birch, who, with her husband, "rendered the public a notable service."

Mrs. Cornwallis-West, "whose conduct has been highly discreditable." — Another portrait of Lieutenant Barrett. — Mrs. Birch, "the other lady in the case."

In January 1917, the scandal of 'The Wicked Woman of Wales' was front-page news in all the newspapers. The caption read:

All England was talking yesterday of "The Lady in the Case" Army scandal, as a result of which Mrs. Cornwallis-West, wife of the Lord-Lieutenant of Denbighshire, was severely censured, with a number of officers of high rank, by a Court of Inquiry appointed by the House of Commons. Today *The Daily Mirror* is able to publish exclusively the photographs of Lieutenant Barrett, the young officer who remonstrated with Mrs. Cornwallis-West over her advances to him, and was the object of her vindictive hostility, and of the other lady in the case, Mrs. Birch, wife of the Cornwallis-Wests' agent, who, with her husband, acted with such public spirit, and courage that Lieutenant Barrett was saved from suffering a great wrong in his military career. Mrs. Birch was complimented by the Court. – (Studies by H. Walter Barnett.)

David Lloyd George. He used the scandal of 'The Case of the Lady' to his advantage, deliberately allowing the story to break to cover up the difficult state of the war. David Lloyd George became Prime Minister in December 1916.

Winston Churchill. Although they were the same age, Churchill became George's stepson and friend.

Edward VII. Edward Albert, who became King Edward VII, was the soul of Edwardian England and particularly of aristocratic society. Those close to him adored him for his dignity and style. He was a lover of many women and father of many children, including, possibly, all of Patsy's.

Stella Patrick Campbell. The second wife of George Cornwallis-West, Stella was the most famous actress of her generation and the lover of George Bernard Shaw. Shaw created the role of Eliza Doolittle in *Pygmalion* for her.

Jenny Churchill. An American beauty, Jenny was the first wife of George Cornwallis-West. A mistress of Edward VII, she had been married to Lord Randolph Churchill and was Winston's mother. She was also one of the great spenders of the age, and had campaigned actively for the foundation of a National Theatre.

Lillie Langtry. The actress and 'professional beauty' was Patsy's friend and neighbour in Eaton Place. They also shared a famous lover, the Prince of Wales.

Patsy: 'The most beautiful woman in all four kingdoms'.

'Now, think carefully before you answer me – I shall ask only once. Have you got a mistress in London?'

'No.'

'I'm going to sit with Patrick.' And she left him and went upstairs.

After all her nursing and care, it was heartbreaking to see Patrick in this condition again. Many people said that there was no such thing as shell-shock, that it was merely cowardice, or weakness – 'lack of moral fibre', they called it. Some even said it was not possible for a British soldier to be so contemptibly feeble. Mrs Birch knew better. Patrick was a strong young man, an honest and straightforward person, who could never have invented such a disability. He wasn't pretending to be ill – he hadn't the imagination for it: it simply was not within the scope of what his mind could create.

The army's treatment of him had damaged him even more than he was already damaged – it might even have destroyed him altogether. Mrs's Birch's feelings for him were complicated, and some of them were those of a mother for a child, despite his age. He was in grave and complicated trouble, which was only partly of his making, and Mrs Birch felt very protective. That emotion fired within her the powerful resilience of a parent, and a determination to see justice done in a case where many would have accepted that they could do little or nothing. A woman of less fortitude would have scolded her son for what had happened, but Mrs Birch was taking upon herself a fight which was not far short of a battle against the whole ruling class of England.

When she realised that, she also realised, quite suddenly, that for many years she had distrusted and been disappointed by her husband. He spent all his time wanting to be part of the Cornwallis-West circle, wanting to be a gentleman. His perpetual journeying to London annoyed her – it was not necessary for the work he did. It seemed that he was trying to be someone grander than a land agent in north Wales. It was pathetic. She now saw that he was a weak person, without substance or morality. She no longer cared to indulge him, but preferred to use him for what he could do for her.

She was suspicious of the relationship between Mrs Cornwallis-West and General Cowans. There was too much influence being used. The quartermaster-general of the British army should be far, far too busy to be indulging the whims of county ladies. What had happened was much worse than the punishment of an innocent and injured young soldier. It was manipulation, for private purposes, of the greatest forces of the realm. She felt she was being called to set these things right.

'Make an appointment to see the best solicitor in St Asaph,' she ordered Dick. 'Then there are telegrams to be sent. I shall write them.' It helped her, venting her anger on her miserable husband.

He had already written to Patsy: 'My dear little Lady, You have seen a bit of what my life is sometimes. I think I shall enlist, or else leave and go to London to be with A. Yours, Dick.'

They sent three telegrams the next day to Mrs Cornwallis-West.

At eight in the morning: 'Military doctor advises Barrett's mental condition extremely poor. Grievous recurrence of effects of shell-shock due to intense pressure. Please reply with actions taken to relieve stress or consequences will be serious.'

At noon: 'Barrett worse by the hour. Delay fatal if you don't clear him immediately.'

At six in the evening: 'Commission less important than his honour, which must be cleared by you or by production of all letters. Cannot keep them back; you must choose; Colonel D-R's treatment of him before other officers is killing him.'

Patsy knew only what she read in these telegrams. She wanted to talk to Patrick and find out whether he really was as ill as the Birches said, but that was impossible. She was upset. She did not know what Delmé-Radcliffe had said. She felt she was being threatened, and she did not know how to stop it all.

She forwarded each telegram to General Cowans, begging her dear Jack to make sure her private letters were taken from this woman and returned to her, as they had wrongly been handed over under pressure by this distraught young soldier.

All Cowans knew was that Patsy had suggested Barrett be moved. He checked, and found that the necessary order had left the War Office a few days before. To ensure that the order was effected, he sent a message to Delmé-Radcliffe: 'It is a mistake for any of us to mix ourselves up in other people's private affairs – unless the man is impertinent or disobedient; but I see you realise this from your letters. Mrs West is pouring letters at me.'

And to Patsy, from the War Office, he wrote: 'Orders have gone by wire for Barrett to be transferred at once to the Third Battalion. It is really all we can do. I will return you all the correspondence on Monday, when I see you. The War Office cannot correspond or bargain with people about letters. I think all has been done that can be done officially; it would never do for us to mix ourselves up in private quarrels and misunderstandings. I am very sorry, but I am sure you will understand. I would do anything for you if I had time.'

Dick Birch made an appointment to see Mr Price of the Denbigh solicitors Porter, Amphlett. Mr Price knew Colonel Cornwallis-West and his wife, of course; he knew Lieutenant-Colonel Delmé-Radcliffe; and he knew Mr and Mrs Birch.

Mrs Birch had made notes about what Patsy, General Cowans and Colonel Delmé-Radcliffe had done, and she tried to explain them to Mr Price. But she grew angry as she spoke, and he had some difficulty in calming her enough to establish the reasons and the evidence for what she said.

She told him about the day when Cowans had come to Bryncelin, and about the discussion of the Americans and supplies of equipment and munitions, which, she said, were topics that should not have been part of civilian conversation. She asserted that

Cowans had been trying to impress Patsy by showing how much influence he had in the War Office, and had been irresponsible in what he revealed. She moved on to Patsy's remarks concerning Brigadier-General Owen Thomas, saying that, in the same way, she was using her views about him to persuade Cowans that Thomas should be replaced.

Then she went through the whole story of Patrick's letters from Mrs Cornwallis-West and how, having found herself in a most compromising situation, Mrs Cornwallis-West had pulled all the strings she could, to make sure that the young soldier did her no harm. The damaging effect on Barrett of Mrs Cornwallis-West's actions, she said, was the evidence of her ruthlessness.

Mr Price made his own notes of all she said. He asked her to go back over what Patrick had said about his interview with Delmé-Radcliffe. The matter upon which he felt there were questions of law was the treatment of Lieutenant Barrett by the army at Kinmel Park. 'There are legal requirements of army officers, even in times of war,' he said, 'and Barrett's treatment sounds open to question. However, I shall need to talk to Lieutenant Barrett myself, and it will be necessary to obtain a medical opinion on the question of his ability to make decisions for himself.

'I make the point to you,' he went on, 'as I shall make it to Lieutenant Barrett, that if one were to take action against the army or particular officers, they would defend themselves vigorously with all the means they felt they required. They would make plain their dislike of a case of this kind when the country is at war, and Barrett would need to consider any future relationship he might have both with the officers concerned and with the regiment as a whole.

'You will need to consider these matters and, if I am to assume that Lieutenant Barrett cannot act for himself, whether you can defensibly act for him. Others may dispute your right to do so, as you may be said to be partial in his favour. I shall have to talk to him.

'If a case of any kind is brought, the army will certainly use King's Counsel, and Barrett would be well advised to do the same. Therefore he is likely to incur a considerable expense, and he will have to bear that in mind. I do not know if any of that cost would be paid by a court, or under what conditions.'

'Lieutenant Barrett is very ill,' said Dick. 'If you question him, he may easily collapse. Would it be in order for my wife to sit with him?'

'For the sake of his health, I understand that proper precautions must be taken. However, it is incumbent upon me to make sure, if we are to proceed with a case of any kind, that that is what he wants to do, that he understands the issues involved, and that you are not exercising undue influence on him. I do not wish to be offensive, but I am obliged to make those points. We are, however, ahead of ourselves.

'For the present time, I must ask you if you will allow me to interview him, in an appropriate way, and whether I may look to you for my fee for this work.'

Mrs Birch ignored the request and said, 'Tell us what you feel can be done about Mrs West and General Cowans.'

'I have great sympathy with what you say, if what you allege is true. If there is a case against General Cowans, it would I think be a matter for an army tribunal, just as is likely to be the case for Lieutenant-Colonel Delmé-Radcliffe. In both those instances, Lieutenant Barrett's case would need to be made. As regards Mrs West, I do not know what action can be taken. She is not subject to the legal requirements of an army officer, nor, on the basis of what you have said, would any of her activities be an infringement of the special legislation in force relating to the defence of the realm. I think my recommendation is that you should approach a member of parliament, perhaps Denbighshire's own member, Sir Hubert Russell. When I have talked to Lieutenant Barrett I will make a recommendation about whether counsel should be instructed, and, if so, perhaps counsel will have a view about the activities of other parties.'

'We have sufficient money to deal with all this, more than sufficient,' said Mrs Birch.

To prevent Patsy writing to or otherwise contacting Patrick, he was moved from Bryncelin to a quiet nursing-home, the Tower, at Llanarmon in the hills above Ruthin, where Offa's Dyke had been built to mark the boundary of Wales and England. Here he would be safe from the chance of a regimental car coming to take him off to war, or an officer's zealous attempt to take him back into the army's care at Kinmel.

Two doctors in St. Asaph confirmed the army doctor's diagnosis: Patrick had withdrawn into a world of fear and confusion. He was able to grant a power of attorney to Mr and Mrs Birch to act in his best interests, but that was the limit of his capabilities. It was essential that he have physical and mental rest and that he be kept away from the stress of army.

Porter, Amphlett and Co.,
Solicitors,
Denbigh,
27 April 1916

Lieutenant-Colonel Henry Delmé-Radcliffe,
Commanding Officer,
12th Battalion, the Royal Welch Fusiliers,
No 1 Camp,
Kinmel Park,
Abergele
<u>In the Matter of Second Lieutenant Patrick Barrett</u>

Sir,

    On behalf of Second Lieutenant Patrick Barrett, who on 21 and 22 March 1916 was an officer attached to your battalion, we beg to apply for a court of enquiry into the circumstances attached to the interviews you held with him on the dates above given and into the whole of the facts that led to those interviews.

Lieutenant Barrett is at present lying dangerously ill at the Tower, Llanarmon, Ruabon, in the county of Denbigh, as a direct result of the treatment he received at your hands.

The grounds of the application are as follows:

1: That he received your censure for an offence which was not within your jurisdiction as his commanding officer.

2: That he was improperly held up to ridicule before other officers belonging to his battalion.

3: That he was not given an opportunity of justifying a letter written by him to Mrs Cornwallis-West, parts of which were most improperly read out to him before two of his brother officers.

4: That, in addition to the above, he has been disgraced by the steps which, we are informed, were taken by you to exchange him into another battalion without his leave or sanction and without his being in any way consulted.

5: That the letter referred to in paragraph 3 is, and can be proved to be, amply justified by the circumstances and by the correspondence which led up to it, and that the said letter was, in the circumstances, a right and proper letter to have been written.

6: That up to the dates mentioned in the opening paragraph of this letter he held an unblemished record during his thirteen and a half years of army service, as borne out by the military records and your recommendation that he be commissioned an officer of the Royal Welch Fusiliers.

7: That the procedures and the whole treatment of this officer were irregular and should be the subject of an enquiry.

8: That the medical board who examined him at Llanarmon on the 15th instant stated that he will not recover from his illness until the stain upon his honour is removed, because his mind dwells upon it continually.

We are sending a copy of this letter of application to the General Officer Commanding, the 14th Brigade, at Kinmel Park, with the request that, for the reasons above given, and particularly for the reasons given in paragraph 8, a court of enquiry be held without delay.

Porter, Amphlett and Co.,
Solicitors

Mr Price sent a copy of the letter, with his invoice, to Mr and Mrs Birch.

Chapter 14

HIGHER GROUND

A s Mr Price had advised, the Birches went to see Sir Hubert Russell. He also knew the Cornwallis-Wests, Colonel Delmé-Radcliffe and the Birches themselves. He listened attentively to their story, but was unsure how to answer. Dick Birch was well respected in Denbigh, and had to be taken seriously. He could not be dismissed as a troublemaker, although Russell felt strongly that none of this was a great help to the war effort.

'I think,' Russell said slowly, 'that I am too closely acquainted with the people involved in this matter, and am therefore unable to be properly objective about it. My suggestion is that I have a word with one or two of my colleagues and see if I can find a member for a different constituency, and perhaps with a particular interest in the War Office and its activities. If this is a course to which you agree, I will put you in touch with this person, and ask him to act on my behalf. It would be very difficult for me to pursue this matter myself, because Colonel and Mrs Cornwallis-West are both very active in the constituency, and I meet them almost every week on one matter or another. I hope you will agree. I cannot otherwise see the right thing to do next.'

The Royal Welch Fusiliers and their affairs were a constant source of gossip in the county. It was part of the proud Welsh effort to support the soldiers being sent off to battle. People in both town and country took a close interest in the comings and goings of generals and colonels. Everyone kept an interested eye on the continual round of orders and commands, and in the misdemeanours and the manoeuvres of the officers and the men.

One choice piece of gossip was about the future of Brigadier-General Owen Thomas. He had been brought out of retirement at the beginning of the war in order to lead the recruitment campaign for the Fusiliers. Everyone thought he was rather old-fashioned, but he was the only Welsh-speaking general in the army and was known to seek Welsh-speakers among his recruits. He was well liked in the county and was acquainted with Lord Kitchener. However, the war was becoming too serious for key matters of logistics and training to be run by popular elderly generals. They were being replaced by younger officers, usually men who had experience at the front but had been invalided home and were unfit for further active service.

Mrs Birch had naturally heard, in conversations with friends around the county, that Patsy Cornwallis-West and her husband were taking a hand, with her friends General Cowans and General Mackinnon, in the attempt to replace Brigadier-General Owen Thomas. Such a move would arouse great anger in the county, particularly as it was rumoured that his replacement might be a Scot. This was good gossip.

So the Birches went to see Owen Thomas and not only told him the story of Patrick Barrett and showed him all Patsy's letters, but also told him of the rumours that he was about to be replaced and that Patsy had considerable influence in the matter. Owen Thomas had all the fine dignity and old polished leather of a very experienced general in the British army. He listened graciously to the Birches, whom he had known for many years. Dick Birch was a good man, a retired officer of the regiment. Mrs Birch was rather clever, and she was an attractive woman, who did good work, and he knew they were both well liked by the Fusiliers' officers and men.

After the meeting, the brigadier-general wrote to Mackinnon.

<u>Private and personal</u>

My dear General,

As a friend, I feel I must give you the following information, which has come to my knowledge from a most reliable source.

From what I know you are already aware of the trouble that has arisen in connection with letters which have passed between Mrs C-W and Lieutenant B. I feel sure you have not seen Mrs W's letters to B; I have, and they are certainly extraordinary; and I am sorry to say B's letter to Mrs W is more or less justified.

The case is now in the hands of a well-known KC. Two actions are likely to be launched, one by Barrett for libel (or some such thing) against you and the quartermaster-general and the other by Mrs B————h against Mrs C-W for slander.

So far as I can judge, the object of the former is public exposure of two generals at the War Office who, it is claimed, have acted unfairly under the pressure and influence of Mrs C-W, thereby causing B to suffer an injustice.

No one knows better than I do that you are the last person in the world to do an injustice to anyone, and I should be more sorry than I can tell you to see your good name mixed up in this case.

Spite seems to be at the bottom of it all and I hear that B has strong backing, financial and otherwise.

I hope you will quite understand my object in writing to you. 'Forewarned is forearmed.'

Yours very sincerely,
Owen Thomas

Within only a few days, as he might well have foreseen, but nevertheless to his great dismay, he received a copy of Porter

Amphlett's letter to Colonel Radcliffe, and a note from Radcliffe asking for instructions.

He gave none except to pass everything on to General Mackinnon's office at Western Command. However, Mackinnon had, only days before, been promoted to the War Office in London, so the matter was dealt with by the new commanding officer, the Scot about whose appointment there had been so much gossip, Sir Pitcairn Campbell.

Campbell refused Barrett's request for an enquiry, and wrote to the brigadier-general in charge of administration.

My dear Caunter,

Re: The Barrett case, which I return herewith

Barrett is no longer under Delmé-Radcliffe's command, so DR has nothing more to do with him. I consider the best course would be, as the correspondence has been sent to me, to inform the solicitors that no court of enquiry is considered necessary.

It would be as well to have 1) a special medical board, or 2) an opinion of an officer (medical) of high rank as to whether Barrett could be moved to the 3rd Battalion at Litherland. I should like him got away from his present surroundings. I fancy Mr and Mrs Birch have taken up the case strongly on Barrett's behalf and Birch has even resigned his agency to Cornwallis-West. They have got Barrett into a private nursing-home, where Mrs C-West cannot reach him. The Birches have letters of Mrs W's to Barrett. There is nothing military about the case, and we must keep out of it absolutely. If you are uncertain of the wording of the answers to the solicitors, wait till I come back on Saturday.

Yours ever,
Pitcairn Campbell

When the rejection of Patrick's request for an enquiry was conveyed to Mr and Mrs Birch, no reason was given for the decision, except that the commanding officer had declined the request. That meant Patrick was being treated even more unfairly, Mrs Birch thought. Someone in the army should have listened to the story; someone should have asked questions about what had happened. Someone should have acknowledged, in particular, that Patsy and Delmé-Radcliffe had not behaved well.

Of course it was the army that she was dealing with, and Society – if that was the right way to describe Patsy. But Mrs Birch still believed that somewhere there would be people embarrassed or concerned or fair enough to listen, otherwise they might as well all be living in Germany. She decided that she and Dick must go to London, and she told him to wire Sir Henry Mackinnon and make an appointment to see him.

Mackinnon of course knew the Birches, and was quite pleased to see friendly Welsh faces in his new London office. He made them welcome, offered them refreshment after their long journey, and then listened to the story. Mrs Birch was quite firm with him, although she was not sure how much he knew of, or would have been involved in, the events she described. Mackinnon was gracious and appeasing, and gradually Mrs Birch realised that his appointment to London to work for Cowans was probably a result of his friendship with Patsy. Her temper began to rise.

Sir Henry said that he really did not know a lot about the events, but since they had come to London he would try to get them an interview with General Cowans, who was certain to have the explanations they wanted. However, he warned them, Cowans was, as they would well understand, one of the busiest men in the world. If Mackinnon could arrange a meeting with him, it would necessarily have to be a very brief one.

He went to see Cowans and explained that the Birches had come to London especially to pursue the matter of Patsy and Barrett and

Delmé-Radcliffe. Cowans said that he simply had not the time to see them, and he was sure Mackinnon could satisfy them.

'They are here in serious pursuit of their aims,' said Mackinnon, 'and I fear they may cause embarrassment. Mrs Birch might even demand to see Kitchener himself — if she gets no satisfaction here she will undoubtedly look for it elsewhere. The things she is saying about Mrs West and yourself may cause you trouble, even though I am certain there is no substance in her story. It would be better if you would listen to her for a few minutes. Then at least she cannot say that no one heard the case. Please, I believe this is important.'

To the Birches, Cowans was charming and pleasant. 'Mrs Birch, Mr Birch, I remember we met at your home in Denbigh. That seems a long time ago. How can I help?'

'We would like to ask for an enquiry into the treatment of Patrick Barrett.'

'I'm sorry, but please explain to me how I can help in the matter.'

'I think you know what I mean,' said Mrs Birch. 'No doubt there are layers of procedure for the army to hide behind, but you know very well what I mean about Patrick Barrett and Mrs Cornwallis-West.'

'I'm extremely sorry, Mrs Birch, but I'm sure General Mackinnon has explained that my time is very short. I should like to help, but I don't know that I can in a case concerning an individual soldier. That must be a question for his regiment.'

Mrs Birch rounded on him. 'Patrick Barrett, whom you met that day in our house, is dying because of what you and Mrs Cornwallis-West have done to him. You had him ordered back to France when he would not perform services for Mrs West, you told his Colonel Delmé-Radcliffe to destroy him, take away his commission and send him to Litherland. You always do what Mrs West wants, don't you? You have also had Brigadier-General Owen Thomas relieved of his command. We want an enquiry into what has been going on, and nothing will stop me getting all these things brought into the open.'

'I am sorry,' said Cowans, 'but I repeat that I am exceedingly busy. I cannot respond to an outburst like this. I have many other matters to attend to.'

'You are responsible for what has happened and you will be brought to account. Admit to us that you influenced Colonel Radcliffe in his treatment of Lieutenant Barrett.'

'Madam,' he said coldly, 'I regret that I must ask you to leave. I cannot have a hysterical lady disrupting the good order of this office. Be good enough to leave at once.'

'Not until you have explained the power Mrs West has over you.'

Sir John took Mrs Birch's arm, led her forcibly to the door and ordered the soldier on duty in the corridor to escort her from the building.

As she left she said, 'You have behaved in an uncivil manner, This whole matter will be brought before the highest authority. If necessary I shall tell the King.'

Cowans bowed slightly and said, 'Good afternoon.'

Mrs Birch was undeterred. She wrote down the whole story of how Patsy had used Patrick for her outrageous, lascivious, physical purposes. When he had the sense to try to stop her, she had used her influence with her friends in the War Office, and with his commanding officer, to have him sent back to France so that he could not cause her trouble. Having lavished letters and gifts on the young man, Patsy had done all she could to get them back and avoid embarrassment for herself. Mrs Birch said Patsy had boasted of her influence, which seemed to extend into the highest quarters, even to a member of the Army Council, the body that now was running the country. It was disgraceful and shameful to all decent people, Mrs Birch wrote, that this woman and her accomplices should be allowed to continue. Nobody was prepared to even look into the matter, though one clear consequence was that a brave young soldier was in danger of dying, and had had to go into hiding from the army and Mrs Cornwallis-West. Mrs Birch very much hoped, she said, that somebody would listen and that she would not be obliged to take the story to the press and explain how the country really was being run in time of war. She described how she had applied for an enquiry at Kinmel Park and how she had travelled to London to ask General Cowans for an explanation but had been rudely told to leave. She also made a list of the letters in her possession and a summary of their contents.

She made Dick Birch type it all out and make several fair copies. She sent one copy to Mr Price and one to Sir Hubert Russell. She also sent a copy to Cowans's immediate superior, Lord Kitchener, at the War Office; one to the prime minister at 10 Downing Street; and one to the King at Buckingham Palace.

Chapter 15

ANXIOUS TIMES

B Y MAY 1916, Stella had become extremely worried about and angry with George. She invited Patsy to lunch. She wanted to tell her that, whatever she decided about George, her decision would not sully or diminish her affection for Patsy and William.

She said, 'He spends so much – much more than I earn – and he earns hardly anything himself. All the time he is away shooting and fishing and spending money. I get angry with him.'

'Poor Stella. I don't know what to say. Boys are so much more difficult than girls – everyone says so. But now look at them all dying in the war. It's very hard. George spends money as if it was his way of stopping the Germans getting it. Poppets gets dreadfully cross with him, but then says nothing because, of course, he adores him. I'm much tougher with George and always have been – we've had such rows. But I fear none of us has been terribly well behaved, so why should we expect George to be better?' She sighed. 'But that's no help to you, is it? I'm just a chattering old Irishwoman.'

'Patsy,' Stella said gravely, 'I don't think you realise how bad things are. George may have to declare himself bankrupt. If that happens, I may have to divorce him, if only to stop the court taking everything I have.'

'Oh no,' said Patsy at once. 'You mustn't let them take anything of yours, still less everything. Poppets has been trying for years to make sure that George's creditors wouldn't get anything that was meant to come to me if Poppets died. Ruthin and Newlands were made into trusts for Daisy and her husband so that George wouldn't have to forfeit them. I don't suppose he told you that, did he?'

'That Poppets had given Ruthin to the Germans? Yes, he told me that – and also that they were setting up a German submarine base at Newlands.'

'I dread what Poppets will say when he finds out how bad things are. You wouldn't think it, but he can be frightening, you know, especially if he gets really angry. I'm sure in the end he will help George, but the trouble is that the estates have made nothing these last two years. You can't hound people for rent when they're away fighting.'

Stella shook her head. 'I don't think Poppets can help – I think it's gone too far for anyone to be able to help. George is very secretive, but I think it's desperately serious. That's why I wanted to tell you about it myself.'

'Bertie would have helped him,' said Patsy sadly.

'Bertie? Who's that?'

'The old King. He adored George.'

'Of course.' Stella had heard stories about Patsy's royal love affair, but Patsy had never mentioned it before. That she should do so was a confidence, a plea for intimacy. She must be deeply upset and troubled, and not only about George.

Patsy went on, 'I don't think Jennie Churchill was a good wife to him. You don't think so, either, do you?'

'He was certainly very unhappy when I met him. You remember, don't you? I think she'd got him deeply into debt. He never told us all the truth about that. I hoped I'd solved most of those problems, but I don't think I can have. There were people he owed money to he has never told me about, to this day.'

'Jennie thought she was marrying a wealthy man, but George is far from rich. I suppose she must have seen other qualities in him, too.'

Stella understood at once that Patsy was telling her something much more complicated than her opinion of Jennie Churchill.

Jennie had been one of Prince Albert Edward's mistresses, vying with Patsy and Lillie Langtry for his affection. She must have suspected that George was the prince's child, and known that, no matter how much affection he gave to other women, his relationship with Patsy was different and special – and it had endured longer. When the widowed Jennie had married George, more than twenty years her junior, it had seemed to Patsy as if she were trying to make a new alliance with the King, as the prince was then about to become. Patsy and Poppets had been strongly against the marriage. Not only was Jennie too old for George, American, unsuitable, and trying to revisit a time and an affair which were long over, but there was a danger that when Poppets died, and George and Jennie inherited Ruthin and Newlands, Jennie would make it impossible for Patsy to live in either house, thereby making her homeless and almost penniless. Patsy had been so worried, she told Stella, that she had even asked Edward Albert to see if he could prevent the marriage, and he had indeed tried.

Patsy was distressed. All her children's marriages were troubled, and the Duke of Westminster wanted to divorce Shelagh. 'Bend Or is a difficult man,' she said, 'just as he was a difficult child. Daisy used to make fun of him because he always wanted to be cleverer than the others, but he never was. The awful thing is that the reason he wants a divorce is because Shelagh's little boy died. He wants an heir – the inheritance can only go to a son. It's barbaric. It's like Henry the Eighth, or some ancient religion. We spent all our childhood with a perfectly good Queen, so why is it that only a son can inherit a dukedom? It's all so cruel for poor Shelagh, as if losing a child weren't enough.'

Emboldened by the trust Patsy had shown, Stella asked, 'But there's something else worrying you, isn't there? Can you not tell me about it?'

'Oh dear, it's so sad. A young soldier in the Welch Fusiliers who was terribly, cruelly wounded in the war came to convalesce near Ruthin. He became attached to us, attached to me. But his mind was affected. He got confused and became obsessive, and we had to ask the regiment to look after him, to tell him to stop. They thought I'd been too kind to him, that I'd favoured him. But, as Poppets said, you couldn't be too kind to a boy like that. He was an orphan, so he was wholly dependent on the support of people like us.'

Stella could not see why that should cause a misunderstanding, but she did not like to probe. 'It must be so difficult in the county with so many soldiers lost,' she said. 'In London they pretend it isn't happening. At any rate, they behave as if isn't.' She waited to see if Patsy would say more.

Patsy longed to tell her friend how much she was in love with Patrick, but could not. She wished he could have been there to meet Stella, the internationally renowned Mrs Patrick Campbell. He would have enjoyed that and she would have been so proud. And the difference in their ages would not have mattered very much. After all, Stella had married a man much younger than herself, and in London, in Stella's circle, it had been all right. But Ruthin was not in London, and the people there were county and army, and that seemed to make everything so dreadful.

Patrick should never have written that letter, but it was the awful Mrs Birch who had made him. That's what Dick had said, that's what he had told her: that Patrick had been made to write the letter. So he could not help it, he did not mean it. Somehow, soon, she would be able to go and rescue him.

As Patsy drifted in thought, Stella thought how astonishingly beautiful she was. She said, 'Patsy, you are so beautiful, I'm so very jealous of you.'

At last, Patsy smiled. 'How exciting, that you should say that.'

George's bankruptcy was entered in the official record: 'Major Cornwallis-West attributed his insolvency to the failure of his firm, the personal extravagance of his first wife and himself and to losses in speculation in copper and on the stock exchange and on a patent rifle. He also lost a large amount through the defalcations of a solicitor whom he formerly employed.'

The official receiver submitted that the major had brought on his bankruptcy by rash and hazardous speculation and by unjustifiable extravagance. The value of the bankruptcy was £170,000.

Mrs George Cornwallis-West (formerly known as Mrs Patrick Campbell) attended the hearing.

Dick Birch was angry with Patsy. He thought she could have resolved the whole problem by using the same power that she had used to create it. She should have asked Colonel Radcliffe to take Patrick back into his care until the boy was fully recovered.

My dear little Lady,

I had another meeting with Colonel Radcliffe tonight, to see if something cannot be done to stop this Barrett business, but he says it is out of his hands and he is merely acting under orders. Now, my dear Lady, at the risk of quarrelling with you I must tell you that I think the letters I have seen that you wrote this poor man were wrong ones and bound to turn anyone's head, let alone the head of a poor Tommy like Barrett. I therefore think it unjust and very wrong that he should suffer for the letter he wrote you. Had you not written to him as you did, his letter would never have been written.

I have, as I think you know, a keen sense of justice and here is a man who fought courageously for his country and lost his health in doing so. He is ill, dazed and absolutely broken-hearted at the cruel way he was spoken to by Colonel Radcliffe, and he knows very well that, unless you save him, his career is at an end. Because of his promotion he has lost his sergeant's pension, and he will have nothing in the world left to him if you take away his honour as an officer.

I beg you, therefore, to write to General Mackinnon and tell him you are sorry you asked for Barrett to be reprimanded, that it was said in a fit of temper, that you know the boy meant no harm; and ask him to forget all about it.

Poor Barrett is, of course, anxious to go to the front, if only he can get this business off his mind, and in four or five months it is possible he will be well enough to do so. But to send him to Litherland now, and then straight to the front, would be murder. He is really ill.

Yours,

Dick

Patsy replied by telegram from Newlands: 'To Head Clerk, Estate Office, Maes Elwy, St Asaph. Send for Mr Birch. Give him following private message. Away all yesterday. You know I would do anything possible for your sake.'

And, again by telegram, 'Commission all right.'

To which Dick replied, still by telegram: 'Repeat: commission less important than honour. Cannot keep letters back any longer so you must choose. D–R's treatment killing him.'

Wire from Mrs West to Dick Birch: 'Can do no more than have done. Sent your wires and letters by Special Messenger to mutual friend in London. I know nothing except through you. Am in no way to blame. Must have documents for his sake. You know I don't wish hurt.'

Letter from Dick Birch to Mrs West: 'Under instructions from the War Office, which he enclosed, Colonel Radcliffe gave orders that Barrett was to join the 3rd Battalion at Litherland at once and report to a medical board there, even though the army's own doctor had certified that Barrett was unfit for any duty for six months owing to wounds and shell-shock. The man is desperately ill, and as you won't stop the persecution we must.'

Wire from Mrs West to Dick Birch: 'Wrote three very important letters to London. Repeat, I hear only what you tell me. Much want to see you. Will come up Tuesday important.'

And another: 'Cannot understand what you want to me to do but think you will agree proposal you should receive Monday.'

The more Patsy thought about what the Birches might do with her letters to Patrick, and to whom they might show them, the more alarmed and afraid she grew. Incoherent with distress, she wrote again.

Dear Dick,

I received your wire last night, and believe me what I wish to do, going straight to the head, is the only way. Now, this is what I will do: see you at Cox's hotel, Jermyn St, on Tuesday, Wednesday or Thursday, at any time you like. You shall bring the original documents, copies not in their original hand-writing are useless. The writer of the documents will write at your dictation, if it is a fair one, which I am sure it will be, a letter to the head of all, Sir J. You shall then enclose all these documents in a letter and post it yourself to him. I think you will see that this is fair, and more than fair as the writer honestly does not recollect what is in them. I think you will realise the writer is doing more than most women would do under the circumstances, but as you know she has never willingly hurt anyone in her life and most certainly never meant to hurt this boy, the writer was absolutely in the dark until you enlightened her, but cannot you realise that the mere fact of a man in the position he now holds, giving private documents to women to do what she likes with, against another person, has done him more harm with the powers that be than anything, particularly as the writer of the docu-ments had gone out of the way with her influence to help this man in every way. Wire me on receipt of this to Cox's hotel, which day will suit you to come up, it ought to be as soon as possible, as I think the head is going to France this week. I also have some very important letters I want to show you on a subject which I cannot put in the post, but I cannot leave someone for too long, he clings to me so, and has a pathetic half-pleading look, such as you see sometimes in the eyes of a faithful old dog, it makes me cry to look at his old eyes filled with tears, as they do sometimes. He is terribly cut up over things lately.

Dear Dick, please let us meet and arrange things quite as I am sure you will wish as we have always done for so many years, as I am sure neither of us would care to lose the other's friendship. I know I personally would be very lost and unhappy.

Bryncelin
St Asaph

Dear Mrs West

I got your letter this morning, but I cannot comply with your suggestion. Your letters are the only thing this poor fellow has in the world to clear his character with, and they are at present in a lawyer's hands. Two sworn and certified copies have been made and one of these I am prepared to show General Cowans, but they must also be shown to General Mackinnon, as the order to Colonel Radcliffe and Barrett's letter to you were sent by him with the orders for Barrett's future treatment. I hold the general in the highest esteem and I am thoroughly convinced that, had he seen these letters and known what led up to Barrett's letter to you, instead of condemning him he would have said he was a 'white man', though uneducated, and it will not be my fault if he does not say so yet. Another reason why your letters cannot be parted with at present is that they are wanted in a lawsuit which is pending.

I mean to see this thing through and to see this man righted whatever happens and whatever it costs. Not for you or for anyone else will I see a man lose his reason or his life – in my house or out of it – through absolutely no fault of his own. The only thing that can save him is a letter from Mackinnon and Radcliffe saying a mistake has been made and withdrawing all aspersions on his honour. If you can get that done, well and good; but otherwise it must be managed another way. It's ridiculous to say you are in no way to blame: you are solely and entirely to blame.

It is now, of course, quite impossible for me to remain in my position as Colonel West's agent. I propose to send him my resignation at the end of this week, and also to ask him to release me from the trusteeships I hold and from the executorship of his will. I am not ashamed to sign my name, though you seem to be.

R. E. Birch

Patsy replied by telegram. To Forder, Estate Office, Ruthin. 'Find Mr Birch privately today without fail. Ask him telephone Western 1847 between 6 and 7 or after 11.30. Most important. Take motor if necessary.'

There was no answer.

It was Patsy's turn to be angry. Dick Birch and his father had been employed by William and his father for many, many years, and no employee could have received greater kindness or more privileged treatment. She had always thought Dick Birch a friend and behaved accordingly. Why, only a few months ago he had begged her not to tell his wife about his mistress in London, and of course Patsy had promised not to say a word. Nor would she, even now. His private affairs were none of her concern, and she would not dream of interfering in them.

Yet now he was behaving not like a friend but like a badly treated, resentful worker. Patsy thought it was not decent of him to be so difficult. He and his wife were causing her a lot of trouble and it was all so dreadfully painful – and embarrassing, too. She was afraid of what they might do with the letters. They seemed to think she wanted to hurt Patrick, which was an utterly ridiculous idea. The whole subject was such nonsense that it was hard to believe that anyone in authority would take the time to listen to them.

Patsy was wrong. By a curious alignment of fates, in the midst of war and the accompanying upheaval of the social norms, the conduct of which she was accused was of disproportionate relevance. A whirlwind was being formed, and its origins lay in the highest places in the land.

Chapter 16

THE DEFENCE OF THE REALM

I N APRIL 1916 the cabinet delegated Lord Reading to visit the United States and negotiate a loan of £1,000 million in order to fund the war effort. The report he submitted to the cabinet when he returned was kept secret.

A few days after our arrival we were convinced that it would be impossible to raise such an amount in a loan, and that it was very doubtful whether we should succeed in raising a loan of even £100 million. We found that our credit in the United States has suffered severely. The Americans seriously question our capacity to win the war. To put it bluntly, they think we have mismanaged our affairs, that we have no generals of real ability, and that our financial resources will not hold out. The German victories in Russia, and the absence of British or French victories in the west, have led them to believe that the Germans are beating us by their greater skills in generalship, management and organisation. In addition, the Americans have an exaggerated impression of the extent and importance of our labour unrest, and were perturbed by the press reports of our domestic troubles. German advice has set afloat the notion that we are approaching bankruptcy.

We were eventually advised that a loan of £500 million, less than half the amount we have identified as a requirement, was the limit of that which could be guaranteed, and that such a loan had to be fully subscribed by individual members of the public with full collateral given by the British and French governments. Such a loan could not be allowed to fail.

In America the banking situation is very different from that which prevails in this country. There are some twenty-five thousand banks and there is a want of cohesion between them, they having hitherto been prevented by law from having branches. There is no single body that represents these banks, hence there is great difficulty in arriving at any agreement or even negotiating with them. The city of New York is the central and most powerful influence, but even there the bankers' outlook is narrow compared with that in London. Banking and financial institutions in the United States are not looked upon with favour by the public, and there are many legal restrictions upon their activities.

Over and above these considerations is the fact that the loans were obtained mainly on the grounds that they were as much or more for the benefit of American trade as they were for the borrowing governments, and this was very expressly stated to us.

I am convinced that £500 million is the maximum obtainable by this form of loan. As time progresses without the war being brought to an end, if in any respect we should fail in our loan commitments or add to our indebtedness, it will naturally become impossible in the future to borrow in America.

This situation fills me with the greatest alarm. Of those who accompanied me I am permitted to say the following. Sir Edward Holden's opinions upon the financial situation in America and the credits obtainable are distinctly less favourable than those I have expressed. Sir Henry Babington Smith and General Sir John Cowans are generally in agreement with my views, except that they think them too optimistic.

Reading

Sir Arthur Markham MP was a wealthy Yorkshire mine-owner and philanthropist, a believer in hard work and generous charity. At the beginning of the war he had organised a co-operative of the country's pit-owners to ensure that the government got the coal it needed, at the best price and as easily and quickly as possible. Coal was crucial, for it was almost the only fuel for transport and heating. It kept the ships and the railways running, and it kept both soldiers and civilians warm and fed. The intention of Markham's coal plan was to prevent profiteering and support the war effort.

The cabinet's and War Office's incompetence, and the realisation of how close Britain was to defeat and impoverishment, filled him with horror and brought him near to despair, for he had great pride in his country. That pride was reflected in his work as an MP. He was respected in parliament, but not greatly liked, because he had a tendency to be right and to be blunt about it. But he suffered from angina and was frequently ill, which prevented him from taking a government post and limited his availability for official extra-parliamentary work.

It was to Markham that Sir Hubert Russell, MP for Denbighshire, had passed Mrs Birch's letter and synopsis, and he had read both carefully. He was acquainted with Dick Birch, who, as a land agent in north Wales, often had dealings with collieries. Therefore he agreed to meet the Birches and their solicitor, Mr Price.

After listening attentively to what they said, he thought for some time. He had many years experience' of both miners and pit managers, and he thought it possible that Patrick had misunderstood Colonel Radcliffe. His instinctive reaction was that the two persons really at fault were Patsy and General Cowans, because of the type of people he believed them to be. Had Radcliffe known the extent of Mrs West's sinfulness, he would surely not have behaved as he had.

Markham suggested that, if Radcliffe were now shown all the letters Mrs West had written to Patrick, and the filth that she had put in them, he would see the situation very differently. He proposed that Delmé-Radcliffe be given the opportunity to re-consider his decision, and perhaps change it, before the matter was taken further.

'I am certain,' he said, 'that the colonel was unaware of the force pressing upon Mr Barrett, and, given the opportunity to do so, will voice his horror when he discovers the real nature of Mrs West's conduct.

'However, in order for that discovery to be made he must be faced with this matter by his superiors. If the senior officers at Western Command do not think this is a subject for enquiry, I believe we must ask them to think again – and we must also ask their superiors to make them think again.'

Markham and Mr Price framed an official complaint to the War Office about the conduct of Lieutenant-Colonel Delmé-Radcliffe, Quartermaster-General Sir John Cowans and Mrs Patsy Cornwal-lis-West in the matter of Patrick Barrett; and about the conduct of General Cowans and Mrs West in the matter of Brigadier-General Owen Thomas.

The complaint contained Mrs Birch's written description of events. It also expressed the view that Lieutenant-Colonel Delmé-Radcliffe might not have been aware of the extent of the activities, in particular, of Mrs West. It might be correct, in the first instance, to show him certain letters she had written, in order to ask him whether, if he had been aware of them, he would still have acted as he had.

On 25 May the complaint was sent, in Markham's name, to Western Command at Chester and to the War Office in London. Markham also sent copies of the papers to the prime minister, of whose party he was a member, and advised him that he had taken these steps 'with grave concern'.

Asquith passed Markham's letter on to Kitchener, who asked Cowans to explain his actions. The prime minister's office sent Markham a copy of Cowans's reply.

2 June 1916

Dear Creedy [Creedy was Kitchener's secretary]

Re: the case of Second Lieutenant Barrett

Mrs Birch appears to think that General McKinnon and myself were the means of ordering him away from Kinmel Camp, where I believe he was, or is, and she has got this delusion fixed in her head. Moreover, she considers she has a grievance against the War Office, which she believes used undue influence to remove Barrett from her care. That is, of course, absolute nonsense; but I gather it is the cause of her actions.

General McKinnon asked if I would grant Mrs Birch an interview. I was unacquainted with the lady and demurred, because of the great amount of work with which I was and am engaged, but he assured me that such an interview might be beneficial in ameliorating her delusion. She came to the War Office and General McKinnon and I interviewed her here. She was in so excited a condition that she was somewhat incoherent, and she appeared to me to be a rather ordinary woman of a neurotic nature. After she had discoursed for about half an hour on the inadvisability of moving Barrett from Kinmel to another battalion, I had to close the interview, and told her that I really could not have my time wasted over things that in no way concerned the War Office. As she was leaving she said that I had treated her uncivilly, and that she would let the King and everybody know. I told her that she was perfectly at liberty to do so, and that I had not, after half an hour's conversation, arrived at an understanding of what her grievance was.

I think it is perfectly atrocious that our time should be taken up on such trivial matters, which, I repeat, in no way concern the War Office. General MacKinnon, to whom you may wish to refer, knows the individuals in the case, I understand. I hope the prime minister and Lord Kitchener will see their way to administering a rebuke to the lady in question if they reply to her; and point out that senior officers cannot be diverted from their war duties to settle a difference of opinion of two ladies.

Of course, I must make it clear that I have known the Cornwallis-Wests for many years and they are great friends of mine.

J. C.

The prime minister's problems were formidable. In April 1916, there had been an armed uprising in Dublin, and there were subsequent parliamentary questions about the methods used by the army to suppress it. In the Near East the British force invading Mesopotamia had been besieged and defeated. In France the reports of the fighting on the Somme contained unbelievable levels of casualties. In addition, Britain's financial problems had grown still worse. Before the war taxes had been less than 10 per cent of people's income and wealth; current estimates showed they needed to be raised to 70 per cent. Then, in June, Asquith arranged for Kitchener and Lloyd George to visit Russia to try to forge a new, purposeful offensive. At the last moment, Lloyd George stayed behind to help handle the Irish crisis. It was well for him that he did. HMS *Hampshire*, the ship carrying Kitchener, was sunk in the North Sea on 5 June. Kitchener's body was never found.

Several cabinet ministers resigned over Asquith's indecisiveness and inability to lead effectively. The public clamour about the continuing crises gave rise to a commission to investigate the losses in the Dardanelles campaign, and all, including Asquith, would be required to give evidence.

Cowans's reply to Creedy about Mrs Birch had not been seen by Lord Kitchener. Knowing full well that Asquith was struggling – and failing – to deal with yet another crisis, Markham wrote to Lloyd George, who had succeeded Kitchener as secretary of state for war. His letter was Lloyd's George's first encounter with the case.

47 Portland Place

London, W

29 June 1916

The Rt. Hon. David Lloyd George, MP
11, Downing Street
London, SW

Dear Lloyd George,

You will ask how it comes about that I am interesting myself in Welsh affairs. I am doing so for the reason that the question has a far wider issue than that of Wales itself, and it profoundly touches the question of War Office administration.

I have furnished the prime minister with full details of a most grave charge which I felt it my duty to make against certain high officials at the War Office, a charge so serious, indeed, that no government could, or I am sure would, defend it. I naturally appreciate that during the last week it has, owing to the cabinet crisis, been impossible for the prime minister to give this matter his personal attention, but I think it only right to let you know that another charge will in due course be formulated and, unless justice is done, will be made in parliament: namely, that an officer of the British army has been made victim by reason of the actions of a disreputable and unscrupulous society woman acting through a member of the Army Council.

I do not wish to embarrass the government regarding officers in high command intriguing with women against an officer in His Majesty's army. Nevertheless, if the War Office think they are going to ignore this question, or treat it as an insignificant side issue, they are vastly mistaken, for in this case I happen to hold every trench fortified with every gun, while the other side has only some poor gas with which to reply.

When I tell you that Mrs Cornwallis-West has been communicating with officers commanding at Chester through a member of the Army Council, to the detriment of the officer I mentioned above, I think you will see that we have reached a stage when it is the duty of a public man who knows the facts to see that a stop is put to this state of affairs.

You are a better judge of public opinion than I am. You will know what the people would think if they but knew the facts.

Yours sincerely,
Arthur Markham

Markham once said that Lloyd George 'never read nor wrote, but he listened and spoke'. In a letter to Lord Reading, the lord chief justice, whom he kept informed about this case, he went further: 'Lloyd George is the only man in the government who has shown real courage and daring during this war. There is no man in the House for whom I would do more.'

Markham continued to pursue him over this case, calling it 'War Office jobbing'. 'Jobbing' meant doing favours for friends and having friends to do favours in return. It also sometimes meant having mistresses. So it was a general accusation of impeachably dishonourable conduct.

Lloyd George had a mistress, Frances Stevenson, who worked in his office. She took an interest in the Barrett case, and alerted him to the way in which the War Office was passing it from department to department in the unspoken hope that it would get lost. They told her they were following normal procedure, but she rather sided with Barrett, and supported Lloyd George in wanting to see the case properly resolved.

Asquith himself had until recently, had a mistress, Venetia

Stanley, and everyone knew that he spent most of his time, especially during cabinet meetings, writing letters to her.

So both Lloyd George and the prime minister – not that they would have agreed about it, for they had little mutual sympathy – were sensitive about attacks on 'jobbing'. They would have liked to hang a 'Treat with Caution' label on Markham's lapel.

In July Lloyd George asked Markham to meet him at the House of Commons, hoping to find a way of resolving the case without a public scandal. Markham was seriously ill, and he told the secretary of state that it took a great effort to prepare himself for days in the House.

Lloyd George expressed his sympathy, then said, 'I have been considering your letter alleging improper behaviour in the War Office.'

'I think there is a need for the views to be heard,' said Markham.

'By whom? That is what I am not clear about.'

'The young soldier should have his name cleared.'

'And?'

'Those who damaged him should be identified, and prevented from doing anything similar in the future.'

'By whom?'

'Those responsible for the actions of the government and its agencies.'

'I don't think the lady in question has broken any laws – not laws of this country, at any rate – and you can't examine a civilian woman in a military court.'

'No.'

'So are you suggesting a committee of the House?' asked Lloyd George.

'I'm not suggesting a mechanism. I'm not able to do so.'

'A committee could come privately to a conclusion.'

'The danger then might be, Secretary of State, that there were no visible justice. These people deserve a public hearing.'

'I understand that, but I am not convinced that even they deserve the attention of the whole country at this time. There are other demands on people just now.'

'That would be true if, with respect, one of the people were not the quartermaster-general.'

'Why have you got so involved in this, Sir Arthur?'

'The letters that were exchanged made me angry. There is a feeling that the War Office answers to no one, and these letters seem to me to support that view.'

'I'm not sure. I sympathise with your young soldier, as you may imagine I would. But I don't want to lose Cowans. I also find him arrogant, and he likes to be seen to have certain friends, but he's more able than you are perhaps aware, and he holds an important position. If somebody takes the blame, I don't want it to be him. Might we agree how to proceed?'

Lloyd George gave Markham a summary of the concerns that faced him. He spoke with respect, knowing that was a wiser course with Markham than an expression of authority or a wielding of wartime secrecy. They agreed that Asquith could not continue as prime minister, and discussed what would be the priorities should he resign or be compelled to resign. Lloyd George, with his inside knowledge of the state of the war campaign, confirmed Markham's observation that the country was in a truly precarious position. But he also gave it as his view that the enemy's position must be as worrying to them as the British position was to the current government. He said he felt that each side was looking for a failure of morale in the other. For that reason, it was necessary to be careful about the way news was presented in the press.

While Markham waited patiently, Lloyd George concluded his train of thought; eventually, he said, 'I think you must pursue your campaign, Sir Arthur. You must see that such wrongful behaviour is put behind us. I shall do nothing to stop what you do. It will be to the good, I shall ensure that.'

Lloyd George had decided what he intended to do.

★　　★　　★

Markham continued on the path he had set for himself. At his request, and on the authority of the secretary of state for war, on 15 July a letter was sent from the War Office to the general officer commanding, Western Command.

Sir,

With reference to your letter of 6 June 1916, forwarding a statement made by Second Lieutenant P. Barrett, Royal Welch Fusiliers, taken down by Lieutenant-Colonel S. Thiele, Royal Army Medical Corps, I am commanded to inform you that it has been represented to the Army Council that Second Lieutenant Barrett is at the present time suffering from a nervous breakdown, due to a sense of injustice at the treatment accorded by his commanding officer, Lieutenant-Colonel H. Delmé-Radcliffe, in relation to a letter which Second Lieutenant Barrett wrote to Mrs Cornwallis-West.

I am commanded to say that it is understood that at the time Colonel Delmé-Radcliffe made the remarks attributed to him he had not seen certain letters which Mrs Cornwallis-West wrote to Lieutenant Barrett and to which that officer's letter was in effect a reply, and in these circumstances the Council have decided that Colonel Delmé-Radcliffe is to have an opportunity of perusing the lady's letters, copies of which are accordingly enclosed herewith.

The Council desire that these (copy) letters be forwarded to Colonel Delmé-Radcliffe, with a request that if, after perusal, he feels that, had he been cognisant of them when Lieutenant Barrett appeared before him at the orderly room, his treatment of the case would have been different, he will be good enough, if he considers that changed circumstances warrant it, to convey to Second Lieutenant Barrett an expression of the opinion which, under the new circumstances, he has formed of the lieutenant's conduct in writing to Mrs Cornwallis-West the letters that formed the subject of Colonel Delmé-Radcliffe's admonitions.

If, however, Lieutenant-Colonel Delmé-Radcliffe adheres to his previous view, he should submit a statement to that effect, which should be transmitted to this department without delay, together with the accompanying correspondence. The Council will then themselves consider whether or not Colonel Delmé-Radcliffe was justified in the action he took.

I am to observe that it should be clearly understood that it is only in the event of Lieutenant-Colonel Delmé-Radcliffe finding cause to alter his opinion, and, having so altered his opinion, of being desirous of conveying to Second Lieutenant Barrett the new impressions he may have gained of that officer's conduct, that he is to communicate direct with Lieutenant Barrett.

I am to request that the matter may be treated as one of urgency.

I am, Sir, your obedient servant,

B. B. Cubitt

Delmé-Radcliffe was much offended by the letter, which he saw as an unpleasant test of his integrity as an officer. It was unseemly to be passing around copies of letters of this kind.

Brigadier-General Owen Thomas advised him to take great care with his response, as 'the whole blame in this might be put on your shoulders, if the War Office feels that need'. But Radcliffe could only say what he thought had actually happened. He could not imagine that anyone senior in the War Office wanted to do anything more than close the file as quickly as possible. In order to do so, they required a letter from him to confirm that he had known what he was doing, and that he would do the same if, God forbid, the circumstances recurred. In his blunt reply to the War Office, he ignored the general's wise advice.

25 July 1916

Sir,

I have the honour to report to you as follows, in answer to the letter, Confidential and Personal, received by me direct from Western Command last week.

My position in the matter may be stated as follows:

I have never contended, and do not contend now, that Second Lieutenant P. Barrett should not have written to the lady; my contention was, and is, that he was not justified in writing her a letter which he must have known was likely to cause her, and in point of fact did indeed give her, very great offence. This is obvious to anyone, and was the cause of my admonition to him that if he could not write to her civilly, as an officer and gentleman should always write to a lady, he should not have written to her at all.

I hoped, when last year I recommended Barrett, then a sergeant, for an officer's commission, that as an officer he would prove a credit to the 12th Battalion, in which he had served with credit under me as a sergeant, and would also, to the other young officers here, prove a good example of what a man from the ranks of the 12th Battalion might achieve. In these hopes I was woefully disappointed, and I therefore consider that I acted correctly in reprimanding him. I had expected much better of him.

He admits having written the letter that gave offence; and the fact that he feels aggrieved by my finding fault with his action in writing that letter shows that he views the position of a young officer in a wholly wrong perspective, and will never see it in a right perspective until he is doing duty with his brother officers in a battalion where he ought to be.

I return herewith all the enclosures sent to me by the adjutant-general, Western Command, Chester, with the request they may now be sent back to him.

H. Delmé-Radcliffe

Denbighshire was boiling with gossip. Either one sided with Mrs Birch, and vowed to protect the young Tommies from the outrages of the aristocrats and the officers, or one was, silently, above that sort of thing and sympathetic to poor old Colonel Cornwallis-West, whose wife seemed only a victim of her own flirtatious kindness. The possibility that the war might be lost was not discussed only in Whitehall. The people were not so foolish as to believe that all was going well, not when they heard every day of thousands more dead, and battles evidently being lost. There was anger and frustration at the inability of those in charge to operate effective and correct policies. In other countries, Russia particularly, the people whose children were dying were rising up against their rulers. In north Wales it was not surprising that a scandal of society ladies and the War Office should be seen as a symbol of all that was wrong, and a cause for great expressions of feeling and anxiety.

Patsy fell ill. The dreadful anxiety about what was happening caused pains in her stomach such as she had never felt before. She stayed at Newlands all summer, avoiding the turmoil of Ruthin.

She was near hysteria when she told George that the Birches had turned against her and were employing an MP to destroy her. She accused George of ignoring her and spending all the family's money and never helping when she needed him. She raged at his mistreatment of Stella and his army debts and screamed of her shame at his behaviour and the humiliation it had brought on his father. He had done nothing to help Shelagh during her divorce from the Duke of Westminster, and nothing to keep in contact with Daisy. All he did was go racing and fishing and shooting and neglect his duty as a husband, while pleading marriage as a reason for not going to the war.

'What have you ever done to help us?' She ranted at him.

He had written two plays and half a novel about himself, which did not sound much. Certainly they would do nothing to help discharge his bankruptcy.

'We shall have to sell Ruthin to pay your debts, and Stella can't help you – she doesn't want to any more.' She sat down and wept. 'The Birches have made up this terrible story about me and sent it to the War Office. After all I've done for both of them. And that poor soldier, Patrick Barrett, they've told him so many lies. She's jealous of me; she can't bear the things I do. She hates me. She said so the day I stayed at their house. She told me I was so much trouble that she hated me.'

'What can I do?' asked George.

She told him to find George Lewis, the solicitor she and Lillie Langtry had used all those years ago: he had been able to solve many problems. But George found that Lewis had recently died. His office, in Ely Place, in Holborn, suggested that George should talk to the MP for Canterbury, Francis Bennett-Goldney, because he had a reputation for working behind the scenes in the House of Commons. Goldney had been a client of George Lewis.

Patsy's illness grew worse. She had trouble moving, and no medicines could relieve her pain. It made her irritable and more and more angry with George.

Arthur Markham, Mr Price and Dick Birch went by train to Chester, then took a car to Llanarmon. Markham had insisted on being present when Patrick's evidence was taken. He wanted to meet the soldier and understand the story fully.

The Tower had been part of the Ruthin estate, and used as a hunting-lodge. It was where William sometimes used to come to be on his own; he had done so when he was standing for election as an MP and wanted to write some speeches about education. Now it had been taken over by Shelagh and turned into a small Westminster nursing-home. It was a little old stone castle in the valley by the bridge. There could hardly be a place with more peace and tranquillity.

When they arrived, Mrs Birch was waiting on the doorstep. She took them inside to meet Patrick. Almost at once, however, a serious difficulty arose. Markham had thought the Tower was a hospital, and that if he himself became ill help and treatment would be available. It was not: the only medical care available was from Welsh birds singing in the trees outside, and rabbits running through the wood. And soon after they arrived he had began to have difficulty breathing. He became worried. The interview would have to be as short as possible.

Cleaned up, fussed over and rehearsed for the visit, Patrick lost his nerve. Mrs Birch had been over with him the drives with Patsy, the letters, the talks, the presents, the night of the pantomime at Rhyl, the visit to the castle, so that he was ready to tell Markham the whole story. But in the room, shaded by the trees outside the window, and faced with the simplest, quietest questions, all he could say, slowly and calmly, was that he wanted to be an honest soldier, and do his duty, for the sake of his friends who had died.

This was only natural, Mrs Birch hastened to explain, because they could see the condition he was in. So they sat, the five of them in the room, while she told the story, and Mr Price wrote it down, and Patrick sometimes nodded in agreement with what she said, when he could concentrate enough. She added, for him, a little about the time General Cowans had visited Bryncelin, because that was when he had arrived home so ill, and he might well not remember it clearly.

When she had finished Patrick signed the writing on Mr Price's sheet, and shook Mr Markham's hand. Mr Markham and Dick Birch signed also to say that it was an accurate record of the evidence given by Second Lieutenant Patrick Barrett, of the Royal Welch Fusiliers, confined to a convalescent home by virtue of the stress under which he had been placed. They were sorry to have to leave so quickly but Mr Markham must immediately be taken back to the station to catch the train.

Markham was moved by what he had seen and heard, and more certain of his purpose.

Patrick, in his own mind, knew he had not told tales about Patsy. He had not broken his promise.

Violet Markham, Sir Arthur's sister, worried terribly about her brother's health. He had told her about the woman who had so scandalous an influence over the War Office, but she was more concerned about the strain he was putting himself under.

He could not let the matter rest. On Tuesday, 27 July, he wrote to Lloyd George again.

Dear Lloyd George,

I have received the message that you propose a debate next week to frame terms for a House committee of enquiry.

I am sorry that I caused you so much inconvenience when we talked. I have not had an angina attack for some months, but now I confess I anticipate one on Tuesday next, because I fear my heart will not stand laying out such a long case before the House.

Such an attack would be most unfortunate, because the statement you have from me was written eight weeks ago, and since then I have collected a great deal of information which neither you nor the War Office have seen or know of.

There are two points about this proposed enquiry which must be made quite clear:

1. Will the committee have power to call witnesses before them and take evidence on oath?

2. Will an indemnity be granted to all witnesses appearing before the committee?

I may be wrong, but I do not see how you are going to get this information without you get the power from parliament to do so. A committee without such powers would be futile, for it could not compel the attendance of all from whom it needs to hear evidence, and I had better say, at once, that I could not possibly accept such a committee.

As regards the composition of the committee, I do not think that two is a satisfactory number. If you appoint a soldier, I think I ought to have the right to nominate an MP, this being the usual parliamentary practice in such cases. I further think that the MP should be an Irish member, but I would not like to suggest a Nationalist.

I am prepared to agree that all proceedings of the committee should be secret, for it is not in the public interest to have these letters made public. Believe me I do not wish to put difficulties in your way. I am, however, firmly convinced that I have a public duty to perform; and nothing will turn me from that path.

It seems to me that the proper course is for me to put down a question next Monday, asking the prime minister whether he is prepared now to appoint a committee of enquiry to report on certain grave allegations made by myself against the department of the quartermaster-general. This would require a bill, but I would point out that, if I make these charges in the House, you may have no alternative but to appoint a committee.

If parliament is prorogued, there will be no opportunity for a discussion; therefore, the matter must be settled before Tuesday.

Yours sincerely,
Arthur Markham

By this devastating letter Arthur Markham had taken upon himself the right to bring the activities of Patsy Cornwallis-West and General Sir John Cowans into the open. His question would be placed on record when he asked it the following Monday, and the government was duty bound to answer it in parliament the next day. There could be no more hiding.

Violet Markham grew even more worried. If her brother, by clever use of parliamentary tactics, forced the government of his own party into a particular and distracting course – and this at a time of great national emergency – he would be extremely unpopular with many of his fellow MPs as well as with the government. But that was the nature of the line Arthur Markham had taken, and she could not induce him to change it.

He was not just making a specific point about this case, although the case gave him the material he needed. He was also making a complaint about Asquith's indecisiveness and lack of leadership as prime minister. In effect, he was saying that situations of this kind should not be allowed to arise. It was a symptom of profound weakness, and the weakness was shown up by Markham's enquiries. That was why Lloyd George had encouraged him to continue his pursuit of the case: they now had another major scandal which with to embarrass Asquith, one which might lead to his downfall.

The newspapers had picked up a scent of the case. They wanted to know what Markham was complaining about. They were sure it was something to do with sex and the War Office, but they had no facts yet. They started hunting for the story.

George Cornwallis-West arranged a meeting with Francis Bennett-Goldney, who was both mayor of and MP for Canterbury. They went together to Ruthin and then visited the Birches at Bryncelin.

Dick Birch had known George since he was a child. George told Dick that Patsy was seriously ill because of the anxiety the case was causing her. He said that she was very concerned that Patrick Barrett should get well, and would do anything to try and resolve the matter, if a way could be found. He explained that she had never wanted Patrick's commission to be taken away, and had only ever tried to work out what was best for his recovery. He brought sincerely expressed apologies for any misunderstandings that might have arisen in the heat of the moment. They all knew how fiery

Patsy could be. The Birches knew, said George, that he himself had often been on the receiving end of her temper. It was her nature, but she never had meant to harm anyone. He also said that his father was lost without Dick's help, and that he was worried about William's health.

They talked about the whole case and how Arthur Markham seemed to have got carried away with the significance of it, and Mrs Birch mentioned that all the solicitors' expenses and costs were now being paid by Lloyd George.

She told George that she had been very angry at what Patsy did. It had been very wrong for Patsy to take Patrick so closely into her affections, she said. It was important that their liaison, whatever its nature, should be stopped, as it was always going to damage Patrick. That was why she had told Patrick what he should say in his letter to Patsy. Of course she bitterly regretted that the outcome was that Patrick was now even more ill. But Patsy had been foolish to involve Colonel Radcliffe. It would have been so much better if they had sorted it all out between them.

She said she would be embarrassed to go to Arthur Markham and ask him to withdraw his request for an enquiry, so Bennett-Goldney offered to do it for her. He said he would try to find Markham at the Commons in the next few days, and see what Markham said. He felt certain he could persuade Markham to drop the case.

George and Bennett-Goldney left the Birches feeling greatly relieved: they had solved the problem. The next day George went to Newlands and told Patsy what Mrs Birch had said. He assured her that the whole matter would shortly be dropped and she need worry about it no more.

She was now quite seriously ill. She could not bear to face people. She hid in her room and would speak to no one. All the things that mattered to her in life were falling apart. Shelagh's marriage had ended. Daisy was far away in war-stricken Germany. George's debts meant that they might have to sell one of the houses to clear them; they were already having trouble paying the bills at Ruthin. Poor Jack Cowans, who had always been such a good friend, seemed destined to lose his job. Only nine months ago she had been as happy as she ever had been; and now all this.

She had grown thin, and her beautiful hair was losing its colour and going grey.

Over the years she had often known unhappiness but had not become depressed – depression was not part of her nature. But this illness had laid her low. She could find no spirit within herself. She began to fear what a doctor might say.

She asked George to tell Poppets what Mrs Birch had said. They did not know, but they hoped this would mean that the ridiculous accusations against Jack Cowans would also be dropped. However, they would still have to prepare solicitors in case Patsy was required to give evidence.

She had been asked to hand over all her letters that might be relevant, which frightened and upset her. It was awful to hand over personal letters. All her life she had written masses of letters, and they were always full of affection. She was shamed by having to hand them over, but she felt too weak to argue any more.

On the day he wrote to Lloyd George, Markham also wrote to Lord Reading, the lord chief justice

> 47 Portland Place
> London, W
> 27 July 1916

Dear Reading

I am very unwell, but I want to open my mind to you for we are old friends and I am always and ever shall be sensible of the support you have always given me. I am writing to you as an old friend and colleague in the House in a strictly private and confidential letter.

I herewith enclose a letter I have today sent to Lloyd

George. Perhaps you will tell him I have sent you a copy of this letter. In the Cowans case all the parties are strangers to me except the Birch family, who have been known to me for many years.

The War Office say this is a quarrel between women. In a sense this is perfectly true. Mrs Birch did strongly object to Mrs X coming to her house and making advances to a soldier she was nursing, and they had high words on the subject. My wife and I turned our house into a hospital, as the Birches have done, and I am certain that my wife would have taken the same view as Mrs Birch if, in our house, any woman had done what Mrs X has done.

Birch is a man whose honesty and integrity I can vouch for. It is clearly most undesirable all these unsavoury details should come before the public at the present time, and an enquiry is the best way out of the difficulty. To hold an enquiry without the committee having the power either to call witnesses or to take evidence on oath, would be futile, and I could not ask my witnesses to put themselves at the mercy of the Army Council. It is essential that they be indemnified against any disciplinary action that might be taken against them.

The adjutant-general has adopted the attitude that it is in no way improper for an officer of high rank to make enquiries at the War Office to ascertain whether a commission or transfer has been made and to hasten the same. I entirely agree, but the case of Barrett is not one in which an officer of high rank is seeking to obtain information, but an attempt to drive an innocent man out of his regiment at the request of a woman.

Cowans has told the War Office – and the adjutant-general has told me – that he did not come into the case until 25 March when he, Cowans, sent a telegram to the lieutenant-colonel of Barrett's regiment telling him that he had better 'wire Chester and act at once'. Nothing can justify the quartermaster-general going outside his department to tell an officer to hasten the transfer of a man out of his battalion at the request of any woman, much less wiring, On His Majesty's Service, that the transfer had been carried through.

I have documentary evidence that Cowans's statement that he did not come into the case until 25 March is untrue: he was in it from the beginning. If I can show, by means of original letters written by Cowans, that he was in the case prior to the 25th, I contend that Cowans's word is of no value whatever.

The adjutant-general does not deny that Cowans admitted showing a schedule of equipment purchased in America to Mrs X, that she showed it to Barrett and that it is therefore likely to have been shown to other people. No minister could stand up in parliament and defend this one point alone.

General Sir Henry Mackinnon and Mr Richard Birch are old friends, and Mackinnon told Birch that when he was staying with Mrs X at Ruthin Castle on 20 February she told him she was in great trouble about Barrett, because he was pursuing her and had attempted to break into her bedroom. That is a most wicked lie, because when the poor fellow broke his journey at Ruthin on his journey to Llanarmon, he was so ill that he had to be carried on a stretcher to his room and was quite incapable of even walking. Yet he is secretly condemned on the basis of this kind of stuff.

When Barrett made an application for an enquiry the papers were actually destroyed, not sent forward to the War Office as they ought to have been. The War Office are fully aware that a military medical board has reported that Barrett has no chance of recovery till his mind is set at rest, and yet, notwithstanding that report, nothing has been done, an enquiry has been refused and not till a member of parliament comes on the scene does this man have any chance of getting a hearing.

Delmé-Radcliffe, the lieutenant-colonel of Barrett's regiment, appears to have acted very foolishly. If your son or mine had written an indiscreet letter to a woman, it would have been proper to take the course that Radcliffe did (though not before Barrett's brother officers), but in the case of a Tommy with no education, and who is a curious kind of creature, but with an extraordinarily high sense of right and wrong, this course was disastrous.

I am an experienced MP. The case I bring against the War Office is founded not on hearsay evidence but on documents which are in existence. If Lloyd George examines them he will have, I maintain, more than sufficient evidence to deal with this officer without holding an enquiry. I know it would be a very bold step for him to dismiss Cowans, but in point of fact nothing would strengthen his position more with the army.

The PM should have dealt with this case weeks ago. I intensely dislike that Lloyd George should be called upon to have to deal with the question, but believe me it will do him good with the army and the country.

As things stand at present I do not know whether or not it will be necessary to bring the case before the House on Tuesday. If I had not had this wretched attack this morning, I could have said what I now put in writing to you, but I did not have the opportunity.

My poor health means that I have written you a very disjointed letter, but what I have got in my mind all the time is this poor fellow who is slowly dying in Wales. He said to me, only last Monday, that he has done his best for his country, that he is quite ready to die, and that, if his case can be the means of saving other men from suffering injustice such as he himself has suffered, he should die quite happy and feel that his life had been not altogether wasted.

Yours sincerely
Arthur Markham

Markham had made clear to his friends in the House that his targets in this campaign were Cowans and a lady whose name he was careful not to give. His attack on the quartermaster-general was not popular. Cowans was particularly angered to be the subject of such blunt words and also to find that, whereas Lord Kitchener had been ready to close the whole subject quickly, Lloyd George seemed not to be supporting him.

Cowans hoped and expected that the whole matter would fade away. It was a waste of everyone's time, and nobody had done anything they should not. His work had hugely increased during the summer because of the failure of the supply lines from India to the army in Mesopotamia. His department had had to move urgently into a whole new sphere of the war, and it had placed them under great strain. The last thing he wanted was a great fuss about a trifling set of letters, which were of absolutely no consequence. Lloyd George should, in his view, have dismissed the whole thing. Cowans was also concerned at how upset Patsy would be when she discovered what they were saying in London about her.

Lloyd George, however, had taken a different line. For one thing he tended to side with the people of Denbighshire – his home at Criccieth was not far from Denbigh – who disliked the way a young soldier had been treated. They felt that soldiers were not expendable at the whim of the War Office, and should not be manipulated by distant, powerful bureaucrats. His political instinct told him that this was an important case and now it was out in the open. To try and prevent the press from covering it would be dangerous. Moreover, he could see it working in his favour with respect to Asquith. All he had to do at the moment was keep the case running.

Bennett-Goldney and George Cornwallis-West had not realised the implications of Mrs Birch's revelation that Lloyd George was paying the Birches' costs. He was doing so because he wanted to achieve something thereby. It was no longer for Mrs Birch to say that the matter could be dropped, or even for Arthur Markham to retreat – not that he intended to. Lloyd George was using the case for his own purposes and these people would not prevent him.

So he did not dismiss the matter. Cowans noted that fact, and began to suspect that Lloyd George was plotting to replace him with a civilian friend, perhaps even a businessman like Markham. After all, most of what Cowans was doing involved buying enormous quantities of food and clothing, the kind of work usually done by someone with commercial experience rather than a career on the parade ground. It was truly disheartening to find himself in this position when he had worked so hard and done absolutely nothing to invite the trouble.

As Markham was leaving the House on Thursday, he was approached by Bennett-Goldney, the MP for Canterbury, whom Markham considered a showman and despised.

'You have the wrong end of the stick over this Barrett case,' said Goldney.

Markham was flustered and his breathing was ragged. He said nothing.

'I have been to see Mrs Birch, and she is sorry for the trouble she has caused the Cornwallis-Wests. She admitted to Mrs West's son that she was behind the letter Barrett wrote. You had better drop the whole thing, because it will fall apart in a court.'

Markham was really upset by this. He went straight to his house and wrote to a letter.

Thursday, 31 July

Dear Mrs Birch,

As I was coming out of the House today I had a most disagreeable encounter with a Member whom I greatly dislike whose name is Bennett-Goldney. He claimed that you told him you had changed your view of Patrick Barrett's case.

I do not know whether that is the truth, but I am sure you will understand that if I am to continue to fight in this matter we must have no secrets from each other: it would be most unfortunate. All our cards must be on the table.

Yours sincerely,
Arthur Markham

Although by now feeling very ill indeed, he went out straight away and posted the letter. As he turned away from the pillar-box, Arthur Markham collapsed on the pavement in Portland Place. He died before help could reach him.

Chapter 17

INQUEST

I T MIGHT THEN have been sensible to let the whole matter of an enquiry drop. So far as anyone knew, Markham was the only person, apart from Mr and Mrs Birch, who wanted it, and he had been unpopular for that reason. Violet Markham feared that her brother's reputation would be damaged by what might be said about him at an enquiry. She begged that the matter be closed for his sake. An awful feature of the war was that people who had died were being blamed for all the evil. Already Kitchener was accused of responsibility for much that was wrong with the army.

But Lloyd George, apparently alone, wanted to press ahead. Like a schoolboy who knows the teacher cannot control the class, he was looking for ways to show up Asquith and his mishandling of the war. Asquith was a supporter of Cowans, and here was a neat way to embarrass the prime minister – on top of all the other things that had been going wrong.

So he followed the path Markham had set for him and, in response to Markham's question of the previous week, on the Tuesday proposed a bill for a special Act of Parliament to create a new form of army enquiry in which civilians could be called to give evidence on oath and in secret. The bill was passed in the House of Commons on Tuesday and in the House of Lords on Wednesday. It gave Lloyd George, as secretary of state for war, the power to appoint a committee to hold an enquiry immediately, which he did. The Army Courts of Enquiry Act (1916) has been used only once. *Hansard* records the short debate in the House of Commons and it is clear that the MPs, who had little idea of what was afoot, merely acquiesced to a request from the secretary of state for war.

The newspapers went wild. During the Lords debate it had become apparent that the enquiry concerned a woman whom no one would name and whose evidence would be given in secret. Nothing could make a better scandal. The editors soon discovered who the woman was, and had to invent a hundred ways of avoiding saying what she might have done – if they could only guess what that might be. It gave them the chance to recall Patsy's former life as a Society Beauty, without explaining why it was newsworthy. The *Evening Chronicle* reported: 'How fascinating to see the charming Mrs Cornwallis-West once again the centre of attention in London society. Many will recall her delightful escapades as a young bride,' and so on. And then there were sinister suggestions of a German link to the case, through 'her daughter Daisy, Princess of Pless, of whom so little has been heard in recent times'.

But no one knew either what was supposed to have happened or what actually had happened between Patsy and Patrick Barrett, still less how the War Office might have been involved.

'We rise quickly and fade away painfully slowly,' Patsy wrote in a note to Jack Cowans.

Asquith was obliged to ask Field Marshal Lord Nicholson, a former Chief of the Imperial General Staff, for an internal enquiry into the actions of the quartermaster-general.

Cowans received an official letter from Nicholson advising him that he was required to attend an army court of enquiry constituted under the Army Courts of Enquiry Act (1916). He was advised that in the course of that enquiry he would be asked about important issues concerning his activities as quartermaster-general and his position on the Army Council. His membership of the Army Council would be suspended until the full outcome of the enquiry was known.

In a private note accompanying the letter, Nicholson advised him to seek representation and legal advice, as the matters raised might affect his current appointment and his career.

Dick Birch had returned from London at the end of July and told his wife that Cowans was going to take legal action of his own to prevent them using his letters as evidence in any lawsuit. She was worried, and on 31 July wrote to Markham. In the letter she said, 'I and I alone am responsible for any mistakes that have been made and any actions that have been taken.'

She received Markham's letter about Bennett-Goldney on 1 August, and was thinking about how to reply to it when Mr Price telephoned and gave her the sad news of Markham's death. She was shocked and distressed. She had liked and trusted him, and with his death she had lost her greatest ally. She, too, supposed that the case would be closed down.

Her first inkling that it might not be came when a reporter came to Bryncelin and asked if she would consider having her photograph taken. He was from the *Denbigh Free Press*, he said, but the request had come to him from the *Chronicle* in London.

A letter from Mr Price informed the Birches that they would be required to give evidence at the court of enquiry to be held at the Guildhall, Westminster. It was too late for them to stop what they had started. Mrs Birch told him what had been said during George Cornwallis-West and Bennett-Goldney's visit, but Mr Price explained to her that the matter was now out of their hands. He had already had to pass all the documents over to the court of enquiry. It was now for them to decide what had really happened and whether any of the parties had behaved improperly. All that could be done now was to attend the enquiry and answer the questions asked.

The Guildhall at Westminster is a court of law. It faces the House of Commons across Parliament Square. It had been rebuilt just before the war, and had fine panelled courtrooms and oak desks.

In the papers circulated to the four members of the commission, including Lord Nicholson, who presided as chairman, were copies of those of Patsy's letters which Mrs Birch had obtained, and her synopsis of the events.

Patrick Barrett was deemed too ill to attend, so his sworn statement, taken from his bedside in Llanarmon, was given to and read to the court.

There were also letters which Cowans had offered in evidence. Since he considered the whole thing ridiculous, he had decided that the simplest course was to allow his files to be searched for relevant correspondence.

When asked by Lord Kitchener's secretary earlier in the summer, Cowans had said he had nothing to do with Barrett until Mrs West had asked him in March to support Barrett's move away from Bodelwyddan Camp. Yet the first letter the commissioners were shown was one in January from Cowans congratulating Barrett on his promotion. Then they were shown those from the previous autumn recommending Patrick for an officer's commission.

Mr Poole, the barrister acting for the commissioners in Markham's stead, drew attention to certain parts of Mrs Birch's synopsis which had been edited and re-composed by Arthur Markham for maximum effect. 'Two grave irregularities therefore appear at this stage,' he said. The first is that Sir John Cowans should have written the letter of 4 January at all, or have interested himself in this case at the instigation of a woman. The second is that he should have used his influence to get Mr Barrett appointed to the 3rd Battalion.

'It is clear that Mr Barrett was posted to the 3rd Battalion through the influence of Mrs Cornwallis-West acting through General Sir John Cowans, who at this time wrote to Mrs Cornwallis-West, on official notepaper, as follows: "Barrett has been posted to the 3rd Battalion. Dear little Patsy, now do be good and don't mention his name to me again. Yours, J."

'It would appear to me that it is, to say the least, irregular that a member of the Army Council should be employing his time writing to "Dear little Patsy" about a soldier of whom he had no official knowledge and who had no connection with his department. Furthermore, pleasing the lady was not confined to the War Office. Upon Barrett's appointment, Lieutenant-Colonel Delmé-Radcliffe wrote the sergeant two extremely flattering letters, in one of which he said Barrett had been "one of the best NCOs among the many good men it has been my great honour to have had under my command". And in the other he said, "The best thing that I can wish for you is that you should remain what you are, a straightforward genuine man." The timing of these letters indicates that Colonel Delmé-Radcliffe received the information about Sergeant Barrett's promotion from Mrs Cornwallis-West before it arrived through official channels.'

Mr Poole went on to describe the increasing contact between Mr Barrett and Mrs West, now quoting from the statements Patrick had made, which were presented to the court.

During my stay at Bryncelin Mrs Cornwallis-West of Ruthin Castle used frequently to visit Mr and Mrs Birch and kindly interested herself on my behalf. I never construed Mrs West's manner towards me as anything but that of a friendly interest until I received certain letters from her in November and December 1915, which letters I have destroyed.

What also opened my eyes to Mrs West's manner, which on many occasions I did not understand, was her reference in my presence, when in the car going to Ruthin Castle on 4 February 1916, to a pierrot she had seen at Colwyn Bay and whom she appeared to know. The reference she made with respect to this man was that when staying with her at Newlands Manor he was very rude to her – that she never forgave an injury – that she was a bad enemy but a good friend and that she would ruin this man, and she further told me that she had asked the colonel to write a letter of complaint about him.

The pierrot was then a sergeant stationed at Salisbury Plain. I understood that his colonel had then written to Mrs West to the effect that the man would not get more forward. This had a great effect on me.

On 3 February 1916 we went in the car to a pantomime in Rhyl. On that occasion Mrs West repeatedly placed her hand on my trousers under the rug.

On a visit to Ruthin Castle, Mrs West showed me into the pink room which overlooks the garden and where there is a tiger-skin rug in front of the fire. She was affectionate with me. Then she took me upstairs saying she had something to show me. Opening a door she said, 'This is my beautiful bedroom, Pat, dear. This is the bed where I have been lonely all my life with no one to share it, darling.' Then she kissed me, which I tried to avoid and she again kissed me in the boudoir.

On 12 February 1916 Mrs West came to stay at Bryncelin and arrived at about four o'clock. Mr and Mrs Birch were out and Mrs West and I were alone for tea and until Mr and Mrs Birch returned at about 6.30. Her conversation was not what I had been used to. She named several prominent men whom I knew and said they were living immoral lives and cohabiting with other women. She included Mr Birch. She spoke of famous people who also lived with younger ladies including the prime minister, Mr Asquith, and Mr Lloyd George from Criccieth, and she said, 'If they do it it can't be wrong, Pat, dear, do you think so?' I said I thought it very wrong and wicked. She asked if I would go with her to Lady Trevor's to meet General Sir Henry Mackinnon. I said it would be very nice but I did not think I could. General Mackinnon is very high up and I did not think it right for a subaltern to stay in the same place. Mrs West also said she would be glad when I got to Kinmel Camp, as she would arrange with my colonel for me to stay at Ruthin Castle at weekends. I said, 'I am afraid that I shall not be able to get leave as I am not well educated and I must study for my promotion exams'. She said, 'Don't

worry about your promotion, Pat, dear. I'll see that's all right.'
I said, 'I hope to get back to France, where I can make a name
for myself.' She said, 'You shall never go back to France. I'll
make sure of that.'

Mrs Cornwallis-West gave me several presents: a large gold
heart, a picture, a scarf, a book of poetry, a photo of herself.

Mr Poole did not look up at the bench as he read Patrick's
statement, but he could sense the astonishment it caused. Lord
Nicholson had to remind all those present that this was a closed
hearing and that no notes or evidence were to be passed to persons
outside the room.

Well satisfied, Mr Poole continued. 'The cumulative effect on
Patrick Barrett of these events caused him to write the letter to Mrs
Cornwallis-West which was quoted back to him and eventually
used against him by Lieutenant-Colonel Delmé-Radcliffe.

'Since the despatch of this letter Mr Barrett has not heard from or
received any communication from Mrs Cornwallis-West. On 18
February 1916, General Sir Henry Mackinnon, then commanding
the Western Division, visited Mrs Cornwallis-West at Ruthin
Castle. On the morning of 20 February, Mrs Cornwallis-West
told him that before he went she wished to speak to him about the
conduct of an officer in his command. She said this officer was
named Barrett, was staying at Bryncelin convalescent home, and
was attached to the 12th Battalion, Royal Welch Fusiliers at
Kinmel Camp. She said he was constantly at Ruthin Castle and
had begun pursuing her, and that she was frightened of him. She
also claimed that he had tried to break into her bedroom, evidently
with the intention of committing an indecent assault. She asked
General Mackinnon to have the officer removed. He obliged her.
He wrote to the commanding officer of the 12th Battalion,
Lieutenant-Colonel Delmé-Radcliffe – directly, instead of through
the proper channels – and ordered that Barrett be dealt with.

'It should be emphasised that Mrs Cornwallis-West's story about

Barrett trying to breaking into her bedroom was an invention from beginning to end, as is obvious from the facts.

'Colonel Delmé-Radcliffe then conducted two interviews with Lieutenant Barrett, the result of which was a serious breakdown of Barrett's fragile physical and mental health. Following Barrett's collapse, and the official certification of his ill health by an army doctor, Colonel Radcliffe wrote to Mrs Cornwallis-West, saying, "I cannot understand what all this to-do is about. I merely applied for Barrett to be sent to the 3rd Battalion and he has been ordered there. There is no disgrace in this – the 3rd Battalion is senior to this one. Now they say Barrett is ill in bed. It is not true that I was cruel to him. I merely took him to task for what he did, and he was quite calm while speaking to me and not in any way upset, and myself I have no fear for his health."

The truth is that Colonel Delmé-Radcliffe, in the face of a medical certificate stating that Barrett was wholly unfit for work of any description ordered him to be sent to Litherland forthwith.

'Unless it has become the general practice of the general officer commanding at Chester to send telegrams to the War Office about the transfer of junior officers, this was the further result of conversations between Mrs Cornwallis-West and General Mackinnon.

'In addition, General Sir John Cowans was instrumental in having Barrett sent to Litherland, from where he would have been sent back to the front in France, although he was utterly unfit for combat duty, in order to ensure that he caused no embarrassment to any of the persons concerned in this affair. The whole of these proceedings, which included concealing the medical report on Barrett, were hole-and-corner methods of a most disgraceful character.'

Thus did Mr Poole unfold Mrs Birch's view of Patsy's behaviour, first as a manipulative, middle-aged harlot, then as a vindictive, scorned woman with the power to influence the highest officials in the land to do her callous bidding. Also implicated were Cowans, Mackinnon and the heartless Delmé-Radcliffe. Each was to be called, in subsequent days, to answer the questions raised by this version of events.

Patsy sat in silence. She was so tense that she felt sick. She knew that none of what Patrick was supposed to have said had come from him. She was horrified that her letters were being passed round these old generals. She had nothing but contempt for any of them. The only thing that consoled her was that, because it was a secret enquiry, witnesses waited outside the courtoom, and no members of the public, apart from her closest family, were allowed to attend.

Nevertheless, press interest was enormous: newspapers wanted photographs of the two women, the villainess and the heroine, and reporters and photographers crowded the front entrance of Guild-hall. Mrs Birch appeared smartly dressed each morning, even showing off several new hats during the five days that the enquiry lasted. Reaction to Patsy was so hostile that George had to ask Bennett-Goldney to arrange with the police and the court for her to enter and leave through a side door.

It was supposed to be a secret enquiry. The court had instructed that nothing of what was said might be repeated outside, and informed all attending that passing information, or any form of message, to a person or persons outside would be treated as contempt of court and punished instantly and severely. All notes were to be handed to the clerk, and were subsequently destroyed. Nevertheless, in the gentlemen's clubs of Pall Mall, tales of scandal and wickedness coloured the conversations of the old men in leather armchairs.

The newspapers complained they were being excluded from a matter of public concern. But those involved now knew why Lloyd George had played it this way. This woman was not only wicked; she was dangerous, too. Who could tell what she might say next?

When she took the stand, Patsy was determined to let these men know what she thought of them. In their world to love someone who needed loving merited disapproval and shame, but to her it was the only thing that mattered.

Mr Poole began by asking, 'Mrs West, will you explain to us the nature of your relationship with Sergeant Barrett?'

'I cared for him.'

'Would you say you cared for him in the same way as you cared for other soldiers injured in the war?'

'Yes, I did.'

'Please describe, in your own words, how your friendship with Sergeant Barrett changed.'

'When?'

'Between, let us say, September 1915 and January 1916.'

'My feeling did not change at all.'

'There are certain letters, written in your hand, which are of a particularly affectionate nature. What were the feelings you were trying to convey?'

'Why are you asking me this? Do you want me to explain to you about feelings? Do you not know about caring for someone?'

'Mrs West, I am trying to help the commissioners understand what happened at this time, so that they can form a view of the events.'

'Do you think they don't understand already? Do we have to describe to them the care that is needed for a poor soldier who is so terribly wounded that he lies on his side all day, weeping for his friends who died?'

'I think it would help to describe that for them.'

'Of course it would,' said Patsy scornfully. 'They don't know. How could they? They've never been near the battle-front. Listen, Patrick Barrett was destroyed. He was mutilated by stupid warfare.'

'Did you feel great affection for Patrick Barrett?'

'Certainly.'

'Did you find him physically attractive?'

'He is attractive, and he is vulnerable.'

'Did you want to have intimate relations with him?'

'Oh yes.'

'Did you in fact have such relations with him?'

'That's a completely different question.'

'Nevertheless, I am asking it.'

'It cannot be answered.'

'I will ask again. Did you?'

'There's no need,' she said. 'Did you ask him the same question?'

'I'm asking it of you now.'

'In front of all these people you ask, as if it were an innocent, matter-of-fact question, what relationship I had with a young soldier so mutilated in this war that he can hardly speak or walk. The question is insolent.'

'Will you answer it?'

'Of course not.'

'I must ask you to explain why you will not.'

'Because you would not understand my answer.'

'In one of your letters to Second Lieutenant Barrett you wrote, "That dear boy we were talking about, will you give him my love and tell him I often think about him? But I can't write to him until I see you on Saturday." Please explain what you meant by that.'

'I have no idea.'

'Was the "dear boy" in fact Lieutenant Barrett?'

'I don't remember that letter, but it's very likely that I would have called Patrick Barrett a dear boy. He is a dear boy, a very dear boy, despite the calamity he has been forced to cause.'

'Will you explain what you mean by that?'

'Well, it's clear to anyone but a fool that this whole charade has been created by Mrs Birch.'

'In what way?'

'Everything that Patrick Barrett has apparently said, he has been put up to by Mrs Birch. It's obvious. Her husband has said so, but anyone of intelligence can see it.'

'You told General Mackinnon that Barrett tried to break into your bedroom at Ruthin.'

'No, I did not.'

'Here it is: "He tried to break into my bedroom, evidently with the intention of committing an indecent assault." '

'I said nothing of the sort.'

'Did Barrett come into your room?'

Patsy was silent. Then she said, 'I cannot recall.'

'I think you must be able to recall whether a young officer came to your room in your own home?'

'Well, I can't.'

'Perhaps he came because you invited him?'

'Don't be ridiculous,' she snapped.

Lord Nicholson addressed Patsy from the bench. 'It might be better if you were to answer the questions,' he said patronisingly.

'Not these questions,' Patsy replied sharply. 'If Patrick Barrett is too ill to answer these questions, it is as well that I do not try to answer them for him.'

'What does that mean? Are you trying to protect him?' asked Lord Nicholson.

'Of course I am – as we all should be. He has done me a great injustice, but I don't blame him for that.'

'Were you in love with him?'

'Yes, of course I was. He's an angel from heaven.'

'Indeed,' said Mr Poole. 'And is General Sir John Cowans also an angel from Heaven?'

'He is, yes.'

'May I ask if you were in love with him, too?'

'I always have been. He's wonderful.'

'Do you love him in the same way as you loved Patrick Barrett?'

'Certainly.'

'Mrs West, I must remind you of the nature of this court. It is not to be taken lightly.'

'Nor shall it be.'

'May I ask whether there are others whom, by love and affection, you have sought to influence, and whose influence you have sought to use?'

'My husband.'

'Well, that is natural.'

'And the old King.'

'Mrs West, please!'

'Well, it is the answer to your question.'

'Is it the truth?'

'Don't ask me again.'

'Do you think your behaviour, your approach to Patrick Barrett, was becoming in a lady of the eminence of the wife of the colonel of the regiment?'

She paused and looked round the courtroom. This was the question she wanted to answer as publicly as she could. She said very clearly, 'As becoming as it would be in a prime minister's behaviour to a young nurse – a Miss Stanley, let us say – or a chancellor's or secretary of state's to a young secretary – a Miss Stevenson, I believe. It's just that I'm a woman and have my own way.'

Even Mr Poole took a moment to recover from that.

Then he turned to Nicholson and said, 'My lord, Mrs West does not appear to dispute the broad synopsis we have of her behaviour prior to Mr Barrett's letter to her asking her to cease. I propose to ask her about the matters relating to Mr Barrett's posting at a later time. With your permission, I should like now to question General Sir John Cowans with regard to his relationship with Mrs West.'

Cowans was called, and took the stand.

'General, I am compelled to follow an unpleasant line of questioning, and I do not in any sense wish to misunderstand your answers, nor to force you to say anything that is not absolutely the truth. I must ask for your co-operation. In your letters to Mrs West and hers to you there is great familiarity. Do you agree?'

'Yes. We have been close friends for many years.'

'Can you describe to us the closeness of that friendship?'

'I was for a time based in north Wales. I, like many other officers, was made warmly welcome at the home of Colonel Cornwallis-

West. I became good friends with Colonel West and all his family. I owe them a great deal for their kindness. That, I think, is the origin of our close friendship.'

'Have there been occasion when you have met Mrs Cornwallis-West alone, perhaps when she has been staying in London?'

'Certainly, sometimes alone, sometimes with her children; they are good company.'

'If Mrs West were to ask you to do her special favours, is there any reason why you should feel obliged to indulge her?'

'In the normal course of good friendship I would certainly feel a special obligation to her.'

'But if she were to ask for something which you, by the nature of your work at the War Office, felt unable to give, would that closeness affect your ability to decline?'

'Of course not.'

'In one of your letters to Mrs Cornwallis-West, you wrote, "You know that I would do anything for you, if I had the time." Please tell us what you meant by that, by saying you would do anything for Mrs West.'

'Exactly that.'

'Do you think it is proper for an officer in your position to say he would do anything for a lady, the wife of a respected senior officer? Might it not make him vulnerable to improper persuasion, or even blackmail?'

'I cannot conceive that, with the people concerned.'

'Can you conceive that, in the light of what seems to have been the relationship that Mrs West formed with Patrick Barrett, and possibly with others, to others such messages may take on a different tone?'

'Apparently, they do.'

'And do you still say your relationship to Mrs West has been close and is reflected in your statement to her: "I would do anything for you, if I had the time."'

'I have already said so.'

'General, forgive my directness, but have you and Mrs West been lovers in a physical way?'

'No.'

'At any time?'

'No.'

'Thank you.'

On 16 October, the *London Chronicle* returned to the attack. 'Is not it quaint to find Mrs Cornwallis-West once again the pet theme of the Society gossips? For she was a famous beauty, the rival of Mrs Langtry, in the remote eighties; and was only a reminiscence to the present generation until now, when the clubs and the dinner-tables have become abuzz over a topic the indication of which must for the present be avoided, until the rights and the wrongs of the matter have been thrashed out. But the lady's personality may, of course, be recalled. It is forty years since she married Colonel Cornwallis-West; and at her beautiful country seat, Ruthin Castle, she is still a great lady.'

That evening, Lord Derby, who had been in court, wrote to Violet Markham that 'The woman is so disgraceful that no one will believe a word she says. One can see perfectly why Arthur felt strongly. There is no fear of his memory being misrepresented.'

The next day Mr Poole questioned Patsy about her influence over Lieutenant-Colonel Delmé-Radcliffe in having Patrick reprimanded for his letter.

'My main feeling was,' she said, 'that he should be moved away from Mrs Birch. I'm sure she meant well, but her influence over him was stifling. He was being prevented from making a full recovery.'

'It is also the case, is it not, that you would have had more opportunity to see him, had he moved from Bryncelin.'

'Yes, indeed. Mrs Birch had made things so difficult that I could not even visit.'

'How often did you wish to see him?'

'All the time. I missed him. I had spent a lot of time with him. We were very close.'

'So why did you ask for him to be sent back to France?'

'I did nothing of the kind – of course I didn't. That shows you how ridiculous are all the things Mrs Birch has said.'

'But you were angry about the letter he wrote to you?'

'I was.'

'You felt you had been scorned by Lieutenant Barrett?'

'No.'

'Then why did you behave so harshly?'

'Because that letter wasn't his, it was Mrs Birch's. She was jealous.'

'But by your actions you punished him.'

'I was angry with him for doing as she told him. But I didn't punish him.'

'That is not quite correct, Mrs West. Effectively you did, because Lieutenant-Colonel Delmé-Radcliffe, responding to your request, punished him so severely as to put him in the condition in which he now lies.'

'Do you think Colonel Radcliffe acted as he did as a result of my request?'

'It seems he did.'

'Don't be ridiculous. Colonel Radcliffe is a wise and experienced officer. He acts, I'm sure, on his own perfectly good judgment. I had no idea what he did.'

'Perhaps you underestimate your powers of influence?'

'They are not as great as your powers of fantasy,' said Patsy.

'Why did you call upon General Cowans for assistance?'

'Because it appeared that Mr and Mrs Birch had, through their hysteria, brought about a situation which had made Patrick Barrett extremely ill. Jack Cowans could have sorted it all out. He has the power.'

'So you sent telegrams to the quartermaster-general asking him to resolve a matter in which you were displeased about what had occurred?'

'Yes.'

'Is that reasonable in time of war?'

'If he had been able to spare just one minute, he could have sorted it out.'

'Is your influence over General Cowans in any way out of the ordinary?'

'I doubt it.'

'Do you think he would have done what you asked because he was pleased to be asked favours by you?'

'I hope so.'

'Was he jealous of Patrick Barrett?'

'Of course not.'

'Perhaps he wished Barrett to be sent back to France to be out of his way?'

'No. Absolutely not.'

'How do you know?'

'The question is so stupid it is not worth answering.'

'Is it not possible?'

'Not in the least.'

Patsy stayed with Stella during the whole wretched drama. Stella was wonderful and listened to all her frustrations and stories of the daily proceedings. Patsy told her friend that no one believed her. The barrister, by his questions and by the reading of Patrick's statement, had created a story that was entirely untrue. Yet how could she say how much she loved Patrick Barrett? That would only have made everything worse. She knew that in the public view she was an even more wicked person than these old men were making out.

The public thought it was wrong for her to have fallen in love with Patrick, whereas she thought it was right, and not immoral at all. She wished despairingly that Daisy were with her – Daisy would have understood it all. Daisy had been very close to Jack Cowans and had always said Jack had so many lovers that he confused even himself. But of course Patsy could not say that in this wretched court. The judges and generals were vile hypocrites, because every one of them would have taken a beautiful young mistress if they had the least opportunity.

Stella listened to it all. She and Patsy had a lot in common.

The two secret enquiries called by Lloyd George, one into the case of Second Lieutenant Patrick Barrett and the other concerning Brigadier-General Owen Thomas, each lasted five days. For those ten days, all the other courtrooms in the Guildhall were empty, and the building was surrounded by police. Although there were no prisoners, as in a trial, the witnesses were kept apart from each other during the day. They were allowed home, or to an address they had given the clerk, each evening.

The two main courtrooms at the Guildhall are beautifully panelled with galleries overlooking the central area. The four commissioners sat at the high, long bench of Court Number 1, looking over counsel and witnesses. The formality was frightening.

'Was Mr Birch jealous of your affection for Patrick Barrett?' Mr Poole asked Patsy on the fourth day.

'Perhaps.'

'Did you deliberately make him jealous?'

'Certainly not.'

'Was Colonel Delmé-Radcliffe jealous of your relationship with Patrick Barrett?'

'I'm sure he was not.'

'Yet would you not agree that jealousy might have been a cause of his extreme and extraordinary behaviour to the young soldier?'

'He treated Patrick in the way he judged best at the time.'

'And might one say that Sir Henry Mackinnon was pleased to be asked to help you because of his affection for you?'

'He was concerned only with the proper conduct of his officers. The picture you are painting is colourful but it is not accurate.'

'But it does account, at all points, for the behaviour of all these people.'

'Only if your imagination works in that way.'

'And does your imagination work in a different way?'

'I see politicians, judges and generals all the time, and I see them use their often undeserved status to manipulate and employ the services of younger women for their own pleasure and self-esteem. It does not require imagination to see that, Mr Poole.'

'And is that how you behaved with Patrick Barrett?'

'I was much more honest with Patrick Barrett than these old men are with the objects of their affection. You may be certain of that.'

'I'm sure we know how certain we can be of everything you say.' He paused, to let his words take effect, then asked, 'Mrs West, is your daughter in Germany?'

'I have two daughters, and I am proud that both of them are nursing and giving care to young soldiers in this dreadful war.'

'But is one of your daughters in Germany?'

'My elder daughter is the Princess of Pless. I have not seen her, and have had scarcely any contact with her, since August 1914. Her children are in Germany and she is with them.' Patsy was upset.

Mr Poole had made his observation, and his point. He said no more.

Instead, he recalled Jack Cowans to the stand.

'General, may I first clear up one relatively small matter? Mrs Cornwallis-West seems to have told Lieutenant-Colonel Delmé-Radcliffe that, so long as he obliged her, or perhaps in return for his obliging her with his handling of Barrett, he might be given the command of a new ordnance depot at Wrexham. Was the command of the depot at Wrexham a post for which you would make the appointment?'

'No.'

'Would you have any influence over the appointment?'

'None whatever.'

'Did you ever discuss the appointment of a commanding officer for that depot with Mrs Cornwallis-West?'

'No.'

'She wrote you a letter in which she suggested that Colonel Radcliffe would be suitable, and that he was flattered when she had raised the subject.'

'Mr Poole, in going through my correspondence, you will have found letters from many people suggesting that appointments should be given to trusted friends. Recommendations of that kind are not only normal but useful and important at such a time as this. There is nothing sinister about them, I assure you.'

'But in this case there was a particular reason.'

'Well, if there was, I had no idea. I believe I wrote back and told Mrs West that the matter was not in my hands.'

'So if Mrs Cornwallis-West suggested to Colonel Radcliffe that you might see him made commanding officer, she would have had no grounds for saying that?'

'None at all.'

'That is important for us, because it gives us an impression of the way in which she used her persuasiveness.' Mr Poole moved on to another subject. 'Sir John, I am concerned about the part you played in the posting of Second Lieutenant Barrett to Litherland. Mrs West sent you several messages, some by telegram and some by letter, in March this year concerning Barrett. Can you recall the substance of those messages?'

'As I recall, Mrs West believed that it was time that Barrett moved on from the nursing-home and got back into training with his fellow officers.'

'And how did you respond to the messages?'

'I merely passed them on to those who were concerned with such postings.'

'Reading the letters, I have the impression that you did more than pass them on. I have the impression that you gave orders for his move to take place.'

'With respect, that is not the case. If you examine the sequence of letters, as I have, you will find the orders for Barrett's move had already been issued from the adjutant-general's office before I asked about the matter.'

'Then you had no influence over the timing of the move?'

'No influence over any aspect of the move. It was not my position.'

'But you took an interest?'

'Out of politeness to Mrs West, yes, I did.'

'This was, in fact, the moment at which you wrote that you would do anything for her. Would you have been pleased if Barrett had been posted to France?'

'In what way?'

'In that you would have done a favour to Mrs West and she would have been pleased with you?'

'That is not the nature of our relationship.'

'Were you ever jealous of Mrs West's affection for Barrett?'

'Certainly not.'

'But would you agree that your actions could be explained by such jealousy?'

'No they could not. I was not aware of the nature of Mrs West's relationship – if indeed there was one – with Barrett. I am not aware of it now.'

'You said that you first became involved in this matter in March.'

'I did.'

'And yet there are letters from you, concerning Barrett, dated January.'

'That is correct.'

'There are letters from several people addressed to you about Barrett's promotion, and they are dated October and November of the previous year. Did you read them?'

'I must have done.'

Bennett-Goldney had requested Lord Nicholson's permission to present some evidence to the court, in view of the sad absence of Sir

Arthur Markham. Since the matter had been raised before the House, and was of concern there, and since Goldney had had considerable discussion with Sir Arthur before he died, Nicholson had granted him permission to make a statement.

Goldney said: 'It should be drawn to the court's attention that Sir Arthur had almost given up this case. He had come to new conclusions since preparing the statement that has been read to the court, and there are important things he would have said to the House, in withdrawing his request for an Act giving rise to this court. He advised me of these before his final illness. The circumstances are therefore somewhat singular, because we are here, believing that it was his intention that we should be, but in fact the opposite was the case.

'In arriving at his new conclusions, he had discovered that the nature of the relationship between Mrs Cornwallis-West and the Birches was very different from that which had been portrayed to him.

'He came in the last few days of his life to believe that Mrs Birch had so constructed the case against Mrs Cornwallis-West that the truth might be that it was just that: a case against Mrs Cornwallis-West. The case, he had begun to believe, arose from envy of Mrs West and her life – and, indeed, her family. In particular, he had come to understand that the letter from Patrick Barrett to Mrs West, upon which so much of this case hangs, was effectively written under the instruction and guidance of Mrs Birch. It reflected her view, not his.

'Whatever the truth of the matter, Sir Arthur had come to believe that it was not a question which should be dealt with by parliament, and certainly not by a court of the stature of this court. He was intending to ask for the request for an enquiry to be withdrawn, and the questions about Patrick Barrett to be resolved by his superior officers.'

Furthermore, Goldney advised the court, as a member of the House he had access to sensitive information which he could have revealed had the court not been bound by strict secrecy. 'There has been,' he said, 'some private and even public discussion as to the loyalty of the Cornwallis-West family. The family has well-known connections in Germany. Under no circumstances should those connections influence anyone. In particular, it should be known that one member of the family has actively, but secretly, been working with great honour and effect to support the essential work of the War Office in the United States. This cannot normally be divulged.'

Patsy smiled at this. When George had accompanied Stella to the USA, he had, it was true, endeavoured to make the case for supporting Britain in as many American newspapers as would listen to him. But he had not found it easy. The newspapers preferred to photograph his wife and speculate about their marriage. Still, it was Jack Cowans who had asked him to go, so perhaps Goldney was not absolutely lying.

He went on, 'There is one further matter which should be recorded. It came to my attention that, while the expenses being incurred by Mrs Cornwallis-West are being met entirely from her own funds, those of Mr and Mrs Birch are being paid by the secretary of state for war himself. Whether such a situation is fair or not is a point I would ask the commissioner to bear in mind.'

With this the court completed its hearing. A narrative of the events as they appeared to have taken place was written. It was presented as a draft in the first instance only to the prime minister and the secretary of state and their very close legal advisers. No judgments were handed down.

Patsy was left to wonder what would be said. She had obviously landed Jack Cowans in deep trouble. George was so distressed that he would not speak to her. William was silent and seemed confused, as if he did not know what to say. Only Stella was still staunch in support; she said it was all rubbish to satisfy a bunch of silly men. They all went down to Newlands. Patsy's health was not improving.

The press and parliament could only speculate what the outcome would be. Asquith was asked repeatedly whether he had confidence in Cowans's actions or whether he would replace him. Day after day he was pressed to make a statement, and though he had far greater worries to contend with, the more he delayed the greater the scandal grew. Lloyd George waited to see what he would do. The end of the enquiries coincided with the publication of the report on the failed invasion of the Dardanelles, which made it plain that Asquith was not competent to manage the war effort. Something had to be done.

For the Cornwallis-West family, the world was falling apart.

Denbigh Free Press
On the evening of Monday the first of November, as Colonel and Mrs Cornwallis-West were motoring from Bournemouth, they met with a very serious accident, about midway from Bournemouth to their residence, Newlands Manor. At Old Milton, there are four cross-roads, and here a YMCA motor transport dashed into Colonel Cornwallis-West's car. Colonel Cornwallis-West was thrown out and was badly cut about the head, three of his ribs broken, and, of course, being a heavy man, he was badly shaken. Strange to say, Mrs West most fortunately escaped injury beyond being badly bruised. Two convalescent New Zealand soldiers were in the car and luckily were not seriously injured; one had his hand slightly injured, the other escaped without a scratch. The car was knocked completely over and much damaged.

First aid was rendered by a convalescent soldier who was walking out at the time, for there is a large camp nearby, and two doctors (Dr Hope and another) rendered every assistance and in the Red Cross transport took Colonel West home, where Dr Bruce, of Milford-on-Sea, and his assistant, Dr Wood of New Milton, did everything possible. Colonel West is going on as well as can be expected, though it must be some considerable time before he can get about again.

Subsequently, a prominent surgeon from Southampton was called in, as further injuries were feared. After the necessary surgical treatment Colonel West was fairly comfortable, but of course it will be several days before all danger is past.

Chapter 18

LLOYD GEORGE

I N VIEW OF the difficulties Asquith was facing, several members of the cabinet suggested that a new War Committee be formed of members of all parties, with Lloyd George as chairman; Asquith would not be included. King George V was furious and would not allow it to be done. He saw Lloyd George as a devious socialist who was not to be trusted with the honour of the country. Lloyd George responded by handing in his resignation as secretary of state, although Asquith begged him not to, 'when so many other matters are in front of me'.

Lloyd George, believing that he had a duty to be resolute, refused to withdraw, and in December 1916 Asquith had to tell the King that he could no longer form a government. Reluctantly and apprehensively, the King was forced to ask Lloyd George to form a coalition and become the new prime minister. Asquith remained leader of the Liberal Party.

Many people remember that Winston Churchill became prime minister during the Second World War at a time when Neville Chamberlain's leadership was evidently inadequate for a country at war. David Lloyd George's rise to office is less well known. However, it is obvious from the documents of the time that, had Lloyd George had not schemed to bring this about, Britain might well have lost the First World War and entered into many years of deep depression. He was forced to manipulate events because his social background made him an unwanted candidate. The King did not want him, and neither did the established elements of the Liberal Party, of which he was a member and which was torn into many factions by his appointment. Nevertheless, he undoubtedly led the country to victory instead of defeat. He wanted Churchill to be part of his coalition cabinet, but the Conservatives refused to permit it. Churchill was seen by them as largely responsible for much of the disaster at Gallipoli, and therefore unacceptable, for the present, as part of Lloyd George's government.

Many wealthy British people disliked and distrusted Lloyd George. He had been involved in personal financial scandals when he was chancellor of the exchequer. He was inclined to be socialist, and he had introduced public welfare schemes; some even said he was a Bolshevik. In 1909 he had made a famous speech which had publicly and notoriously upset Edward VII. Arguing for a budget in which he introduced the state pension, and substantially increased spending on the navy in order to build more Dreadnought battleships, and announced that he would fund these measures by taxing the very rich, he had said caustically: 'A fully equipped duke costs as much to keep up as two Dreadnoughts; and dukes are just as great a terror and they last longer.' The King was incensed, for he saw the statement as an attack on the House of Lords, and even on the monarchy itself, and he made his feelings known.

Becoming prime minister in the midst of a war was a very difficult ascendancy, which Lloyd George said he did not want, but felt he had to make. He could hardly have been faced with a worse predicament. The country was close to defeat, and at the time of his appointment the Treasury had only sufficient funds to survive the two weeks to Christmas 1916. At that point the government would not have been able to pay its bills, salaries or other commitments.

The assistant secretary to the chancellor of the exchequer, John Maynard Keynes, prepared the following paper for the new cabinet at its first meeting on the morning when Lloyd George became prime minister.

> There are two sets of circumstances which exercise us. One is the inability of our principal ally (France) to continue the war. The second is the power of the United States to dictate our actions.
>
> In the course of the past three months I have spent more hours than I care to recall in the company of the finance ministers of our allies. There is no likelihood of their furnishing us with any further quantity of gold. None of our existing loan agreements extends beyond March, and it is possible that at that time absolutely all the available assets of the British Empire will be pledged in loans. If all our liquid resources are exhausted by our military commitments, dramatic reductions in our credit and our incomes will be the consequence.
>
> We ought never to be so placed that only the possibility of a further public loan in America within two weeks stands between this country and insolvency.
>
> And in order to support such a request, the Americans would have to lend us the whole of their annual savings and refrain from building a single house or railroad and from every other form of capital expenditure within their own country.
>
> If things go on as at present, I venture to say with certainty that by next June, or earlier, the president of the American republic will be in a position, if he wishes, to dictate his terms to us.

On the chancellor's copy of the paper, he added a handwritten note: 'If we all throw in our watch-chains, we might last a few days longer.'

Britain's indebtedness to America was unbearable, but so were the debt and impoverishment of Germany. The new prime minister could not tell the level of pressure on the German chancellor, but in his rational moments he knew it must be even greater than that on himself.

Moreover, listening to Keynes's advice, he speculated that there would come a point at which the Americans could not afford to let Britain lose the war: they would lose too much money, and would stand no chance of recovering it. This, he gambled, would make the American financiers force President Woodrow Wilson to bring the USA into the war on the British side. The choice for the president would be either to join the fighting and ensure victory or else to watch Britain go bankrupt and lose the war, in which case America would lose its money. Lloyd George calculated that, having accepted this next loan, Britain would owe America more money than there was money in the whole world.

So for Britain to survive the war it was vitally important to keep borrowing, and Jack Cowans was the best borrower Lloyd George had – 'a real Edwardian', he thought him. If Cowans were removed from his position at this juncture, it would certainly arouse the suspicions of American financiers that there were even more problems in the British government than they had thought. Cowans had to stay, and he had to be told to maintain, or increase, his rate of borrowing. It was an appalling way out of the predicament, but it was one Lloyd George had to keep pursuing.

He wished he could share his concerns with parliament.

Lloyd George believed above all in the importance of parliament. As Markham had said, Lloyd George was at his best in the House of Commons in debate. It concerned him a great deal when the quality of debate was lower than he believed it should be. He worried that so many good people had died and there were no longer as many good parliamentarians as he would have wished. If parliament did not debate properly, power fell into the hands of theorists rather than realists. For now, however, he could not concern himself with the structures of democracy: his only concern was to survive the war.

He had to increase the strength of the Allied blockade on

German imports as best he could, at all points, and he had to make sure that Britain bought as much as possible from the Americans.

He influenced American public opinion in favour of Britain as best he could.

It was good fortune for him that German military action in Mexico brought the American press finally against the Germans. President Wilson, against the advice of Congress, but under great pressure from the merchant bankers, decided that his role in creating peace in Europe was more likely to succeed if he were to join the war on the side of the French and the British.

The president's decision coincided not only with the Treasury view that Britain was bankrupt, but also with the final defeat of the Allied armies in Gallipoli and Mesopotamia and the humiliating withdrawal from both those theatres of war. Britain was on the point of defeat.

When the Americans joined the war, an important reason was to recover their loans to Great Britain. The first thing they did was provide submarine cover for all the gold Britain could find, to be shipped to Morgan Stanley's bank, first in Edmonton, in Canada, where the attention was not so great, and thence to America. It was the final condition for joining: that debt repayment could begin at last. This also meant that the German U-boat campaign to starve Britain into surrender was countered by a mass of American submarines in the Atlantic.

Most of the gold in the British Empire was not in London but in South Africa. In order to ensure that the South African government was content to ship gold to America, Lloyd George invited two South African leaders, Jan Smuts and Louis Botha, to join the British war cabinet. It was a diplomatic decision, the reasons for which were not broadcast at the time. Nobody was told how much Britain owed America.

Chapter 19

THE CASE OF THE LADY

I T WAS FOR all these reasons that Lloyd George used the Cowans enquiry to suit his purposes. He had kept his promise to Arthur Markham. The case had been so heavy a straw on the back of the camel Asquith was riding that it had helped bring about his downfall. It allowed Lloyd George to keep Cowans in his post, but firmly under the control of the prime minister, not of Asquith's supporters. And now it enabled him to give the press something to distract them from following his efforts to survive the war. He could release the story in the way he wanted it told.

The press was longing for a major scandal. The British press has always been tenacious in the pursuit of moral wrongdoing, and has caused the downfall of many a politician. Many of the victims are quickly forgotten, but we remember the enormity of some cases. We recall Charles Parnell and Kitty O'Shea in one century, John Profumo and Christine Keeler in the next. To be the cause of such scandal is to be the centre of a mighty tornado. It is history of a most popular kind, when politicians plead that there are more important matters, yet the newspapers have a story which enthralls their readers.

Lloyd George called the new secretary of state for war, Lord Derby, and the lord chief justice, Lord Reading, to a meeting to discuss how to handle the press as regards the Cowans affair. His object was to make sure that Cowans's reputation was unsullied. He suggested that the matter should no longer be 'The Affair of the War Office', but rather 'The Case of the Lady'. He had altered the account produced by the court of enquiry, and removed the sections of evidence given by Patsy and Bennett-Goldney. He left in a certain amount of material about Cowans, so that the story remained authentic.

They agreed that *The Times* should be asked to publish an article about Cowans's contribution to the war; and that the other newspapers should be allowed to comment on the Lady, but not to write any more about the military aspects of the tribunal. They announced that they would publish a synopsis of the events, implying that, for military reasons, not everything could be revealed.

Patsy was to be the focus of outrage.

On 23 December the editor of the *Daily Express* received a letter.

Dear Blumenfeld,

I do hope you will as far as possible drop what is known as the War Office Mystery. We are going to publish the findings with a certain synopsis of events but I shall certainly resist the publication of anything further as I can assure you that, although it does not affect the military people, the Lady story is not one which anybody would like to see published. The only people I think it is hard on are the military people, because I genuinely think the evidence did not justify some of the things the commissioners say in their findings. Of course, personally I think the whole thing is a mistake. It would have been much better to have it out in open court, but it is all very well to be wise after the event.

Anyhow, I do hope you will be able to please me at the present moment by giving as little publicity to it as possible.

With the compliments of the season to you,
Derby

The commissioners issued a statement which was intended, in a military way, to clear Patrick Barrett's name:

Second Lieutenant Patrick Barrett
Second Lieutenant Barrett entirely merited the grant of the commission made to him in December 1915. There has been nothing in his conduct since that date which has been in any way unbecoming to an officer and a gentleman. Any censure that has been passed upon him in connection with the circumstances of this case has been wholly undeserved.

This statement resulted in a frenzy of press speculation. The *Denbigh Free Press* reported:

The findings of a special court of enquiry will, it is expected, be published very soon but meanwhile the public has been more mystified than enlightened by the partial official statements already made. 'At present the position of Second Lieutenant Barrett is ambiguous', says the correspondent of the *London Evening Chronicle* in an article bearing the title 'Lifting the Veil on the War Office Enquiry'. It is evident that that he was victimised because he thought more of his duty as a soldier than the patronage of a great lady.

His character is cleared and his illness officially regretted, but only a few know of the nature of the charge against him or of the sufferings he has undergone through the conduct of 'The Lady in the Case'.

In a parliamentary statement it was earlier said that the lady is outside military jurisdiction. She is not, however, beyond the scope of public opinion and should not be screened from the condemnation of that tribunal.

On 1 January *The Times* printed an article of two full pages describing the heroic achievements of the quartermaster-general. It was full of praise for his meticulous organization and ability to cope with the ever-changing theatres of war. No mention was made of the recent court of enquiry.

On 5 January the *Daily Mirror* obtained copies of the judgments on the other participants in 'The Case of the Lady'. It published handsome photographs of Patrick and of Mrs Birch, which took the whole of its front page. It also showed an unhappy and unflattering picture of Patsy. The case, the paper declared, had been that of her wicked advances and then her vindictive hostility towards the young soldier, whereas Mrs Birch had 'rendered the public a notable service' with spirit and courage, and 'had been complimented by the court'.

That day every headline, every front page, reported on 'The Anger of a Woman Scorned', 'The Revelation of the Lady in the Case', 'The Wicked Woman of Wales'.

The *Daily Mirror* outlined the whole story and reported some of the official findings of the court of enquiry.

Quartermaster-General Sir John Cowans

The quartermaster-general must have known that the case was one of discipline, with which he had nothing to do, and that the proper War Office official to deal with such matters was the director of personnel services under the orders of the adjutant-general. In spite of this, Sir John saw fit to intervene by addressing Lieutenant-Colonel Delmé-Radcliffe by telegram and letter. He disclosed official information to Mrs Cornwallis-West and he implicated the War Office by informing Mrs Cornwallis-West that the War Office had done all that could be done officially, the War Office at that time being entirely ignorant of Mrs Cornwallis-West's complaint and having sanctioned Second Lieutenant Barrett's immediate transfer on the disingenuous pretext put forward by Colonel Delmé-Radcliffe. Sir John revealed his frame of mind by telling Mrs Cornwallis-West that he would do anything for her if he had time. In our opinion, this correspondence indicates on the part of Sir John Cowans not merely indiscretion but a departure from official propriety

Lieutenant-Colonel H. Delmé-Radcliffe

We find that Lieutenant-Colonel Delmé-Radcliffe treated Second Lieutenant Barrett unjustly by censuring him without giving him full opportunity of justifying his conduct. Colonel Radcliffe should have informed him without delay of the complaint preferred against him by Mrs Cornwallis-West. Colonel Radcliffe adopted an unusual and unfair procedure, inasmuch as on receipt of Mrs West's complaint he took steps for Barrett's transfer without making an investigation of the conduct complained of. We are of the opinion that entering into a private correspondence with Mrs West on the subject of the complaint, and discussing with her the steps he proposed to take to deal with it, requires severe reprobation. We are also of the opinion that he showed want of humanity in ordering Barrett to proceed forthwith to Litherland when he had good reason to know that the officer in question was seriously ill. We find that Lieutenant-Colonel Delmé-Radcliffe acted hastily, harshly and improperly. We regret to think that, acting under the influence of a lady of position in the county, he denied justice to one of his junior officers.

Mr and Mrs Richard Birch

We noted a tendency in some of the witnesses and in speeches of counsel to regard this case as the result of a quarrel between two women, one being as bad as the other. Such a view does not do justice to Mrs Birch. We believe that her conduct was dominated throughout by the desire to protect Lieutenant Barrett, whom she had nursed in her house and who was still in her charge, from a gross injustice. In this she was wholeheartedly assisted by her husband from the time when he became acquainted with the full facts. It seems certain that, but for the exertions of Mr and Mrs Birch, there would have been little possibility of the Army Council being placed in such possession of such facts as enabled them to secure the investigation that has now taken place. In view of all the circumstances, it is not surprising that the case put forward by Mr and Mrs Birch may have been, to some extent, overstated. We think it right, however, to express our opinion that there are inadequate grounds for some of the allegations in what has been called the 'synopsis', which was circulated by Mr and Mrs Birch. In particular, we have to condemn a charge made against Sir John Cowans, which proved to be without justification, namely, that: 'Acting on instructions given directly, and also most improperly, by Sir John Cowans, Colonel Delmé-Radcliffe had this officer transferred without his sanction to the 3rd Battalion, the Royal Welch Fusiliers, with a view to his being sent back to France, although he was physically unfit.'

Mr Birch himself has admitted the injustice of the charge. In this respect we are obliged to report indiscretion on the part of Mr and Mrs Birch. But, taking their conduct as a whole, we find that by their action in defence of a friendless young officer they have rendered the public a notable service.

Mrs Cornwallis-West

With regard to the matter of Second Lieutenant Patrick Barrett, in view of the findings which we have arrived at and expressed in our statement of facts, it becomes unnecessary to criticize at any length the conduct and discretion of this lady. If discretion alone had to be considered, we think that, whatever the influence Mrs Cornwallis-West may have had over Quartermaster-General Sir John Cowans, the lady exaggerated it. We have no doubt that her injudicious boasting of the power she wielded at the War Office, which was, however, confirmed to an appreciable extent by the wording of some of General Cowans's letters, was calculated to bring him and the administration at the War Office into disrepute.

Unfortunately, we have not had to consider only a question of discretion, and we feel obliged to record our opinion that this lady's conduct, as revealed in this case, has been highly discreditable, in her behaviour towards Second Lieutenant Barrett before his letter of 14 February, in her vindictive attempts to injure him afterwards, and in the untruthful evidence she gave before us. It appears from the evidence given before us that Mrs West holds positions of some importance in the county of Denbighshire in charitable associations of a public character for assisting in war work. In our opinion it is to be regretted that she should hold such positions.

It was widely reported that 'The prime minister has instructed that a letter should be sent immediately to Second Lieutenant Patrick Barrett advising him of the finding of the court concerning his appointment as an officer.'

Lloyd George also instructed that an interim finding of the court be published in parliament. It was printed on one sheet of paper and deposited in the parliamentary archive, among the Blue Books recording official history. The finding recorded, in two short sentences, the fact that Patrick Barrett was innocent of the offence of which he had been accused, and that the work of the commission of enquiry was now complete.

Now at last the newspapers had their story. They were merciless.

The *Daily News*: 'Mrs Cornwallis-West has now to pay a heavy social price for her meddlesome folly, and the officers, presumably her friends, who consented to share in it all suffer more or less heavily with her.'

The *Daily Graphic*: 'The prime minister adds enormously to his standing in the minds of his countrymen by the unflinching determination with which he caused this matter to be probed and justice to be done, directly it was brought to notice.'

The Times: 'We are at war and have no time to waste on minor incidents which, when all is said and done, savour more of personal intrigue than of solicitude for the efficiency of military administration.'

The *Manchester Guardian*: 'The very gross scandal has had an ending which is highly salutary. For the offenders, especially the chief among them, no formal penalty could have equalled the punishment of this publicity.'

Punishment it certainly was. Patsy was pursued everywhere by journalists. She was now seriously ill. The pain in her stomach was worse, and she suffered from bleeding which caused her great distress. Stella advised her to give one interview to the local newspaper in Hampshire and allow them to make her comments available to any other papers which wanted them. Patsy took her friend's advice, but she gave little away: the anger she had expressed at the hearing had given way to weariness.

The *Hampshire Chronicle* duly carried the story. 'Seated in her boudoir at Newlands Manor, Hampshire, yesterday, Mrs Cornwallis-West said in an interview, "I know the truth and my friends know the truth. I have had an abundance of evidence that they will believe in me. I have nothing to say. The whole thing is beneath contempt. I prefer to remain silent. It is the only dignified way. I am too ill, in any case, to make a press statement."'

George tried to help by explaining what he thought had happened: 'Captain George Cornwallis-West, son of Mrs Cornwallis-West and husband of the actress Mrs Patrick Campbell, in a statement in the *Pall Mall Gazette*, said, "Neither the press nor the public have been allowed to appreciate the political intrigue which lies behind the whole of this case. A distinguished member of parliament, entirely on his own initiative, came forward and gave evidence on this particular point. It is no exaggeration to say that it fell like a bombshell on the court. Is it not very extraordinary that no mention was made of this in the findings of the court? Or is it because his evidence was conveniently disbelieved, like my mother's?" '

In fact, Bennett-Goldney had not been quite the trump card for which George had hoped. Some years before, when he was on service in Ireland, the Irish crown jewels had been stolen from their closely guarded chamber in Dublin Castle. The matter became the subject of a major parliamentary enquiry. Although the matter was never resolved, there was a strong suspicion that Bennett-Goldney had been involved in the theft. The commissioners had taken the same view as Arthur Markham: that Bennett-Goldney was not a reliable witness.

Poor William Cornwallis-West decided that he had to come to the aid of his wife:

Interviewed at his home at Ruthin Castle by a representative of the *Weekly Dispatch* was Colonel William Cornwallis-West. Colonel West is the husband of Mrs Mary 'Patsy' Cornwallis-West who has become known in the newspapers as 'The Lady in the Case'.

'In the circumstances,' he said, 'we should have much preferred an enquiry in a court of justice, so that the public, through the press, might have known what were the charges made against my wife. I consider that Mr Lloyd George and Sir Arthur Markham were misinformed as to facts, and I have good reason for believing that Sir Arthur, shortly before his death, was on the point of withdrawing from the case.

'The circumstances are of a most extraordinary character. The whole gravamen of the charge against my wife was that she was too intimate with this young man, Lieutenant Barrett. I should explain that Mr Birch was my land agent, as his father had been before him. My wife and I showed nothing but kindness and consideration to Mr and Mrs Birch, putting various opportunities of a social and pecuniary advantage in their way, and helping them at every turn. Mrs Birch is a woman under forty, and it was she who first brought Lieutenant Barrett to my wife's notice.

'Mr and Mrs Birch had turned their house into a hospital, and Lieutenant Barrett, then a sergeant, was one of their patients. He was a strange young man with something of a "mystery" in his life. We understood that he was an orphan, never having known either his father or his mother. We never discovered what he did before joining the army as a private. He had been at the front, and there had received serious injuries from which he was recovering at the time the Birches introduced him. He was always sickly and ailing and the doctor said his heart was wrong. He was anaemic and miserable, but he had friendly, gentle ways. Mrs Birch took him up enthusiastically and often spoke to my wife about him. She suggested that Mrs West should also take him up and "bring him out" among the county people – our acquaintances in Denbighshire. It would do him a world of good and get him among the right set.

'My wife is Irish to the marrow, enthusiastic and emotional. Emotion and compassion, particularly compassion, are apt to carry her away, occasionally to the point, perhaps, of indiscretion. She acted as a mother to him – nothing more. Her sympathies were aroused by his loneliness, and her maternal instinct was moved by his bad health. She visited him from time to time, and she found him generally in tears. Once he said he thought he was dying, and she kissed him on the forehead, and said, "It's all right, Pat. Don't be afraid." That was a motherly action, surely, from a sympathetic woman of almost sixty to a boy in his twenties. I believe it is not uncommon for a nurse to kiss the forehead of a soldier who is dying. She implored him to try to be a man and to pull through. Her letters, like her ministrations, were motherly and kind. But they were impulsive, emotional and – like herself – Irish.

'It was at this time that Mrs Birch's attitude to Mrs West entirely changed. She accused her of wrongfully influencing Barrett. The whole matter then came to a head and the case was laid before Sir Arthur Markham. Can it be believed that a woman of this age could be capable of any affection for this young man other than motherly solicitude? It is incredible and monstrous that my wife should be said to be guilty of telling untruths.

'It is also monstrous that General Sir John Cowans should be implicated in such a case. It is ridiculous to make so much of the fact of the correspondence between him and my wife. People who have friends in positions of authority naturally write to them if they have recommendations to make. Everybody does it, and General Cowans is a friend of the family of long standing. I can say also that in spite of all this miserable business Denbigh people are as loyal as possible. They know the truth of the imputations that have been cast against my wife. It is a great consolation to see so many people rallying around us. As to the suggestion that my wife should withdraw from her public positions, I cannot understand it. As wife of the lord lieutenant of the county she has certain duties, and in addition she used to do a great deal of war work. She has not, however, been able to work for the last six months, having been very ill owing to the worry and anxiety of this affair. I dispute the power of those gentlemen to prohibit my wife from doing war work. I have no intention whatever of allowing her to withdraw from it.'

Colonel Cornwallis-West also said, 'I wish to add that the extraordinary number of letters we receive daily proves that the public consider the reflections on Mrs Cornwallis-West to be unjust and unmerited, coming as they do, not only from personal friends but from persons with whom we have no acquaintance and, in a number of cases, from soldiers in hospitals both in Wales and in Hampshire, which is most gratifying. They are so numerous that it will be impossible to reply to them all at once, though we hope to be able to do so before long.'

In another interview, with the *Liverpool Evening Express*, Colonel Cornwallis-West stated his view that his wife's case had not been handled in accordance with normal principles, in that only certain findings and only selected items of evidence from the enquiry had been made public.

'It seems a pity,' he said, 'that this storm in a teacup should be raised in the middle of such a great war, and that all these distinguished generals and officers should have had to give up their time in connection with the matter.'

The newspapers, though, were thriving on the scandal and wanted to prolong it as long as they could.

On 17 January the *London Chronicle* reported: 'It now seems certain that there will be a debate in the House of Commons on Lieutenant Barrett's case as soon as parliament reassembles. The *Birmingham Post* yesterday said: "The present position is regarded by sober citizens as profoundly unsatisfactory. It has been plainly evident to the readers of certain London newspapers during the past week, even before the findings of the court were promulgated, and especially to the purchasers of the Sunday journals today, that the whole of the evidence is in the hands of certain persons and that extracts from it are freely available. Ministers will be pressed to allow minutes of the full proceedings to speak for themselves." '

William Cornwallis-West pleaded for this not to happen; the family had taken more than they could endure.

On 3 February 1917, a Welsh member of the House of Lords, Lord Aberconway, wrote to Andrew Bonar Law, leader of the House of Commons.

Dear Mr Bonar Law

Colonel Cornwallis-West, who is seriously ill at his Hampshire home, has asked me, on his behalf, to communicate with you regarding the recent case, and, knowing that your time is greatly occupied, I think it best simply to forward to you his letter and the accompanying papers.

Although it is obvious that there are many matters connected with the case which he would like to have brought before you, the main object, I believe, of his interview, had it taken place, would have been to ask you, as leader of the House, to prevent, if possible, the details of this unpleasant case being raked up for parliamentary discussion.

I may say that I feel very strongly myself on the desirability of letting the case be forgotten as soon as possible. I say this as a resident in Denbighshire, and as a man with much experience in the affairs of life, and I am sure that you will agree with me that in these days of national crisis subjects like this are best left alone.

I do not wish to express an opinion on the other points raised in Colonel Cornwallis-West's letter, as I am only partially acquainted with the facts, but I am fully prepared to believe in his contention that evidence might have been adduced which could not be brought before the special tribunal, but which might have modified public opinion with regard to Mrs Cornwallis-West.

I remain,

Yours sincerely

Aberconway

Enclosed, written in a very shaky hand, was a letter from William Cornwallis-West. It said:

Mr Bonar Law has kindly promised me an interview, before parliament meets, in respect of those matters which are being gloated over by the gutter grass [sic]. I know how occupied Mr Bonar Law must be. If this disgraceful conspiracy against an innocent woman should be made the subject of discussion, as well as the conduct of distinguished generals, that will really be a greater scandal than the thing itself in the midst of war. Parliament meant the whole thing to be private, but the tribunal has overridden that.

Yours very faithfully

W. Cornwallis-West, Colonel

There follow some details of the matter which I had intended to draw to the attention of Mr Bonar Law:

The great injustice to Mrs Cornwallis-West, who was tried as a sort of culprit and disbelieved by the tribunal, though never brought face to face with her accuser, Second Lieutenant Barrett.

She was nearly two full days under examination and Barrett examined privately in Wales in the presence of Mrs Birch.

Mrs West's letters were given up by someone, probably Mrs Birch, and lately published in all the newspapers, whereas Barrett's sincere thanks to Mrs West for all her kindness to him were never given. (The letter is attached herewith.)

The horrible charges made by Mrs Birch and adopted by Barrett in this respect were utterly repudiated by her, speaking on oath, and would anyhow be believed only by persons of vile minds.

The charge made in the 'yellow press' that Mrs West's asking Barrett to apologise for a letter he had written to her was the act of a vindicative woman, and done to injure him, is strongly repudiated. Mrs West realised that Barrett had, under outside influence, entirely misunderstood her attentions to and sympathy for him, and in consequence asked him to explain and apologise for his letter

A copy of this important letter was seen on Mrs Birch's table by Mr Birch, who told my wife that it had been put there on purpose but that he pretended not to see it. Mrs Delmé-Radcliffe gave evidence on oath in court that Mrs Birch had told her she made Barrett write it, and Mr Birch, on seeing it, said to Mrs West, 'Of course, my wife did it.'

The enquiry entailed my incurring heavy expense. The injustice of expecting me to find the money for the conduct of a trial not sought by me or any member of my family, but instituted entirely on the initiative of the government.

Though according to the Act the proceedings of the enquiry were secret, no sooner was it over than its report was published and much evidence, such as that of Captain Bennett-Goldney, MP, is omitted and never referred to.

In conclusion I wish to add that I daily receive letters from all parts of England from perfect strangers strongly rejecting the enquiry's cruel aspersions on my wife, and especially from a number of soldiers, both at home and at the front, entirely disbelieving the evidence on which the case was founded and offering the warmest sympathy to my wife and myself for the success which has attended a mischievous conspiracy against her good name and fame as a warm-hearted woman.

Lloyd George and Bonar Law agreed that, they having achieved what they had intended from the case, it was now time to close the matter down. The papers of the enquiry, those which had not yet been destroyed, were gathered in a box and sealed in the archive. Lloyd George ordered that they should not be opened for a hundred years (in fact they were released after seventy-five years). Patsy Cornwallis-West, who had done and said far too many awkward things, had been damned and he wanted no more interference from her. The days when her class and kind could dictate what was acceptable had gone, unless, to his mind, one wanted to provoke a revolution.

Lloyd George had been angered by several of Patsy's statements during the enquiry. He contacted officials of the King and warned them that during the course of the secret hearings mention had been made of the relationship between the Prince of Wales, later

King Edward VII, and Mrs Cornwallis-West. His advice was that a number of archives should be searched, and any letters referring to these matters should be destroyed. His advice was carried out. Later, the Cornwallis-West family papers were also searched, and evidence of the affair was removed and burnt.

That is why there is no record of Patsy Cornwallis-West in any official or private archives. She wrote letters every day of her life, but almost none have survived. She is rarely mentioned in histories of the time. She has been removed.

It is only in Daisy's diary and in George's and Stella's autobiographies that there is a fragmentary record of her last few years.

Chapter 20

AN END OF WAR

BERLIN, IN 1918, still resolute and Prussian, was no place for an English princess. Daisy was forty-three. Her eldest son, Hansel, was already an experienced soldier and had won the Iron Cross, and her second son, Lexel, was nearing the age at which he might have to fight. Princess Daisy's movements were restricted by the military police, and her nursing was confined, by edict, to a safe distance from the battlefields. Like her mother, she had shown her concern for the welfare of soldiers, irrespective of their nationality. This, of course, brought conflict with authority. Trying to contact British prisoners of war because they were friends, or children of friends, was near treason. War demands unreasonable loyalty – in fact, loyalty to one's country is an idea invented by soldiers fighting war.

Her friendship with the Kaiser kept her out of most serious trouble, but even that was less of an advantage than it once had been, as his power ebbed. She was a symbol of enmity and suspicion, and her husband was away for long periods. She spent the early part of the war in Berlin, but in 1915 moved, to be less visible and for the safety of her third child, Bolko, to Garmisch-Partenkirchen in Bavaria and to Berchtesgaden near Salzburg.

She knew what had happened to Patsy and Jack Cowans, from the letters like this one that Poppets had managed to send.

Newlands
14 January 1917

My darling Daisy,

If you have lately received the English papers you must have read about a certain lady being accused of all sorts of things. Do not believe a word of it, and rest assured from me that the charges are wicked and vile fabrications and the accusers are cruel and vindictive, but they managed to give an entirely wrong impression of what passed on certain occasions, as well as misconstruing what the poor soul meant to the miserable creature who was the cause of all the trouble. The public realise this now and write innumerable letters to her, all strongly deprecating the judgment as in every way based on false testimony uttered by persons of corrupt minds. Do not think any more about it. I will send you a newspaper about it and hope it may reach you. How are you, dear soul? I trust enjoying the snow and the sunshine. Happily, we have no snow here, but it is cold.

Good bye, darling,
Your ever devoted
Poppets

Patsy's health had worsened again. She thought she had ulcers caused by stress, but her condition was much more serious: she had cancer. It was not, however, in her nature to consider anything so depressing worth talking about. In March, as the newspaper reports began to quiet, she wrote to Daisy.

We managed at last to get a butler. He is dreadfully old and once served the Archbishop of Canterbury and his name is Maycock, I'm not sure, or Woodcock, or Paycock. Well, his wife calls him Maycock, and he calls her Mrs Maycock. 'Mrs Maycock, bring the parsnips,' he says. And believe me she wears the trousers in their house. Well. We had a lunch for poor Shelagh who came home for a few days from the hospital in France. Winston has arranged for her to be awarded the CBE, you know. Did I ever tell you that George Lewis died? He was Winston's solicitor since W was a boy, and also he had always looked after George. Anyhow, Shelagh has had such a rotten time with Bend Or – he made her go in front of the newspapers, which was awful of him, and we know why (that's why I thought we needed George Lewis to help her, but of course I could not find him). Well, the lunch. Poppets somehow bribed a farmer's wife for a shank of lamb, and Maycock was bringing it majestically and slipped on the polished floor. He caught the edge of the table-cloth (a table-cloth, Daisy, the first we'd used in two years) and everything flew, especially his teeth. Everyone laughed, of course, and the poor man would not move because he did not want anyone, particularly Mrs Peacock, to see him without his dentures. Oh Daisy, I had to poke him with my stick.

Oh my Daisy. I can never tell you how wonderful Poppets is, or how wonderful we think your darling letters, and how he grasps the truth of everything. My pet, how you must have suffered. Oh my Daisy, how I long to have you home and the precious boys doing just what they like with their old Granny.

To tell you about old Poppets. We just make him lead the life of an old country gentleman since his accident: that is, not letting him be going constantly to meetings and taking the chair in hot stuffy rooms. Well, last Friday there was a big meeting at Milford about growing War Food. He had a bit of a cold, so I sent down a message to say we were coming, but that I did not want him to take the chair and speak.

Up we marched through a mass of people, when I found placed by the platform an armchair with a cushion. Poppets made one dash at the cushion, threw it back over his shoulder, where it hit a poor old lady's bonnet, making her look drunk to the world, and exclaimed, 'Good Heavens who put that cushion there?' Then he sat down.

Mr A, a very little man quite crooked because he had been trying to cut down a tree and put himself under it when it fell, and fat B, who looks a cross between an old actor and a eunuch, began dancing and bowing to each other like two mad goats, arguing as to which should take the chair. In the end, the fat man <u>stomached</u> the little thin man into it with a flop. When the thin man recovered his breath he began a long-winded speech by saying, 'Ladies and Gentlemen, I know very little about this subject. I never fed a pig in my life.'

At last the fat man's turn came, and he got up, his arms full of papers, which he kept quoting from and then dropping. I saw Poppets drumming his fingers as he does when he's thinking, and humming to himself. Then he attacked one side of his head – the bad side – and scratched it hard. Before I could say one word, he was up on his feet, knocking all their silly arguments flat, giving them <u>facts</u> on every subject. He spoke for twenty minutes, without a single stop or stammer, and sat down amid loud applause.

Then at the top of his voice, 'Now, my dear little Patsy, I think we will go.' And out he marched, people still clapping; he ate a huge dinner, slept like a top, and insisted on going to a concert the next day. But now I must tell you another of his strange freaks. His hair all over is turning <u>quite black</u>. I swear he is putting nothing on it.

God bless you, darling precious one. Oh God, how I long to see you. Geoffrey Brooke was lunching with Miss Paget the other day, who was so nice and said she had heard from you. I heard from Jack Cowans yesterday, he said he was writing to 'that dear child Daisy'.

In June Poppets wrote again to tell Daisy that Patsy had been unwell, but it was nothing serious and not to be concerned. At the beginning of July, he died.

The Germans were triumphant on their eastern front. The Bolshevik revolution was making possible the defeat of the Russian army, and allowed the German Imperial Government to turn and look for victory in the west. Twelve million Russians died during the Great War.

Socialism, Daisy felt, could change the world for the better. Peace, if it ever came, might be fairer, but the Russian immolation created a much greater fear of the power of the Communists. There was an expectation that, whatever was going to emerge from the war, the peace was not for the aristocrats and royalty, who had allowed such turmoil to start. Everybody knew that, in every country. New governments, however they formed, had to listen to the will of more ordinary people. But the Communist revolution, as anyone could see, was a real terror and appalling and would be chaotic anarchy. In Berlin, and in Pless which gave Daisy her title, the horror of a Bolshevik world consumed the old families and they had deep anxiety about what the treaties of the end of the war would bring.

War on the western front had sapped the very strength that Germany needed, for everyone's sake, to guard against the threat in the east. A strong, united German empire, as Bismark had intended, was a good thing. What Great Powers would be left if the Bolsheviks were injected into the bloodstream of Europe?

Daisy, Princess of Pless, saw all that. Yet she saw, too, the headstrong determination of the self-willed Germans, who, in clinging to their traditions, had allowed the country to be divided and eventually defeated. The generals in the west became independent of the advisers to the Kaiser; the long war began to wear out the strong ropes of military cohesion. With the country under blockade, Berlin became an irrelevant centre of power. Only in

Bavaria was there a remnant of nineteenth-century civilisation, and even a hope that the end of the war might bring back the loveable Bavarian royal family. Daisy stayed there quietly in hiding, wishing that she could somehow leave and get back to Britain. In 1918 she travelled with friends to Belgrade and stayed there until the end of the war. As she watched the torture of Germany and society, so, too, she witnessed the saddest days of her own family.

Ruthin is a dignified and honourable place: in July 1917, the local newspaper reported:

We regret to record the death of the Lord Lieutenant of Denbighshire, Colonel W. Cornwallis-West, which occurred early on Wednesday morning at Ruthin Castle, to the great sadness of the members of his family and a very large circle of friends in north Wales and in Hampshire.

Colonel Cornwallis-West, as was recorded in our columns, met with a serious motor accident some months ago, near his Hampshire residence, and for a time his life was despaired of. His splendid constitution, however, aided the surgical skill and the best of nursing and he so far recovered as to be able to perform in a limited degree his many public duties. Only two weeks ago he was in Denbigh attending the governors' meeting of Howell's school. His death was, therefore, a great surprise and grief to the many residents of the district, by whom he was so well known and so highly respected.

His death cast a gloom over the town. He had been out and about in the borough during the previous week, and was able to sit on the castle lawn on Sunday. Flags are flying at half-mast on the town hall and several other premises.

Patsy was too ill to leave Ruthin Castle and go to William's funeral. She watched from the front door as the hearse and carriages departed.

The *Denbigh Free Press* reported that 'Colonel Cornwallis-West was buried facing the castle at Ruthin, in a plot of land which his father had given to the church. The grave is unusual in facing away from all the others, but it was his special request, that, on the day of judgment, he should wake and see, first, his much-loved castle, in which he and his family have lived for several generations. For the funeral, at the request of Mrs Cornwallis-West, who was too ill to attend, a choir of soldiers from Kinmel Park sang the hymn 'Cyfaill yn Angau'.

> *Cyfaill yn Angau*
> Yn y dyfroedd mawr a'r tonnau
> Aid aes neb a ddeil fy mhen
> Ond fy anwyl Briod Jesu
> A fu farw ar y pren:
> Cyfaill yw yn afon angau,
> Ddeil fy mhen I uwch y don:
> Golwg arno wna imi ganu
> Yn yr afon ddofon hon
>
> O anfeidral rym y cariad,
> Anorchfygal ydyw'r gras
> Digyfnewid yw'r addewid
> A berg byth o hyn I maes;
> Hon yw f'angor ar y cefnfor
> Na chyfrewid meddwwl Duw
> Fe addawodd na chawn farw
> Yny nghlwyfau'r Oen y cawn I fyw
>
> *My Companion in Death*
> In the waters and the waves
> There is no one to hold my head
> But my dear companion Jesus
> He who died upon the wood
> Friend he is in death's river

He holds my head above the wave
To look upon him let me sing
In this deep flood

Oh how infinite is the power of love
Invincible is the Grace
Immutable is the promise
That will last for ever
This is my anchor upon the ocean
That unchangeable is God's will
He promised that we would not die
But that in the wounds of the lamb
We will be allowed to live

It was Poppets's favourite hymn for a funeral. Shelagh said they had talked about it. 'If you knew what the words meant, in English, it was about going sailing at Cowes. That's what he wanted heaven to be: Cowes week at Ruthin.' But sung by the soldiers, with all the people from the town, and the county, and the regiment, in that cemetery down from the church, where his father had given the land, and where he'd always said he wanted to be buried, it made her cry. You could hear the men's choir up at the castle. Daisy, in Germany, wept bitterly when she heard about her father's death and could not get home.

The *Hampshire Chronicle* was less generous than the Denbigh newspaper: 'He was well respected in north Wales,' it said, as if recent events had affected their view and, whatever the residents of north Wales might think, people in Hampshire should make up their own minds about the family.

George was worried as well as sorrowful. As the only son, he inherited all his father's property at Ruthin and Newlands, and everything of value would be taken to repay his creditors. Daisy and Shelagh would lose access to their homes, and his mother would have nowhere to live.

Besides, Stella was furious with him because she had discovered that he had a girlfriend in Hampshire whom he had been seeing since before he married Jennie Churchill, and whom he still visited quite often.

Public schools do not teach about the necessities of money. Bankruptcy is a fact of life which is not found on the timetable at Eton. It is a very adult moment. So to George Cornwallis-West, who, like many Englishmen, retained the enthusiasms and perspectives of an eleven-year-old all his life, bankruptcy was merely a nerve-testing but endurable visit to the headmaster's study.

The people to whom he owed money insisted that, whatever devices his parents might have tried to contrive, all his father's property now belonged to George and could be sold to pay his debts.

It was only a week after the funeral that the bailiff came to Ruthin. 'There can be no question,' he pronounced, 'that an arrangement made to benefit a German prince should outweigh that law of inheritance by which this estate now correctly belongs to George Myddleton Cornwallis-West, and will therefore be seized by those acting on behalf of his creditors.'

Patsy listened with more anger than she had felt through all the matter of Patrick and Mrs Birch. Poppets had made these arrangements, with Dick Birch advising him, to ensure that Ruthin could never be taken away because of George. And now, when she again needed William to be there and defend them, the poor soul was lying in his grave down in the churchyard. She cried again, as she had cried each day, and became very ill.

Shelagh wrote to Daisy that Patsy had suffered a haemorrhage and the doctors from Liverpool had come and taken her to hospital. They decided she did not need surgery, but, being in a state of collapse, must be moved away and not try, on her own, to fight the case for Ruthin.

A sale document was therefore drawn up for Ruthin, describing all the lands and tenancies, all the furnishings and furniture. The castle itself was sold and became a hospital, and the beautiful gardens were left to decline. Patsy asked the head gardener to take some of the old statues she had positioned around the garden and hide them in the dungeons before they could be removed by the auctioneers.

Stella's anger with George and his childlike inability to face real things made her reconsider her position. As the creditors put more and more pressure on him, she realised that it was preferable not to grant him a divorce. In this way he was forced to repay her whatever money he had, even after the bankruptcy was eventually removed. She did not tell Patsy about the pathetic woman in Milford, but she did say how sad she was about what George was letting happen to the houses and that in the end she had decided that divorce was too easy an escape for him. Patsy supported her in this. She and Stella had become very close during the hearings at the Guildhall.

George deeply resented his mother's siding with Stella. He wanted to divorce Stella and no longer be in her debt. He felt his mother should support him, whatever happened, as he had supported her. But Patsy was thinking not so much of herself as of Shelagh and Daisy: both needed homes, and George had lost everything for them, too.

'Like an army in retreat,' said Patsy to Shelagh. Ruthin was abandoned, and they moved to Newlands, leaving Wales for ever. Then the bailiffs came to Newlands as well. This time Patsy was not at all friendly, she refused them entrance and covered her ears, so that whatever they said was not heard – she could tell herself it had not been spoken. The tenancy agreement made with the Prince of Pless was for Newlands and the grounds. It did not include the fittings and furnishings, which were the work of thirty years' collecting and design by Patsy. She would not leave them and would not allow solicitors to argue that they belonged to William's estate and had therefore been inherited by George. They were hers, and when the time came they would be left to Daisy and Shelagh, not to George.

George was forced to comply with an instruction to evict his mother from Newlands. This is how it appeared in the newspaper:

A motion was brought before the court by the trustees in the bankruptcy of Mr George Cornwallis-West against Mrs Mary Adelaide Thomasina Eupatoria Cornwallis-West, widow.

The court was asked to declare that an agreement made in 1909, whereby a lease of Newlands Manor, Milford, which prevented Mr George Cornwallis-West from taking possession of the premises, was a fraudulent device.

The lease had made Prince Henry of Pless the permanent tenant of the property, but the court found that this was not a valid agreement, having been made without the consent of Mr Cornwallis-West, who was the rightful heir.

Mrs West was occupying Newlands and preventing its inspection by the trustees of the bankruptcy. Counsel for the petitioner said that the summer was a most important time to sell this class of property.

The court declared in favour of the trustees and Mrs West was required to undertake not to interfere with the sale.

Poor Patsy had to move from Newlands to her sister's house, Clouds, in Wiltshire. From there, in a series of frantic notes she tried desperately to reclaim the beloved items from Newlands.

On the inventory of goods for Newlands she wrote anxious comments: 'My son knows these items belong to me, he came with me to the bank and asked that they be protected. I paid for them myself. I have the bills.'

The inventory gave an idea of what a delightful home it had been, with Venetian glass panels and chandeliers and glassware; silver 'engraved to the designs of Mrs Cornwallis-West'; and wool rugs and family portraits in the boudoir. The music room had three pianos and a harp.

Everything was sold to appease George's creditors. Everything they owned.

On 11 November 1918, the Great War ended. Twenty million people had died in fighting around the world. In Munich and Vienna crowds took to the streets, angry with the governments which had capitulated to the American decrees at the armistice. National Socialism was the cry. Czechoslovakia declared itself independent of the Austro-Hungarian Empire. The Austrian prime minister, blamed for his participation in the commencement of war, was taken out of parliament on to the streets and murdered.

Daisy still could not get home. With her German connections, she was regarded in England with grave suspicion. She found that nearly all her society friends disowned her. Eventually only Queen Alexandra, the Queen Mother, lent a helping hand: 'Poor Daisy, your mother has been so ill, and your brother has been forced to do such horrid things. Please call on me as soon as you can'; and with this letter Daisy managed to get back into the country in September 1919. No wonder Daisy recalled that there had been no jealousy among the women who surrounded King Edward, and that they had supported each other in difficult times.

She found Patsy at Clouds, desperately ill. For the sake of her health, Daisy took her to Cannes, where she had rented a flat in exile from Germany. Hans Heinrich now no longer wished to see her. He had paid for the flat and for her to leave Bavaria. He wanted a divorce. 'According to an article in a Berlin newspaper the Prince of Pless is seeking an order for the nullity of his marriage in 1891 to the Princess Daisy, who is the elder daughter of the late Colonel Cornwallis-West and Mrs Cornwallis-West of Ruthin Castle, in north Wales. The prince, we are told, is in love with an Austrian Catholic lady, who could not defy her Church by marrying a man whose wife is still living. So the nullity suit is to clear the way for his second marriage. The princess is a sister to Shelagh, Duchess of Westminister.'

Patsy's painful illness confined her to a chair by the window of Daisy's apartment in Cannes. While she gazed out at the sea, she worried about being beautiful when she died. Eventually, the doctors advised her to return to England, and she spent her last days at Arnewood, near Newlands, in the New Forest. She died on 21 July 1920, and is buried in the churchyard at Milford, where her mother-in-law, Theresa Cornwallis-West, is also buried. Her grave is marked with a simple cross which bears only her name. There is no mention of her family and no phrase of loving memory.

Sir John Cowans was the only general in the British army to remain in the same post throughout the war. He died not long after Patsy, also of cancer, having spent his last days alone in the South of France.

The Birches continued living at Bryncelin until they died. They had no heirs and the house fell into disrepair.

As a result of what had been said at the court of enquiry, Lieutenant-Colonel Henry Delmé-Radcliffe was retired from his post as commanding officer at Kinmel Park.

Patrick Barrett never recovered fully from his wounds and shell shock. He remained in convalescence for a long time, but in the 1920s he became a teacher and lay minister in St Asaph, where he died when he was forty. The war had destroyed his life as it had those of the Cornwallis-Wests and so many others.

Shelagh kept the title Duchess of Westminster.

After living for years in France and Bavaria, and turning her diaries into books, Daisy eventually returned to Silesia. The years between the wars brought a terrible feud between her sons and her husband, and much unhappiness. Daisy died in 1943, but her grave was plundered for jewels, to the deep sadness of her family and those with whom she spent her last days

By January 1920 all the family property had been sold and George had paid sufficient of his debt to be discharged from bankruptcy. Stella and George remained married until she died in 1940, although they never again lived together. She continued to tour as one of the most famous actresses of the time. George wrote charming books about fishing and gentlemanly living. He never forgave his mother for her behaviour and in his will asked that he should not be buried near her.

Patsy bore the burden of many harsh judgments made against her. It had always been her object to give pleasure and never to hurt, yet she fell victim to all the disapprovals the world could muster. To be removed from history is a heavy punishment, for it prevents those who might like to forgive, or even those who might enjoy hearing about her life, from exercising such kindnesses.

Patsy neither broke families nor murdered people. She is remembered with real affection. She played no part in the annihilations that became a feature of the years that followed her death. She did not consciously repress or exploit others in the way of many of her contemporaries. Patsy's sins do not compare with those of many people in much higher places.

She was forgivable, as her husband was admirable. He forgave her, for whatever she had done.

SOURCES

Books

Debrett, 1910

Hansard, 1916

The History of Ruthin Castle Hotel

Beatty, Laura, *Lillie Langtry: Manners, Masks and Morals* (Chatto & Windus, 1999)

Bateman, Audrey, *The Magpie Tendency* (Audrey Bateman, 1999); about Francis Bennett-Goldney

Campbell, Stella Patrick, *My Life and Some Letters* (Hutchinson, 1922)

Cornwallis-West, George, *Edwardian Hey Days* (Puttnam, 1931)

Cornwallis-West, George, *Edwardians Go Fishing* (Puttnam, 1932)

Daisy, Princess of Pless, by Herself (John Murray, 1928)

Daisy, Princess of Pless, *From My Private Diary* (John Murray, 1931)

Daisy, Princess of Pless, *What I Left Unsaid* (E. P. Dutton, 1936)

Graves, Robert, *Goodbye to All That*, 4th edn (Cassell, 1966)

Grigg, John, *Lloyd George: From Peace to War 1912–1916* (Methuen, 1985)

Koch, W. John, *Daisy, Princess of Pless* (Brightest Pebble Publishing Co., 2002)

Koch, W. John, *Schloss Fürstenstein* (Bergstadtverlag Wilhelm Gottlieb Korn. Würzburg, 1989)

Leslie, Anita, *Jennie: The Life of Lady Randolph Churchill* (Hutchinson, 1969)

Lloyd George, Frances, *The Years that are Past* (Hutchinson, 1967)

Luke, Michael, *Hansel Pless, Prisoner of History*, ed. Patrick Scrivener (Cygnet Press, 2001)

MacDonald, Lyn, *1914: The Days of Hope* (Michael Joseph, 1987)

Peters, Margo, *Mrs Pat: The Life of Mrs Patrick Campbell* (Bodley Head, 1984)

Collections and Archives

Art and Design Collection, Westminster Reference Library, London

Bodleian Library, Oxford: the papers of Herbert Asquith, and others

Canterbury Cathedral archives

Churchill College archives, Cambridge

County Record Office of Hampshire, Winchester: papers relating to the Cornwallis-West family

Denbighshire Public Record Office, Ruthin: papers and articles relating to the Cornwallis-West family

Flintshire Reference Library, Mold

Hampshire Record Office, Winchester: papers of the Cornwallis-West family

House of Commons Library: Field Despatches of World War I from the *London Gazette* (also published in the Uncovered Editions series, as *Battles of World War I*) Review of the Enemy Press (November 1918); papers relating to the outbreak of the Great War, Command Paper Cd. 7860 (also published as an 'uncovered edition', *War 1914: Punishing the Serbs*)

House of Lords Library: various papers, including those of David Lloyd George

Imperial War Museum, London

King's College archives, Cambridge: the papers of J. M. Keynes

Lillie Langtry Museum, Jersey

London School of Economics Library: the Markham papers

National Army Museum Library, London: the papers of Sir John Cowans

National Library of Wales, Aberystwyth: papers relating to the Cornwallis-West family in the Longueville collection

National Newspaper Archive, Colindale: published articles from 1870 to 1922

New Milton Historical Society records: extensive papers relating to the Cornwallis-West family and to the Newlands estate

Public Record Office, Kew: papers relating to Army Courts of Enquiry and to the War Office

Royal Welch Fusiliers' Museum and archives, Caernarfon Castle

Victoria and Albert Museum, London

A NOTE ON THE AUTHOR

A former bookseller, Tim Coates is the editor
and publisher of *Uncovered Editions*, a series of
historic official papers from the British and
American governments. This is his first book
for Bloomsbury.

A NOTE ON THE TYPE

The text of this book is set in Bembo. This type was first used in 1495 by the Venetian printer Aldus Manutius for Cardinal Bembo's *De Aetna*, and was cut for Manutius by Francesco Griffo. It was one of the types used by Claude Garamond (1480–1561) as a model for his Romain de L'Université, and so it was the forerunner of what became standard European type for the following two centuries. Its modern form follows the original types and was designed for Monotype in 1929.